Unifying the Mind

Unifying the Mind

Cognitive Representations as Graphical Models

David Danks

The MIT Press
Cambridge, Massachusetts
London, England

MIT Press books may be purchased at special quantity discounts for business or sales promotional use. For information, please email special_sales@mitpress.mit.edu.

This book was set in Stone Serif Std by Toppan Best-set Premedia Limited, Hong Kong. Printed and bound in the United States of America.

Library of Congress Cataloging-in-Publication Data is available.
ISBN: 978-0-262-02799-1

10 9 8 7 6 5 4 3 2 1

To Mara and Kiera, for their endless patience and support

Contents

Acknowledgments

Although I did not realize it at the time, the core of these ideas was formed over a decade ago, when I was a graduate student and started thinking (at Clark Glymour's suggestion) about whether human causal learning could sometimes be fruitfully understood using Bayesian networks. The idea seemed a bit crazy to me at first, but it gradually came to seem more plausible over time. From that starting point, the picture has gotten broader and more general, eventually resulting in the view that I articulate in this book. As with any project that unfolds over this length of time, the debts I owe are many, and there will undoubtedly be influences that I inadvertently fail to recognize and acknowledge.

Many audiences were gracious with their time, comments, and criticisms as I worked out these thoughts and arguments in talks over the years. The ideas in chapter 2 were explored in talks at the 2013 Marshall M. Weinberg Cognitive Science Symposium, the University of Pittsburgh Center for Philosophy of Science, and the University of Geneva; those in chapter 4 at Colorado College, Carnegie Mellon Philosophy, the 2004 International Congress of Psychology, and the 33rd Carnegie Symposium; chapter 5 at the Center for Advanced Study in the Behavioral Sciences, a 2004 NIPS workshop on probabilistic models, and a summer workshop at the Institute for Pure and Applied Mathematics at UCLA; chapter 6 at the 2009 meeting of the Eastern Psychological Association, the Center for Behavioral Decision Research at CMU, and UC–Berkeley Institute of Cognitive and Brain Sciences; and chapter 7 at Caltech, Georg-August-Universität Göttingen, Carnegie Mellon Psychology, the Center for Advanced Study of Language at Maryland, and the Air Force Research Laboratory.

Along the way, many people also provided feedback in conversation or on various written pieces. I suspect that many of them think that I am still wrongheaded in my ideas, but I deeply appreciate their attempts to steer me correctly. Particular thanks are due to Jeremy Avigad, Joe Danks, Frederick Eberhardt, Noah Goodman, Alison Gopnik, Tom Griffiths, York Hagmayer, Charles Kemp, Tamar Kushnir, Tania Lombrozo, Edouard Machery, Tiago Maia, Jay McClelland, Bob Rehder, Steve Sloman, Josh Tenenbaum, Michael Waldmann, and Annika Wallin. Many of these ideas were also explored or worked out in collaboration with some of my wonderful students, notably Patrick Beukema, Steve Fancsali, Conor Mayo-Wilson, William Nichols, Sarah Wellen, and Huichun (Joy) Zhu. In particular, Steve did much of the coding for the simulations in section 6.2, and discussions with Sarah influenced many of my ideas about minimalism in chapter 7.

A James S. McDonnell Foundation Scholar Award was crucial to this entire effort, as it has provided me and my students with both time and resources to fully make sense of the role of graphical models in our cognition. They trusted that I could make this somewhat crazy idea work, and I hope that this book repays some of that trust.

I have had the extraordinary luck and pleasure to conduct most of this work while in the warm and supportive confines of the Carnegie Mellon Department of Philosophy. I have never encountered a group with such a strong commitment to intellectual rigor, coupled with complete open-mindedness about what might be the best way to tackle a problem. There is much rhetoric about the desire to be interdisciplinary, but I would argue that no department is more truly interdisciplinary, in the sense of using whatever methods, frameworks, models, and techniques are necessary to address and solve the truly hard, and truly interesting, puzzles. I could not wish for a better, more supportive, but still deeply rigorous and challenging environment in which to do my work.

Two people deserve special mention. Clark Glymour taught me graphical models, introduced me to problems in human causal learning, and was one of the first to openly suggest the "graphical models in the mind" idea. His work has provided me with an ideal of how philosophy, psychology, and machine learning can be used together to help us understand the human mind just a little bit better. Perhaps most importantly, he has been a tireless supporter and relentless critic of all my views. Almost every idea in this book has been worked out partly through discussions and arguments with Clark, and they are better as a result.

Finally, my deepest thanks and gratitude go to Mara Harrell, who has been the sounding board and critic for every thought I have had over the past years, whether good or bad, interesting or banal. She has also had the unenviable task of putting up with my periodic bouts of insanity, both in writing this book and in life more generally. This book simply would not exist without her help and support, and words alone cannot express my gratitude to her.

1 "Free-Range" Cognition

1.1 Thinking across Boundaries

Suppose you find yourself in the wilderness, hungry and lost. The particular reason you ended up there is relatively unimportant; perhaps you were hiking through a cloud bank and lost your bearings, or perhaps you were a contestant on a popular game show. The key challenge, regardless of what previously happened, is to figure out how to survive. More precisely, you need to engage in different types of cognition to, for example, determine which objects might potentially be food, observe other animals' eating habits to determine what is possibly safe, and make decisions (possibly involving hard trade-offs) about what exactly to eat. Moreover, all this cognition must take advantage of disparate pieces of knowledge: you have to use your beliefs about the physiology of other animals both to determine whether their food choices are informative, and also to decide whether they might think that *you* are food. On top of all of these separate cognitive challenges, you are in a highly dynamic environment. You must be able to learn from the outcomes of your choices, revise your understanding of what is edible, and adjust to changing circumstances around you. More generally, you must be flexible in learning and reasoning, bringing many different cognitive resources to bear on each problem that you confront.

Everyday cognition obviously involves much lower stakes (at least most of the time), though marks of these more hostile environments might persist in our cognition (Sterelny, 2003). Despite the difference in stakes, our ordinary, everyday thinking similarly requires an astonishing range of cognitive activities, even in familiar environments: we categorize objects, make inferences about them, learn causal relations between them, make plans and take actions given causal beliefs, observe and categorize the outcomes of our actions, learn from those outcomes, and so on. Despite this variety, though, our cognition seems to be quite seamless. We move between cognitive processes and representations with ease, and different types of cognition seem to readily share information. Consider a simple example: I notice that my dog is limping, which leads me to reason that her leg must be hurt. As a result, I decide that I will not take her for a walk, since I do not want to risk further injury. This sequence of thoughts is utterly unexceptional; we have similar trains of thought many times every day. If we stop to consider all the different types of thought and knowledge that went into such a sequence, however, then we quickly realize that much of cognition must be unified in important ways. My reasoning and decision in this case require knowledge about my dog's physiology, her normal state, the likely effects of certain actions, the costs and benefits of those outcomes, and so on, and I must deploy all these different types of information—seamlessly and in a coherent manner—to succeed in my goals.

These examples, both everyday and more fantastical, also serve to highlight a quite different, but just as striking, feature of our cognition. Despite our substantial limitations and need to think in many different ways, we seem to be able to navigate successfully through the world, accomplishing many different goals along the way. It is a banal, but nonetheless correct, observation that the world is exceedingly complex along many dimensions, including the physical, social, and causal. At the same time, our conscious cognition is, by all appearances, a relatively slow, limited input information processor that seems quite inappropriate for the complexity of the world. Any particular inference, decision, or explanation almost always involves more factors that are (potentially) relevant to our cognition than conscious thought appears to be capable of handling. And yet, despite all these challenges, we are astonishingly successful in predicting, understanding, and controlling our world in all its complexity. We manage to forecast snowstorms, establish universities, raise children, and generally succeed in navigating our world. We regularly achieve many of the ends that we desire, all without blindly simplifying our world or operating solely on unconscious cognition. We instead somehow manage to ignore just the complexity that does not really matter for (consciously) determining how to reach our goals in each particular situation (at least most of the time).

This book attempts to make sense of these two different features of our real-world cognition: the relatively seamless way in which we shift between seemingly distinct cognitive operations; and our ability to (correctly) attend precisely to the information, features, and possibilities that are relevant to our goals, perhaps only loosely or indirectly. These two aspects of cognition are rarely viewed as connected in any significant way, when they are studied at all. In fact, much contemporary cognitive science essentially ignores both of these features, either implicitly or explicitly. Standard practice is to focus on particular cognitive processes in relative isolation. For example, papers on causal learning often start by noting the importance of causal knowledge for decision making but then never examine exactly how such learning and decision making interact. Similarly, category acquisition/application and decision making—two other foci of this book—have been explored relatively independently. Moreover, the research in these areas has focused on situations in which it is quite clear what information is important and relevant. Laboratory experiments are obviously one such situation, as we (as cognitive scientists) all typically use simplified materials so that we know just what our participants see. But even many field experiments explore situations in which the available information is easily specifiable, such as studying an air traffic controller who has access only to the information in the console in front of her. As a result, researchers rarely ask how we manage to focus our attention largely on the relevant aspects of the world (though there have been many philosophical arguments about how and why relevance is so hard to explain, as detailed in Samuels, 2010).

I began with vivid, real-world examples, but little in this book will touch directly on complex cognition in realistic situations. I instead aim to determine some of the aspects of the general structure of our cognition that make successful thought possible in our complex world. That is, my goal here is to advance our understanding about the basic building blocks from which complex thought is built; actual models, built from those elements, of cognition in fully realistic and highly complex real-world situations will have to wait for future work. To expose those building blocks, I turn to what is sometimes called computational cognitive science: using precise computational models to describe, predict, and, most importantly, explain human behavior, at least in limited laboratory settings. In particular, I advocate an empirically well-supported cognitive account in which a mind has a shared store of cognitive representations that are structured approximately like graphical models, a computational framework that has been developed in machine learning over the past thirty years. Both of the salient features of cognition discussed at the outset—seamless cognitive integration and appropriate focus on relevant factors—are naturally explained if our cognitive representations are graphical models.

While I will have much more to say about graphical models throughout the book, the key insight is that the "graph" part of them—objects like *Switch* → *Light* as a representation of my knowledge about the causal structure of the lights in my office, though typically more complicated—encodes relevance relations in a way that is easy to store and easy to use. Moreover, graphical models are rich enough to contain the information required by multiple cognitive processes. Relatively simple conscious cognition can lead to successful navigation of a complex world when we have graphs that encode precisely this type of (correct) information about what matters for what, and when those graphs are available to multiple cognitive processes. That is, we successfully navigate the world—predict, infer, explain, classify, and decide—because we have graphs in our heads.

1.2 Cognitive Representations, Graphical Models, and Cognitive Unification

Two different features of cognition are the focus in this book: the relatively seamless way that we move from one type of cognition to another, and our ability to quickly attend to the information that is (usually) most important in a particular situation. I contend that both of these features can be explained (at least partially) if I can demonstrate—both theoretically and empirically—that multiple cognitive processes can all be understood as distinct, though related, operations on a common store of cognitive representations structured as graphical models. Seamless, free-ranging cognition arises because the different types of cognition have a shared informational base of cognitive representations. Use of relevant information occurs because graphical models directly represent notions of relevance.

The nature of cognitive representation has generated substantial debate, but arguably more heat than light. I will use a natural, but relatively imprecise, understanding of the notion: our cognitive representations are the internally encoded information that our cognitive processes use, manipulate, and modify. That is, cognitive representations are the "content" in our head, however it might precisely be structured or instantiated. More will be said about this issue in chapter 2, including how we might distinguish between representations and processes. We can already see, however, how seamless, free-ranging cognition could occur if the necessary information (i.e., the cognitive representations) is shared by multiple cognitive processes. Consider the simple challenge of turning on the lights in an unfamiliar room. Success requires both causal learning to determine which switches control lights, and means-ends decision making to determine what action will achieve my goal based on causal reasoning about the causal system. At least three different types of cognition are engaged in this simple problem, and yet we solve it seamlessly. In my account, this success is explained as the causal learning generating a cognitive representation (structured as a graphical model), which is subsequently accessed by the processes for both decision making and causal reasoning. Of course, many critical details remain to be provided about this picture, including an explanation of how this account is actually novel in an interesting way. However, this brief example gives us hope that an interesting explanation of seamless cognition might be possible.

The other piece of the puzzle is explaining our use of relevant information in terms of shared cognitive representations being structured as graphical models. A graphical model consists of two components: (i) a graph encoding qualitative information about the structure (causal, informational, or other) among various factors; and (ii) a quantitative representation of the relation strengths. Roughly, the qualitative component compactly represents relevance, and the quantitative component encodes the strength and nature of that relevance. Of course, relevance is a dynamic relation that depends on the particular cognitive agent and particular context. The stable graphical model is thus not quite sufficient, since relevance depends on the particulars of our situation. The key is that the elements in the graphical model structure can have different values in different situations. For example, to use the causal graphical model *Switch* → *Lights*, we also need to know something about the state of the *Switch* or the *Lights*. When we know the values of the graphical model elements (e.g., when we know what is active), then the graphical model can guide our inferences appropriately. That is, the context and cognition sensitivity of relevance arise completely naturally from graphical models, when one includes the particular values of elements in the graph. Graphical models were originally developed partly to improve elicitation of human expert knowledge about causal and other relevance relations. They are now widely used by machine learning researchers to encode complex information in a wide variety of domains. However, despite being a rich computational framework with powerful representational and algorithmic resources, graphical models have only recently begun to appear in cognitive science research (e.g., Glymour, 2002; Gopnik et al., 2004; Griffiths, Chater, Kemp, Perfors, & Tenenbaum, 2010; Sloman, 2005).

The upshot of the observations in the previous paragraph is that arguments that our cognitive representations are structured (approximately) like graphical models are actually arguments for a particular explanation of our ability to (usually) focus on appropriate information in real-world cognition. My primary focus in much of the book will thus be on graphical models more specifically, rather than relevance relations in general, since the former are arguably a subset of the latter. If I can show that the graphical models framework provides an appropriate model for many of our cognitive representations, then our ability to focus on the relevant information comes along "for free." Of course, we presumably use representations like graphical models partly *because* they directly encode relevance relations, but I will not try to give the type of evolutionary story required to defend that particular claim. I instead focus on the smaller, but still substantial, challenge of showing that our cognitive representations have this structure and so can serve an appropriate explanatory role in understanding our ability to attend to relevant information in complex situations.

To meet this more focused challenge, I will argue that different types of cognition can each be understood—both theoretically and empirically—as operations on graphical models. That is, in many particular areas of cognition, the relevant cognitive representations appear to be particular graphical models. Very few theories in cognitive science are expressed in terms of graphical models, and so a major part of my effort will involve showing that multiple cognitive theories can actually be fruitfully expressed in the graphical models framework. That is, these theories can be (re)interpreted as operations on graphical models, though this is not the language that has been used by the cognitive scientists who developed the theories. Much of chapters 4, 5, and 6 will be taken up with providing these (re)interpretations. In fact, I will even show that multiple incompatible cognitive theories—ones that make directly conflicting predictions—can be expressed as operations on graphical models. Sometimes they differ about the particular *type* of graphical model that is appropriate for the cognitive representation; sometimes they differ only about the process used for learning or reasoning, rather than the underlying representation. The key point, though, is that we can translate all these theories into the graphical models framework, and so we can understand much of our cognition as operations on graphical models, though many empirical details remain to be figured out by cognitive scientists.

Given the ambitious nature of my goals, it is important to be clear about what will count as success. First, I make no claim to universality in this account. I am not trying to explain every aspect of cognition, nor do I think that every cognitive representation is structured as a graphical model. In fact, section 4.4 includes an argument that one type of causal cognition—specifically, causal perception—produces cognitive representations that are almost certainly *not* graphical models of the sort that I use elsewhere in this book. I instead focus on, and make claims only about, several types of cognition that play significant roles in our everyday lives. Graphical models are appropriate in these areas and perhaps others, but almost certainly not always and everywhere. Second, because I focus on areas of cognition that have been studied extensively over decades, I can often build on previous research. If I can show, for example, that a particular cognitive theory can be understood as operations on a graphical model, then my view can "inherit" much of the empirical support for that other theory. That is, if an empirically well-supported theory can be expressed using graphical models, then we immediately know that the graphical models framework can account for those empirical data.[1] I will thus not talk in significant detail about experiments and empirical findings, but will instead show how to understand different theories, including references to papers that articulate the empirical data supporting them. Third, I would suggest that the language of "truth" is not the best way to evaluate cognitive theories, at least given our current state of knowledge. Instead we should ask whether an account is interesting, explanatory, coheres with other knowledge, and is likely to be empirically and theoretically fruitful in the future. I contend that the graphical-models-based view expressed here meets all these criteria, though it will take a book to demonstrate it.

1.3 Where Are We Going?

My goals in this book are obviously quite ambitious and require that we cover quite a lot of ground. A complicating factor on top of all of this is that the graphical models framework is itself quite mathematically complex.

Entire books have been devoted just to explaining the computational and mathematical aspects of graphical models (e.g., Koller & Friedman, 2009), without even beginning to engage with cognitive issues. It turns out, however, that we do not need many of the mathematical details about graphical models to understand the view I advocate here, and most of the arguments on its behalf. We only need to understand 5 percent of the graphical models framework to do 95 percent of the work in this book. I have thus structured things so that the main thread of the book focuses on the important, and more qualitative, parts. Where possible, I have tried to omit mathematical details that distract from the main points. Of course, those details are not irrelevant: at some point, we need to make sure that all the computational pieces line up appropriately. I have thus separated out the formal mathematical details into distinct sections marked with an asterisk (*). It is important that nothing is being hidden here; all the qualitative claims can be precisely expressed in the full mathematical framework of graphical models. At the same time, readers who are less mathematically inclined or interested can skip the marked sections without loss of understanding, as those sections focus on the details, not the overall picture and arguments.

Before diving into the heart of the story, we have some conceptual and mathematical groundwork to do. Chapter 2 considers the question of what it really means to say that my cognition involves shared representations structured as graphical models. Numerous recent debates in cognitive science (e.g., Griffiths et al., 2010; Jones & Love, 2011, and accompanying commentary; McClelland et al., 2010) have turned partly on what exactly is intended by a particular cognitive model or set of models. The question of commitments is not simply an idle philosophical one. At the same time, many philosophers and cognitive scientists have proposed conceptual frameworks to capture the commitments of a cognitive theory, or the ways in which different cognitive theories relate to one another (e.g., Marr's levels, neural reductionism, or cognitive autonomy). I argue that all of these fall short: they all fail to provide the theoretical resources needed to capture the particular claims that I will defend throughout this book. We instead need a subtler understanding of (a) theoretical commitments in terms of a multidimensional space, and (b) intertheoretic relations based on one theory constraining another. I provide such an account so that the reader can properly interpret the claims of later chapters. In chapter 3, I then provide a primer on the formal computational framework of graphical models.

There are actually multiple types of graphical models, so this chapter provides an introduction to the different ones that will be used in later chapters. Although the focus is on a formal framework, much of the chapter is written qualitatively, though the mathematical details are provided for interested readers in clearly indicated sections.

I then turn to the hard work—building on results from myself and many others—of showing that the graphical models framework can help us to understand single areas of cognition. Chapter 4 focuses on causal cognition of many sorts, ranging from learning which switches control which lights, to reasoning about the likely causes of a car accident, to directly perceiving that my hand's push caused the door to close. Graphical models have already played an important role in our understanding of causal cognition, and so this domain provides a good starting point to see how we can interpret cognitive theories as operations on graphical models. Chapter 5 turns to the many types of cognition involving concepts, broadly construed. We learn how to divide the world into groups or categories; for example, we learn that there are different species of animals. We categorize objects as belonging to particular groups, such as deciding that the animal at my feet is a dog. We use information about an object's category to make further inferences about it (e.g., that this animal probably barks). And these concepts and knowledge are integrated in important ways to support further inferences (and decisions), such as the expectation that this particular animal likely has four legs. I show that the cognitive representations underlying these operations (i.e., the concepts) can be represented as graphical models, and the different uses correspond to different operations on those representations. Finally, chapter 6 focuses on decision making, ranging from deciding how to leave my office to deciding what kind of candy to share with my daughter. I argue that many different types of decisions depend on means-ends or social reasoning that is naturally understood as operations on graphical models.

At the end of these three chapters, we will have a coherent picture in which each of these disparate cognitive domains can be understood, in isolation, as operations on graphical models. Of course, these theoretical similarities and identities might simply be a mathematical oddity. Chapter 7 thus explores different possible cognitive architectures that could explain this theoretical unification. After surveying the relevant "theory space," I argue that the empirical data about the nature and extent of integration of cognitive processes suggest that the most plausible cognitive architecture (again, given our current knowledge) is one comprising a single, shared representational store that different cognitive processes access in a relatively serial fashion. That is, the data suggest that the same cognitive representations are used and modified by multiple cognitive processes, and so we have an explanation for the relatively seamless nature of our cognition. Moreover, this particular architecture makes a number of distinctive predictions, particularly about distinctive learning and goal effects. I thus provide a number of future experiments that will both test and explore the unified model.

At that point, I step back to consider other proposals for unifying cognition. I am certainly not the first to propose a unifying account, but I argue in chapter 8 that the spirit of my architecture is importantly different from (though complementary to) many previous proposals. More specifically, other accounts have unified cognition either by providing a small, shared set of processes or operations underlying all cognition (e.g., ACT-R, Soar) or by arguing that all cognition is of the same type in some sense, though there need not be any actual sharing or overlap (e.g., connectionist networks, Bayesian models). In contrast to both of these types of unification, I focus on the role of representations (not processes) that are truly shared (not simply of the same type). Finally, chapter 9 considers some of the broader conceptual or philosophical morals that can be drawn. For example, typical definitions of cognitive modularity do not fit cleanly with the idea that cognition might be unified through shared representations rather than shared processes or schemata, and so we must rethink our understanding of modularity. A different issue arises from the observation that relevance is not necessarily a univocal relation in the world; there are different types of relevance. Graphical models are typically understood to represent only a single type of relevance in each model (though the type can differ across models), which raises the question of how to understand—theoretically, empirically, and cognitively—"mixed" relevance relations. The cognitive architecture presented in this book also raises challenging issues about the common positions of both neural reductionism and the autonomy of the cognitive sciences.

We move smoothly between categorizing objects in the world, making inferences about them, using those inferences to reason about the causal structure of the world, making plans given that causal structure, taking actions based on the plan, observing and categorizing the outcomes of our actions, learning from those outcomes, and so on. And in many cases, it is not even clear where one cognitive operation ends and another begins: if I am learning about a new type of object and I learn that objects of that type have a distinctive causal structure, it is unclear whether I have done category learning, causal learning, both, or some hybrid that is not really either. The representations and processes of conscious cognition—however they might be individuated—are integrated in real-world cognition and together enable us to (usually) focus our cognitive energy on the factors, events, and aspects that are relevant to successfully achieving our goals. And all of this, I contend, is based on different cognitive operations on a shared representational store of graphical models. Now I begin the hard work of articulating, explaining, and defending that claim.

2 Computational Realism, Levels, and Constraints

2.1 What Is a Computational Cognitive Model?

This book argues that we can fruitfully understand significant parts of human cognition as different processes operating on a shared representational store of graphical models. My approach throughout is unabashedly computational: cognition will be understood as precise operations on mathematically well-specified objects. More precisely, a background assumption of this work is that it is appropriate to think about aspects of cognition as fundamentally involving learning, transforming, making inferences using, and manipulating structured representations about the world.[1] One challenge with computational models of the mind is that it is often unclear just what commitments—metaphysical, epistemological, and methodological—are intended for a particular theory. The mathematics of a cognitive theory are insufficient to know exactly what the theory does and, often just as importantly, does *not* imply, whether about the world, the cognitive scientist, or future experiments. As a result, we are often left in the position of not knowing whether some empirical data confirm, disconfirm, or are simply irrelevant to a particular computational cognitive theory. Whole debates in cognitive science (e.g., Griffiths, Chater, Kemp, Perfors, & Tenenbaum, 2010; Jones & Love, 2011; McClelland et al., 2010; Melz, Cheng, Holyoak, & Waldmann, 1993; Shanks, 1993) sometimes revolve around questions of commitment: what (beyond "fitting the data") is implied or required for the proponent of a particular cognitive theory?

I attempt to bring some clarity to these issues in this chapter, as it will be particularly important for me to be clear about the commitments of my account. As we will see in chapter 7, my commitments differ in important ways from other cognitive theories with similar computational structure (such as Griffiths et al., 2010), and so I want to ensure that the relevant distinctions are clear. Because I aim to develop an account of theoretical commitments, differences, and constraints that applies to cognitive theories in general (rather than just my own), this chapter is also the most explicitly philosophical one in the book. Discussion of graphical models will have to wait until chapter 3, and extended discussion of specific cognitive theories will start in chapter 4. Sections 2.1 through 2.4 take various philosophical detours to provide clarity about the relevant "possibility spaces," and then I put everything together in section 2.5 to state the particular commitments of my view. That last section is thus the most important in the chapter; the other sections provide the machinery to understand the statements there.

One important dimension of variation between different cognitive accounts is their relative abstractness; some terminology is helpful here.[2] Starting at the most specific, a cognitive *model* offers a computationally well-specified account of a specific aspect of cognition. For example, a cognitive model of categorization provides a function that takes as input both a novel case and various possible categories and then outputs some type of categorization behavior (e.g., probabilities of placing the novel case into each of the categories). In practice, almost all cognitive accounts that actually make concrete predictions are cognitive models. Moving up in abstractness, a cognitive *architecture* specifies the basic building blocks for cognitive models, as well as the ways in which those components can be assembled. Cognitive architectures describe aspects of our cognitive structure that are relatively constant over time (Langley, Laird, & Rogers, 2009), and so a single cognitive architecture encodes a set (usually infinite in size) of cognitive models. Many well-known cognitive theories—for example, cognition should be modeled using neural networks (Rogers & McClelland, 2004)—are best understood as cognitive architectures. Any particular, fully parameterized neural network is a cognitive model; the set of all (appropriately structured) neural networks constitutes the cognitive architecture. Understanding the mind as a Bayesian learner is similarly a cognitive architecture (Oaksford & Chater, 2007), while each specific Bayesian account is a cognitive model. Newell (1990, p. 80) described cognitive architectures as the "fixed" parts of cognition—that is, the basic pieces that do not change and generate flexible behavior by being assembled in particular ways. Similarly, Anderson (2007, p. 7) focuses on cognitive architecture as the abstract "structures" that make cognition possible.

Most abstractly, a cognitive *framework* is a general approach for understanding the nature of the mind. Frameworks do not specify the precise computational pieces that are used to construct a model, but rather indicate a general approach to modeling the mind. For example, attempts to construct symbolic models of cognition (as opposed to neural models, or embodied models, or others) together form a cognitive framework, though architectures within that framework might use quite different elements. Finally, one might note that I have not used the word "theory" in this division. That term is used in many different ways, but in this book, a cognitive *theory* will include a cognitive account at any of the three levels just discussed; that is, a cognitive theory can be a framework, architecture, or model. When we consider how to connect different cognitive accounts, we will often not care about the level, so it will be useful to have a term that encompasses all three. When it actually matters whether the theory at hand is a model, architecture, or framework, then the appropriate term will be used.

This trichotomy is useful in understanding the level of abstractness at which a cognitive theory is offered. It does not, however, provide strict distinctions between the levels; no "bright lines" separate frameworks from architectures, or architectures from models. For example, one might offer a cognitive theory that looks like a cognitive model but has free parameters that must be filled in for a particular domain or for a particular individual. Such an account is not, strictly speaking, a cognitive model as defined earlier, as we cannot generate precise predictions without specifying the relevant free parameters. At the same time, this particular theory is clearly more specific than a stereotypical cognitive architecture, as it does not simply provide a set of building blocks and ways to assemble them. Rather, it shows how those pieces are (mostly) put together for a particular type of cognition. There will inevitably be borderline cases that could be categorized in different ways by different individuals, but most of the cases that we will consider adhere reasonably cleanly to the model/architecture/framework distinction.

This trichotomy provides significant guidance in understanding the methodological commitments implied by advocacy of a particular cognitive theory. In particular, accepting a theory at one level imposes methodological commitments at the levels below. For example, if I advocate a specific cognitive architecture, then I am committing myself (at least for the purposes of that investigation) to constructing cognitive models within that architecture. As a concrete example, the cognitive account offered in this book is a novel cognitive architecture based on shared representations expressed as graphical models. I am thus committed (methodologically) to developing specific cognitive models using these components, at least within this book. This commitment is obviously nonbinding: a researcher can entertain other possibilities or can come to realize that a particular higher-level commitment (e.g., to a particular architecture) is incorrect. Moreover, one can advocate different architectures or even different frameworks for different aspects of cognition.[3]

At the same time, this trichotomy is relatively uninformative about the epistemological and metaphysical commitments implied by advocacy of a particular cognitive theory. The specification of a cognitive theory—whether framework, architecture, or model—almost never (in isolation) commits one to any particular picture of the world, or constrains the ways that theory could be implemented, or determines how we could confirm or learn about the truth of that theory. One could, for example, propose a cognitive model but claim that it is just a useful computational device for generating predictions given inputs. Alternately, one could propose *exactly the same* computational model (more precisely, something with the same mathematics that makes the same input-behavior predictions) but claim that every process and representation in it should be interpreted in a strongly realistic manner. More generally, the mathematical/computational specification of a cognitive theory significantly underdetermines the commitments that are implied by it. We thus need something more than this trichotomy to understand the full commitments of the cognitive architecture advocated in this book. In other words, we need to do some philosophy to really understand what the cognitive science means.

2.2 A Proliferation of Levels

We need some way to talk about the different metaphysical and epistemological commitments that arise for different mathematical/computational cognitive theories, or even for the same theory in different researchers' hands. The (close-to-)dominant language used in contemporary cognitive science is Marr's (1982) three levels for characterizing information-processing devices in general and processes in the human mind more specifically. The *computational* level focuses on the challenge faced by the cognitive agent; more specifically, one identifies the appropriate input and output of the process, constraints on the possible types of computation, and features of the agent's environment. The *algorithmic* level (also called the representation level) specifies an implementation—invariably only approximate in various ways—of the computational theory, including representations of the inputs and outputs. Finally, the *implementational* level describes the physical realization of the representation and the algorithm. Roughly speaking, the computational level specifies what problem is being (appropriately) solved; the algorithmic level explains how it is solved; and the implementational level gives the details of the physical substrate that does the solving. As a concrete (noncognitive) example, we can think about a word-processing program as (i) a process for entering, editing, and rendering text documents (the computational level); (ii) a bunch of lines of code that produce the appropriate behavior (the algorithmic level); or (iii) changes of 1s and 0s in the internal memory registers of the computer (the implementational level).

Marr's levels are helpful for providing a quick characterization of the commitments of a theory,[4] but they unfortunately conflate at least three dimensions along which cognitive theories make commitments: extent of realism, tightness of approximation or scope, and (importance of) closeness to optimality. In Marr's levels, these three dimensions of variation must change in lockstep, though they can actually vary independently. That is, Marr's levels project a complicated, three-dimensional (at least) space of theoretical commitments down to a single dimension of variation; at the end of this section, I give the precise projection used to generate Marr's levels. Moreover, many more than just three levels exist for each dimension, as theories can differ in their commitments in relatively fine-grained ways. To understand what is intended by the cognitive architecture offered in this book, we need to examine these three dimensions of metaphysical and epistemological commitments in more detail.

The first dimension of theoretical commitment is arguably the easiest to understand: the *extent of realism* for a theory is the parts of the theory that are intended to refer to objects or processes that "really exist." Many aspects of the traditional "levels of description" hierarchy (e.g., physics is lower level than chemistry) can naturally be understood as varying the extent of realist commitments of the theory. As a simple cognitive example, consider a model of someone computing $2 + 2 = 4$, that is, a model of an individual being asked to add two plus two and then responding with four. A completely minimal realist commitment for such a model would be to regard it instrumentally: the model offers only a correct characterization of the input–output function for human addition. A substantially more realist commitment would claim that there are representations of the numbers 2 and 4, as well as some process by which the former representation (perhaps with a copy) is manipulated to yield the latter representation. As we see here, the mathematical specification of a theory is insufficient to determine the realist commitments; those are, in an important sense, outside the scope of the computational part of the model. Nonetheless, important empirical questions turn on those realist commitments, and so we need to be clear about how to understand them.[5]

Cognitive objects and processes are arguably unobservable and so it is not always clear what it means to attribute "reality" to such things. An enormous literature exists about the nature of representations, their content, what it means to have processes that are distinct from representations, and so forth (a tiny sample of writings includes Churchland, 1981; Dretske, 1981, 1988; Lycan, 1981; Millikan, 1984; Ramsey, 2007; Stich, 1983, 1992). I will not directly engage with that literature, however, since many, perhaps most, aspects of those debates are orthogonal to the dimension of realist *commitments*. All I require is that there be something structured and somewhat persistent, which can be functionally or operationally identified as a representation. These properties hold for aspects of almost all cognitive theories (Shagrir, 2012), including seemingly nonrepresentational accounts such as connectionist (e.g., Eliasmith & Anderson, 2002; Rogers & McClelland, 2004), embodied (e.g., Barsalou, 2008), and dynamical systems (e.g., Port & van Gelder, 1995) theories. We can generally draw a rough distinction between representations and processes: representations are the relatively stable, persistent objects that encode information, and processes are the dynamic operations involving those objects that can potentially (but need not) change the state of those objects.[6] Of course, representations are partly determined by the uses to which they are put, but they are importantly not identical with those uses (Grush, 1997). Rather, representations are whatever encodes information (perhaps for a purpose) stably over some reasonable timescale, and processes are whatever manipulates that information (perhaps differently depending on the form of the representation).

Given this division, realism implies different epistemological commitments—in part, licensing different predictions[7]—for realism about processes and about representations. Realism about a representation implies commitments about stability of predictions for different types of cognition that use the information encoded in that representation. If the representation "really exists," then the same object is used for (potentially) many purposes, and so predictions in these different contexts should reflect that shared informational basis. For example, realism about the concept DOG implies that behavior in a categorization task involving dogs should be correlated (in various ways) with performance in a feature inference task involving dogs. More generally, representation realism licenses us to use behavior on one task to make predictions about (likely) behavior on different tasks that use the same representations, at least ceteris paribus. Importantly, representation realism does not imply that every representation is available for every process; it is certainly possible that we have multiple representational stores, some of which are process specific. But when the same representation is supposed to be available to multiple processes, then representation realism implies a set of epistemological commitments about correlations or stabilities between predictions about the behaviors generated by the different processes.

Process realism similarly implies epistemological commitments of interprediction correlations and stabilities, but this time for the same task given different inputs, backgrounds, or environmental conditions. That is, if one is committed to the reality of a given cognitive process, then that process should function similarly across a range of inputs and conditions. For example, realism about a particular process theory of concept learning implies that the same process should be active for a variety of inputs that trigger concept learning. Whether I am learning about the concept DOG or the concept CAT, the same process should be engaged (since that is the process that is "really there"). Of course, process realism does not imply that every process is triggered for every input or in every condition; rather, process realism is the more minimal claim that correlations and stabilities should exist for predictions about the different performances of the same task, ceteris paribus.

Moreover, the epistemological commitments of process realism and representation realism are separable, at least in the abstract. One could think that the appropriate predictive correlations obtain within a cognitive task, but not between them (i.e., process realism without representation realism): for example, performance on a categorization task involving dogs might imply stable correlations about categorization involving cats but not anything stable for predictions about feature inference on dogs. Alternately, the appropriate stabilities might obtain across tasks for the same information, but not within a task (i.e., representation realism without process realism): for example, there might be prediction correlations for categorization and feature inference involving dogs, but not between categorization involving dogs and cats.

Crucially, one can be selectively realist about the representations or processes in one's theory; process realism and representation realism are not all-or-nothing affairs. To take a concrete example, consider associative models of contingency (or causal) learning, such as the Rescorla–Wagner (1972) model. At a high level, these models posit that people learn correlations (possibly including causal strengths) by updating associative strengths between various factors. Computationally, they use a two-step process: given a new case, one (i) predicts the state of some factors based on their associative connections with observed factors and then (ii) changes the associative strengths based on the error in that prediction. Most standard interpretations of associative learning models are realist about the associative strengths, but not about the predictions generated in step (i). That is, associative strengths "really exist" somewhere in the mind/brain, while the "predictions" are just a computational device rather than being encoded anywhere. On the process side, most are realist about the update process in step (ii), but not about the prediction process from step (i).

A second dimension of variation in theoretical commitments is the intended scope or *degree of approximation*. All theories are approximate in that they exclude certain factors or possibilities. Variations on this dimension correspond to variations in which factors have been excluded, and thus the intended scope of the theory. As a concrete example, suppose one has a cognitive model of human addition that predicts that people will respond "93" when asked "What is 76 + 17?" A question arises when someone responds (erroneously) "83": what does this behavior imply for the model? One response is to hold that we have a (partial) falsification of the cognitive model, as it made a prediction that was not borne out. A different response is to argue that the behavior is due to some factor that falls outside the intended scope of the model (e.g., the individual was temporarily distracted), and so does not constitute counterevidence. The mathematical or computational specification of a theory does not include what is (deliberately) omitted from the theory, but we can only know how to respond to an apparent mismatch between theory and reality if we know what is being excluded.[8] This dimension is obviously related to the extent of realism, but they are importantly different. Realism is about how to interpret elements within the theory, while approximation/scope is about the elements that are not in the theory, specifically whether the absent factors are included but simply do not matter (according to the theory) or rather fall outside the intended scope of the theory.

This dimension is related to the performance/competence distinction, but it is not identical to it. Roughly speaking, a competence theory aims to characterize what people are capable of doing, while a performance theory aims to describe what they actually do. Typically, a competence theory explains and predicts people's ideal behavior if they did not face, for example, limits on memory and attention, cognitive processing errors, and other deleterious factors. A performance theory is supposed to account for these various factors so as to (approximately) capture actual human behavior in all its messy glory. The mathematical specification of a theory does not entail that it is either a performance or a competence theory; that distinction instead arises from one's commitments about the theory's intended scope. One could have many intended scopes in mind besides performance and competence theories, including ones that arise from abstracting away from only some human cognitive limitations and peculiarities, rather than all of them (as in competence theories). The performance versus competence theory distinction marks out two important points along this dimension of commitments but fails to capture the full range of possible commitments.

The third dimension of variation in a theory's commitments is the *intended optimality* (if any) of the theory: that is, is the theory claimed to be optimal (or rational), and if so, for what task(s) and relative to what competitors? We are often interested not just in *how* some behavior occurs (i.e., the underlying representations and processes that generate it) but also in *why* that behavior occurs; claims about optimality underlie these so-called why-explanations. Actually tracing the causal history (whether ontogenetic or phylogenetic) of a process or representation is often remarkably difficult, if not impossible. An alternative path to reach a why-explanation is to show that (i) some cognition is optimal relative to competitors, and

(ii) there are sufficiently strong pressures on the individual (or lineage) to push the individual to the optimal cognition (and those pressures actually obtained in these circumstances). If these elements can be shown, then we can conclude that the cognition occurs *because* it is optimal. This alternative path is a standard way to demonstrate, for example, that some physical trait constitutes an evolutionary adaptation (Rose & Lauder, 1996). In practice, many putative optimality-based explanations fail to show that there are actual selection pressures that would suffice to drive an individual toward the optimal cognition, or even to maintain an individual at the optimal cognition (Danks, 2008). Nonetheless a theory's closeness to optimality (relative to alternatives) is an important aspect of the theory, though not part of its mathematical/computational specification. Variation in this dimension clearly induces different metaphysical and epistemological commitments, as optimality claims imply constraints on the causal history of the cognition, and how the cognition should plausibly change under variations in the environment or learning history.

For all three of these dimensions of variation, there are many levels within each, rather than just three or four (as one typically finds in various accounts of "theoretical levels"). One's realist commitments, intended scope, and relative optimality of a theory can all vary relatively smoothly, or at least with sufficiently fine granularity that one can have many different levels of commitment within each dimension. This is one reason that Marr's levels are insufficient: three levels (or four, as in Anderson, 1990; or five, as in Poggio, 2012) are just not enough to capture all the different ways in which we can vary our commitments. More importantly, as noted earlier, Marr's levels conflate these three dimensions of variation. The computational level implies (a) weak realist commitments (particularly about processes); (b) significant approximation (since the theory is about how the system should solve a problem, rather than what it actually does); and (c) a high degree of optimality. At the other end, the implementation level implies (a*) strong realist commitments, (b*) little approximation, and (c*) very little optimality. There simply is no good way to use Marr's levels to describe, for example, rational process models (e.g., Denison, Bonawitz, Gopnik, & Griffiths, 2013) that have both strong realist commitments and significant optimality.

As a result of this conflation, the use of Marr's levels can be a mixed blessing. On the one hand, Marr's levels encourage more precise specification of a theory's extracomputational commitments, which is a positive compared to the bare statement of a computational model. On the other hand, use of Marr's terminology can force proponents of a theory into particular commitments that they would prefer to deny, as the levels bundle together commitments that should be kept separate. The usefulness of Marr's levels principally depends on whether the theory's proponent happens to endorse one of the limited sets of possible commitments that can be expressed in that trichotomy. None of those levels work for my case; the three dimensions introduced in this section will, however, do the job.

2.3 Previous Accounts of Intertheoretic Relations

The previous section focused on commitments as relatively abstract entities, rather than something that has a direct impact on scientific practice. We can operationalize these different types and levels of commitments by thinking about the relations that they induce between the cognitive theory *T* and other (possible) theories in both the cognitive and other domains. For example, if *T* is advocated as being purely instrumentalist (i.e., essentially no realist commitment), then a neural theory of the same phenomena need only generate the same input–output function as *T* (if *T* turns out to be true); the truth of *T* places no other constraints on the neural model. More generally, the different positions in this multidimensional "commitment space" imply different constraints that *T*'s being true (or accurate, or useful, or meeting whatever one's standard is for scientific theories) places on other theories. As one might suspect, the philosophy of science has long studied intertheoretic relations, particularly the question of which relation is most appropriate for cognitive theories; work on just that one question could fill a whole book (and has, as in Schouten & de Jong, 2012). Most of that work understands theories as falling on different levels of description, and so I will sometimes adopt that language, though such talk is really shorthand for theories occupying different points in the multidimensional commitment space. This section focuses on the two most prominent accounts—autonomy and reduction—and argues that neither can do the work that we require here. This argument will involve surveying a wide range of different possibilities, and it is important not to lose the forest for the trees: the key moral is not any particular objection against any particular account, but rather that the extant accounts do not seem particularly promising, and so we must develop a different account of intertheoretic constraints (as I do in section 2.4). Readers who already agree that reduction and autonomy are insufficient characterizations of intertheoretic relations are welcome to skip to the next section.

One possibility is that the proper intertheoretic relation, at least for theories in the cognitive sciences, is actually autonomy (Fodor, 1974, 1997): advocating a theory T at one level places (almost) no restrictions on theories U that have different commitments (i.e., are not direct competitors). That is, perhaps different theories are essentially independent, though they must agree on the relevant observable facts. In particular, if one advocates a higher-level theory, then perhaps the only resulting constraint on lower-level theories is that they generate the same (or approximately the same) input–output function.[9]

At least three different types of arguments have been offered in defense of autonomy. The first is an appeal to multiple realizability in the cognitive sciences: if a cognitive state can be realized in many different ways (e.g., in neurons, in silicon in a computer, etc.), then there is seemingly relatively little that we can infer from a theory at one level about theories at a different level. In these cases, commitments at one level would be essentially autonomous from commitments at a different level. A second argument depends on the (methodological) behaviorist claim that there is no real difference between two theories that predict the same behavior given the same stimulus. For example, Anderson (1990, p. 26) holds that "if two theorists propose two sets of mechanisms in two architectures that compute the same function, then they are proposing the same theory." If this claim is correct, then advocating a theory at one level clearly imposes only the constraint that theories at another level must match its input–output function. A third argument focuses on so-called rational analyses, some of which seek (roughly) to understand the ways in which human behavior can be understood as the rational solving of some task (Danks, 2008). For these analyses, one must show that "behavior can be ... described as conforming with ... some rational calculation" (Chater, Oaksford, Nakisa, & Redington, 2003, p. 67). But if such a demonstration is all that is required, then advocating a particular rational analysis (of this type) imposes no constraints on *how* that behavior is generated. The only constraint on lower-level theories is that they must somehow generate this behavior (see also Anderson, 1991a);

that is, the only relevant intertheoretic relation is one of input–output approximation.

Many objections to the autonomy position focus on the argument from multiple realizability (e.g., Bechtel & Mundale, 1999; Bickle, 1998; Kim, 1992). In particular, these responses aim to show that higher-level theories are not metaphysically autonomous from lower-level ones (though see Aizawa, 2009). I focus here on two different challenges, both stemming from scientific practice. First, as argued in the previous section, cognitive scientists can and do make realist commitments for a theory *T* that include more than just the input–output specification. The intertheoretic relation of autonomy does not, however, enable us to pass those commitments along to lower-level theories. Suppose, for example, that our theory of decision making includes a realist commitment to explicit, separable representations of outcome probabilities and outcome utilities. If autonomy is the only relevant intertheoretic relation, then any theory with the same input–output relations will be acceptable, even if it does not share those representational commitments. Moreover, the autonomy advocate can only allow the "downward flow" of representational or process commitments by giving up exactly on the motivating desire to be agnostic about the reality of theoretical elements. That is, a fundamental tension exists between the philosophical claim in the autonomy response that one should not (in general) attribute reality to cognitive representations and processes, and the methodological reality that cognitive scientists do this all the time in a seemingly justified manner.

A second, more practical concern about the autonomy response is that it fails to provide any guidance or insight for scientific practice. If one accepts a particular theory, then (on the autonomy account) no constraints are placed on theories at higher or lower levels, besides the bare constraint of a particular input–output pattern. In particular, if I accept a theory that posits a particular mechanism *M*, then I have no reason to look either for higher-level theories that posit a coarsened version of *M* or for lower-level theories that postulate a potential refinement of *M*. Even if such theories exist, the intertheoretic relation of autonomy does not accord them any privileged status with respect to *M*. Any theory with approximately the same input–output relation is equally acceptable, and so our acceptance of *M* provides only the weakest guidance to our search for, or acceptance of, theories at different levels. But cognitive science is filled with examples in which theories at one level are used to guide the search for theories at different levels. The autonomy response fails to give any explanation or justification for this practice (and, in fact, implies that no such justification is possible).

The other intertheoretic relation that has been extensively proposed in the philosophical literature on the cognitive sciences is *reduction*.[10] Roughly, a higher-level theory *H* reduces to a lower-level theory *L* when *L* is a finer-grained version of (something approximately equivalent to) *H*.[11] That is, as a first pass, *H* reduces to *L* when *L* "gives the details" of *H*. For example, many cognitive theories are thought to be reducible (at least in principle) to neuroscientific theories that show what is "really going on" that generates the behaviors that are captured by the cognitive theory. Theoretical commitments arise from an assumption that seems to be widely, but implicitly, shared: acceptance of *H* commits one to believe that *H* will ultimately reduce to true (lower-level) theories L_1, L_2, ... ; acceptance of *L* commits one to accept any (higher-level) *H* that reduces to *L*. Of course, these commitments turn critically on what exactly counts as a reduction. Different notions of reduction can be placed into two (rough) groups depending on whether they focus on equivalence or replacement.

Equivalence-based notions of reduction view the intertheoretic relation as one of identity of some sort. In the canonical version of "reduction as syntactic equivalence" (Nagel, 1961), a theory is a set of sentences in some logical vocabulary, and *H* reduces to *L* just when one can logically derive the statements of *H* from (i) the basic statements of *L*; (ii) "bridge principles" that tell us how to translate the basic predicates of *H* into the language of *L*; and (iii) perhaps some initial or boundary conditions in *L*. That is, *H* reduces to *L* just when one can derive *H* from *L*, given a translation of *H* and *L* into the same language (using the bridge principles) and potentially a restriction of the scope of application of *L*. There are various subtleties here, such as allowing for the possibility that *H* is false in certain respects and so the derivation should be of some corrected version *H** of the reduced theory (Dizadji-Bahmani, Frigg, & Hartmann, 2010; Schaffner, 1967). Alternately, the derivation of *H* from *L* might obtain only at some asymptotic limit or under a suitable approximation, but there are well-known adjustments that preserve reduction as syntactic equivalence in these cases (Batterman, 2002; Rueger, 2001, 2005).

The reduction-as-syntactic-equivalence view has been immensely influential over the past sixty years, but many problems arise when using it as a model of implied intertheoretic constraints. First, we are often interested in theoretical claims that are not readily expressible as equations or logical statements, such as "graphical models provide an architecture for describing representations in a common cognitive store." This statement does not correspond to any particular equation or logical statement; at best, it corresponds to a (very large) family of models. It is thus excluded from participating in any reduction-as-syntactic-equivalence relations, even though it seems to place constraints on other theories. Second, as argued earlier, an individual can have varying realist commitments about different parts of a theory. The syntactic equivalence approach treats all parts of the theory similarly and so cannot capture the possibility that some parts of a theory imply strong intertheoretic constraints while others imply only weak ones.

One natural way to try to salvage the reduction-as-equivalence idea is by modeling theories semantically, rather than syntactically. Arguably, the best-developed nonsyntactic view of scientific theories is the structuralist or model-theoretic account (Balzer, Moulines, & Sneed, 1987; Sneed, 1971; Stegmuller, 1976), and the corresponding account of reduction has been applied in the cognitive sciences (Bickle, 1998, 2003). At a high level, structuralist reduction is semantic containment: *H* reduces to *L* just when there is a mapping from the models of *H* into the models of *L*, where the models of a theory are not necessarily defined by any syntactic expressions.[12] Structuralist accounts of scientific theories use substantial set-theoretic machinery, but that is largely irrelevant to the resulting account of reduction; see Moulines and Polanski (1996) for the relevant technical details.

One problem with this account is that models are defined purely structurally, and so theories about quite different domains can seemingly reduce to one another, even though we ordinarily think that reductions should only occur between theories in the same domain (Moulines, 1984; Schaffner, 1967). The cross-domain problem can be solved by requiring "ontological reduction links" that identify the objects of possible models for *H* with at least some of the objects of possible models for *L* (Moulines, 1984). These ontological reduction links clearly block many spurious cross-domain reductions; Bickle (2002) argues that they block all of them. However, they do so by violating the motivating intuition of the structuralist program that the only relevant properties of elements in a model of a scientific theory are structural ones (Moulines, 1996). The structuralist is thus forced to choose between two intuitions: (i) structure matters, not domain;

and (ii) only within-domain reductions are acceptable. Regardless of choice, the structuralist account of reduction will not be left intact, so it cannot provide us with a suitable guide to capturing the intertheoretic constraints on commitments.

A third way to (try to) understand reduction in terms of equivalence is to incorporate both syntactic and semantic concerns by modeling reduction as "implementation": *H* reduces to *L* just when *L* implements *H* (Danks, 2008). One natural understanding of implementation is suggested by the common analogy between cognition and computer software. A computer language (e.g., C, C++, Java, Prolog, LISP, etc.) is defined by a set of basic methods and functions (and an acceptable syntax). Basic functions are defined solely by input–output relations (and the permissible inputs and outputs), and so they determine the "level of description" for computer programs written in that language. A computer program in one language can sometimes be *compiled* into a program in a different language. At an abstract level, compilation can be understood as replacing each higher-level basic function with a (possibly quite complex) sequence of lower-level basic functions. The only necessary constraint on a compiler is that each sequence of function calls (in the lower-level language) must have the same input–output relation as the particular higher-level basic function that is being replaced.

If cognition is essentially a computer program running on the hardware of the brain, then we should plausibly expect that higher-level cognitive theories could be compiled into lower-level theories about cognition (Danks, 2008). This general notion of reduction as implementation is arguably implicit in the use of box-and-arrow or data flow diagrams in areas such as cognitive neuropsychology. Importantly, however, box-and-arrow diagrams can tolerate ambiguity about the precise input–output function for each box and thus are more general than this notion of compilation. The precise mathematical details of a box are often (relatively) unimportant for understanding and using such a theory but are crucial for the compilation relation. The proposal that reduction is compilation requires our scientific theories to exhibit a degree of specificity that is simply absent from many theories that plausibly imply intertheoretic constraints; that is, the intertheoretic relation of compilation cannot provide the full story of intertheoretic constraints.

Instead of thinking about reduction as equivalence, we could think of it as replacement: *H* reduces to *L* just when *H* can be replaced (in some sense) by *L* or special cases of *L* (Churchland, 1985; Dizadji-Bahmani et al., 2010; Hooker, 1981a, 1981b). Of course, *H* might continue to be pragmatically useful—the equations might be easier to compute, the ontology might provide a handy shorthand, and so on—but *H* does not do any "real work." More precisely, there must be a structure or substructure within the language and framework of *L*, call it L^H, whose theoretical power is appropriately analogous to that of *H*. Consideration of canonical cases naturally points to three central aspects of theoretical power: (1) the explanatory scope of L^H should be approximately the same as *H*; (2) the ontologies should be approximately similar, with a (rough) map from *H* to L^H; and (3) there should be some (not-always-clear) similarity of structure between *H* and L^H. For all three of these aspects, the similarity between L^H and *H* can range over a continuum of values, and so this notion of reduction is not a binary relation but rather a "space" of reductions: identity (syntactic or semantic) between L^H and *H* arguably provides an origin point for this space, and other regions of the space correspond to reductions, significant theoretical corrections, and even eliminations.

This notion of reduction can clearly capture many different facets of the interactions between theories at different levels. The risk, however, is that it does so by being so flexible or vague that it loses all practical content. In particular, saying "*H* reduces to *L*" is supposed to license novel inferences, support novel connections between theories, permit novel claims about the presence or absence of theoretical objects in the world, and so on, but this notion of reduction does not (yet) support such novelties. For example, one dimension is ontological overlap, which can occur to various degrees and should presumably provide us with a guide to what we should do with the ontology of *H*: (i) if it provides a shorthand for the ontology of L^H, then retain it; (ii) if it can be adjusted slightly to result in a shorthand, then amend it; and (iii) if it is sufficiently different, then eliminate it and find a more appropriate, upper-level ontology. This decision thus depends on our ability to actually locate the reduction somewhere along this dimension, but no principled method of doing so has been provided. It may be possible both to make the account precise and also to retain the underlying intuitions, but that has not yet happened, and many promising accounts have foundered precisely when people tried to make them precise (though Dizadji-Bahmani et al., 2010, suggest that perhaps precision can be attained only through domain-specific inquiries).

Moreover, even if this account of reduction could be made to work, there are extremely general reasons to worry that reduction cannot provide the full story about intertheoretic constraints and commitments. First, the statement "*H* reduces to *L*" implies that one has definite, positive theoretical proposals to serve as the relata. Scientific practice, however, rarely involves such precise proposals, at least in many domains. One might find, for example, a claim that two variables are associated, or some functional relationship falls in some (perhaps large) family, or some previously considered theoretical possibility is incorrect (but without any further information about which theoretical possibility actually is right). These different types of theoretical claims can all imply commitments at other levels even if there is no particular broad theory in which they fit (and so no appropriate relata for reduction). Second, essentially all accounts of reduction imply that it is a transitive relation: if *H* reduces to *L* and *L* reduces to *S*, then *H* reduces to *S*. Intertheoretic commitments do not, in general, seem to be similarly transitive. *H* can constrain *L* and *L* can constrain *S* without *H* constraining *S*; for example, *H* could constrain *L* to explain phenomenon *P*, and *L* could constrain *S* in terms of truth (perhaps via a reduction), but without *H* constraining *S* in any interesting way (Putnam, 1975). *Some* implied intertheoretic commitments might be grounded in the relation of reduction, but it does not seem that all can be understood in this way.

Third, and perhaps most important, reduction is a between-level relation in the sense that *H* and *L* are presumed to be theories at different levels about roughly similar phenomena.[13] Intertheoretic constraints can arise, however, between theories that do not stand in this type of "hierarchical" arrangement. Consider, for example, theories of causal learning and reasoning (see chap. 4) and the causal model theory of concepts (see chap. 5). These two types of theories investigate different phenomena—learning the causal structure of the world in the former case, and grouping individuals based on shared causal structures in the latter case—and so cannot possibly stand in a reductive relationship in either direction. Nonetheless they clearly constrain each other; at the least, they both depend on representations of causal structure, and so information about one theory can be informative about the other. We thus need a more general account of intertheoretic constraints to allow for constraints between theories that do not stand in a "higher-versus-lower-level" relationship.

One final defense of the centrality of reduction is that it can serve as a methodological guide to the intertheoretic commitments that scientists *should* make in practice. That is, perhaps the importance of reductions is that scientists will do better if they actively seek to find them, rather than depending on other types of intertheoretic relations to guide their inquiry (Barendregt & van Rappard, 2004; Bickle, 2003). There have certainly been instances in which the search for a reduction has led to scientific progress, but the general methodological stance is overly limiting. In general, *any* intertheoretic connections—whether reductions or not—advance our scientific understanding, and so we should seek all of them. Of course, reduction is arguably the strongest possible interlevel constraint, so it can sometimes make sense to focus on finding reductions of some theory *H*. But any interlevel constraints can advance scientific understanding, and so we should aim to understand the full scope of constraints, where reduction is a special, though particularly salient, case.

2.4 Connecting Theories through Constraints

The previous section concluded that scientific theories are connected, both in theory and in practice, by constraints, rather than reductions or autonomy. This section aims to flesh out just what these constraints could be. At a high level, one theory *S* constrains another theory *T* if the extent to which *S* has some theoretical virtue *V* (e.g., truth, predictive accuracy, explanatory power) matters for the extent to which *T* has *V*. More colloquially, *S* constrains *T* just when, if we care about *T* along some dimension, then we should also care about *S* along that same dimension. The intertheoretic relations in the previous section focused almost exclusively on the theoretical virtue of truth, but there are many other dimensions along which constraints can apply, and constraints along one dimension need not track constraints along a different dimension. For example, *T* can reduce to *S* (and so truth-constrain it[14]) while not imposing any constraint on its explanatory power (Putnam, 1975).

This rough statement of "constraint" is quite high-level and vague in important respects, but it implies certain properties. First, between-theory constraints are nonsubjective: the beliefs of the scientists are irrelevant, unless the relevant theoretical virtue involves those beliefs in some irreducible way (as on some analyses of explanatory power). Of course, scientists may not realize that a particular constraint exists and so might fail to exploit it in their theorizing. But whether a constraint exists is a matter of mathematics, the structure of the theories, and so forth, rather than any knowledge or reasoning by particular scientists. Second, this notion of constraint is agnostic about almost all aspects of *S* and *T*: the theories need not be in different, comparable levels (i.e., one being higher-level than the other) or even be full-fledged theories. Rather, *S* and *T* can be qualitative claims or other partial theories, as long as one is relevant for the other (for the particular theoretical virtue). We can thus capture cases such as causal learning theories placing constraints on causal model theories of concepts.

A third, less obvious implication is that constraint is comparative in both relata. That is, whether *S* constrains *T* depends not just on *S* and *T* but also on the alternatives to both *S* and *T*. For example, suppose that *D* is a theory of case-by-case changes in causal judgment and *A* is the asymptotic (or equilibrium) characterization of *D*; in other words, *D* is one way to implement *A* (in a step-by-step manner).[15] As in all cases of implementation, the obvious truth constraint here is "if *D* is true, then *A* must be true," and by contraposition, "if *A* is false, then *D* must be false." A less-obvious constraint is: "if *A* is true, then all dynamical models *D** with non-*A* asymptotics must be false." Thus, at the extreme of only one dynamical model for each asymptotic theory, we get an additional constraint: *A* being true implies that *D* must also be true.[16] Similarly, if *D* is false, then *A* is less likely to be true and, at the "one dynamics per asymptotics" extreme, can actually be rejected immediately. In general, the spaces of alternatives for both relata shape the constraint relation—both whether it exists and the particular form it takes. This relativity to alternatives implies that uses of constraint in actual scientific practice may be dependent on history and context: whether we say that *S* constrains *T* (and how) can depend on the recognized alternatives, which are partly a function of the history of the scientific domain. Of course, whether *S* constrains *T* (relative to possibility sets **S** and **T**) is not *actually* historically determined; rather, what can be history dependent is whether the scientists focus on possibility sets **S** and **T** that exhibit a useful constraint relation, or sets **S*** and **T*** that exhibit no such useful relation.

Aspects of the constraint relation between S and T are, however, sometimes relatively independent of the spaces of alternatives. For example, the "obvious" truth constraint mentioned in the previous paragraph—if D implements A, then: if D is true, then A is true—does not depend on the alternatives to D and A. Only the converse truth constraint is alternative dependent, which perhaps helps to explain why the obvious one has received more attention in discussions of implementing theories. More generally, reduction and autonomy imply constraints that are typically alternative independent, though in different ways. Reduction usually implies that S and T are, in some sense, interchangeable, regardless of the alternatives. In contrast, autonomy typically implies that there are (almost) no constraints between S and T, regardless of the alternatives. But although these two constraints are largely alternative independent, many are not.

More precise statements about the nature of constraint require focusing on particular theoretical virtues. For concreteness, I will focus for the remainder of this section on an admittedly speculative and programmatic account of constraints relative to the cognitive virtue of "truth," as it is closely connected to the issue of commitments. I use scare quotes around the word "truth" because the argument is frequently made that all theories are idealizations of one sort or another (Cartwright, 1983; Kitcher, 2001), and so it does not make sense to speak nonmetaphorically about the truth of scientific theories. If one endorses such a view, then the word "truth" should be read for the remainder of this section as referring to the preferred dimension(s) of evaluation for a set of competing, mutually exclusive theories (e.g., accuracy with respect to the features of the world that influence our predictive and control capabilities, as in Kitcher, 2001).

For a formal model of this notion of truth constraint, we start with the relevant dynamics: if S truth-constrains T, then (by definition) learning about the truth of S should change how one thinks about the truth of T. This formulation naturally suggests using probabilities: perhaps S constrains T with respect to truth if and only if $P(T \mid S) \neq P(T)$. That is, one theory S places truth constraints on another T whenever the probability of T changes when we condition on the truth of S. This idea generalizes to Jeffrey (1965) conditionalization, in which we condition on S having some probability, rather than being definitely true. Despite the superficial appeal, however, a model of truth constraints using probabilities faces significant challenges whether we interpret the probabilities subjectively or objectively.

A subjective interpretation of probabilities is that they represent degrees of belief, either actual or rational. Probability distributions assume that the possibility space is exhaustive: we need to articulate the space of all possible theories in **S** and **T**. In many actual scientific cases, however, we want to allow for the possibility that the truth is "something else," and it is unclear what are or should be (a) the probability of something else, and (b) the probability of other possibilities given that something else is true. Relatedly, a definition in terms of probability distributions presumes that the space of alternatives is fixed through time: we cannot account (in a principled way) for the introduction of novel theories that were not previously included. If the probabilities are supposed to represent actual degrees of belief, then this condition almost certainly cannot be met, as new scientific theories are constantly introduced. If we instead interpret probabilities as rational degrees of belief, then we must have some notion of what the probabilities should be for theories that no one has ever considered. Finally, the task of assigning complete, consistent probability distributions to rich spaces (such as the space of scientific theories in some domain) requires that one solve uncomputable functions (Gaifman & Snir, 1982). That is, a suitable probability distribution sometimes cannot be generated by *any* computational device (though perhaps this problem could be avoided by using distributions that are not too incoherent, according to one of the measures proposed in Schervish, Seidenfeld, & Kadane, 2003).

One might instead interpret the probabilities objectively, but it is unclear just what it would mean to have objective probabilities of the truth of scientific theories. The laws of the universe are presumably set in a "one-shot" event, and there is no clear understanding of what a "limiting frequency" would be for them. Similarly, symmetry or other physicalist considerations will offer no help here. More generally, scientific theories seem to be either true or false, not varying in probability (though our judgments or confidence can obviously vary).

We can instead model truth constraints using the general framework of rational belief change: *S* truth-constrains *T* if and only if a change in belief in *S* from time t_1 to time t_2 would, for a fully knowledgeable agent, rationally produce a change in belief in *T* from t_1 to t_2. There is no assumption here that the change in belief in *S* is rational. Rather, this account of constraint essentially models it as a conditional: if belief in *S* changes (for whatever reason), then belief in *T* should rationally change as well, assuming that the individual understands the implications of her beliefs. This final clause is important, as the existence of a constraint does not depend on whether an individual scientist actually knows about the connections between the theories. This account thus has the (correct and natural) implication that one productive scientific activity can be the discovery of intertheoretic constraints, as this can enable us to change our beliefs more intelligently.

An enormous variety of models of rational belief change have been proposed that approach the problem from a corresponding range of perspectives. (A hopelessly partial menu of options includes Alchourrón, Gärdenfors, & Makinson, 1985; Bovens & Hartmann, 2003; Gärdenfors, 2003; Levi, 1991, 2004; Teller, 1976.) Crucially, many of these accounts are qualitative in nature rather than requiring quantitative probabilities, and they allow for changes in the possibility space (i.e., the set of possible theories) over time. As a result, these accounts are not necessarily susceptible to the same types of objections as probability-based accounts. One might be surprised that the resulting notion of truth constraint is relative to a particular standard of rationality, but this rationality-relativity is actually a natural property for a theory of truth constraints. The original core intuition was that the truth of *S* should matter for the truth of *T*, and we must incorporate a normative theory to capture the "should" in that statement. If one's theory of rationality says that one ought not change one's beliefs about *T* in light of new information about *S*, then it is completely natural to say that *S* does not truth-constrain *T* (relative to that standard).

To help make this more concrete, we can provide the formal analogues to various truth constraints that regularly arise in scientific practice. If *H* reduces to *L* given conditions *C*, then an increase in belief in *L*&*C* should rationally also increase belief in *H*. At the limit of full acceptance of *L*&*C*, one should rationally also accept *H* fully. If *H* is instead fully autonomous from *L* (including differing inputs and outputs, so there is no constraint on that front), then belief in *H* should rationally not change in response to changes in belief about *L*. In addition to these two standard intertheoretic relations, scientists also frequently talk about one theory *S* being inconsistent with another theory *T*, which implies that changes in belief in *S* should rationally prompt the opposite change in *T*. At the limit of full acceptance of *S*, *T* should rationally be rejected. This account even extends to more qualitative types of constraints, such as two theories mutually supporting each other. For example, causal learning theories and causal model theories of concepts use the same representational framework and so can be understood as mutually supporting: each makes the other more probable. More generally, arguments based on converging evidence from disparate domains, measurement methods, or processes are completely standard in psychology[17] and correspond here to the symmetric constraint that increases (or decreases) in belief in *S* should rationally lead to increases (or decreases) in belief in *T*, and vice versa.

This proposal clearly exhibits the properties previously identified for intertheoretic constraints. First, whether *S* constrains *T* is a nonsubjective matter, as the scientists' local, particular knowledge or beliefs do not influence whether a fully knowledgeable agent rationally ought to change her beliefs. Second, many models of rational belief revision require only that we be able to talk coherently about beliefs, rather than focusing on fully developed theories. This account of truth constraints can thus be appropriately agnostic about *S* and *T*; we need only be able to specify them clearly enough that we can capture (and derive) their relations to each other from the perspective of rational belief revision. Third, in this account, truth constraints are clearly comparative in both relata, since questions of rational belief revision can turn on the alternative beliefs that one has available or considers plausible (or even just possible). Thus this model provides a reasonable initial model of truth constraints. Moreover, even if it turns out to be wrong in details, it points toward a way to generalize our understanding of intertheoretic relations beyond the simple ones of reduction and autonomy.

2.5 Putting the Pieces Together

The previous two sections took a significant detour through philosophical issues, but that was necessary to make sense of the commitments that one can have about a cognitive theory. In particular, claiming realist commitments for a theory is essentially shorthand for a complicated set of intertheoretic constraints, including constraints on future empirical observations and manipulations. The standard language used in cognitive science is insufficient to express these complex commitments. The choices are not just minimal instrumentalism versus full-blooded realism versus complete theoretical autonomy; rather, there is a continuum of commitments that cannot be determined solely by the mathematical or computational specification of some cognitive theory. Having made this detour, I now have the language and resources to be clear about the commitments of the cognitive account presented in the remainder of the book.

I propose a particular cognitive architecture in which many of our cognitive representations are well modeled by graphical models. This account is committed to the realism of these representations but is largely agnostic with regard to realism about the processes (though there must be suitable processes that can use the information encoded in the representations). More specifically, the account proposes that there are persistent objects in the mind that subserve a wide range of cognitive processes, but where the precise processing method might, but need not, be identical in all domains or all contexts. The account thus places both upward constraints on accounts of human behavior (e.g., about the effects of learning context on subsequent choices) and downward constraints on neural accounts (e.g., there should be some persistent neural object, state, or disposition that is the representation). It also points toward various formal questions that are neither higher nor lower level (e.g., can distributed representations capture the types of transformations that are an important part of the power of graphical models?). And finally, precisely because the proposed architecture is wide-ranging in scope, the data to support it will come from many different domains. I do not propose this architecture because it works for just causal learning, or just categorization, or just certain decision phenomena. Rather, I propose this architecture because it is the best account that explains all these domains, and others.

3 A Primer on Graphical Models

3.1 Graphical Models as Representations of Relevance

The previous chapter laid the philosophical groundwork for the cognitive architecture that I will present. This chapter introduces and explores the framework of graphical models, the computational and mathematical basis of that architecture. The main thread of the chapter focuses on a conceptual introduction, with mathematical details provided in sections marked with an asterisk (*); the reader can skip those sections with little loss of (qualitative) understanding. Section 3.1 explores the common elements shared by all graphical models, with subsequent sections examining the details of specific model types. As with many formal frameworks, a high-level grasp of different graphical model types suffices to understand most uses of them. The technical details are important to ensure that nothing is swept under the rug, but are often largely irrelevant to many uses of the framework. Readers interested in additional details about graphical models should consult one of the many available introductions, both for graphical models in general (e.g., Koller & Friedman, 2009; Lauritzen, 1996) and for specific model types (see references cited in the specific sections of this chapter).

At their core, graphical models can be understood as compact representations of relevance relations, where different types of graphical models represent different types of relevance (e.g., informational, causal, probabilistic, communicative). They thus address a key challenge for any cognitive agent: namely, determining what matters and, often equally importantly, what can be ignored. The term "graphical model" encompasses many different types of mathematical models, including Bayesian networks (also called Bayes nets), structural equation models, random Markov fields,

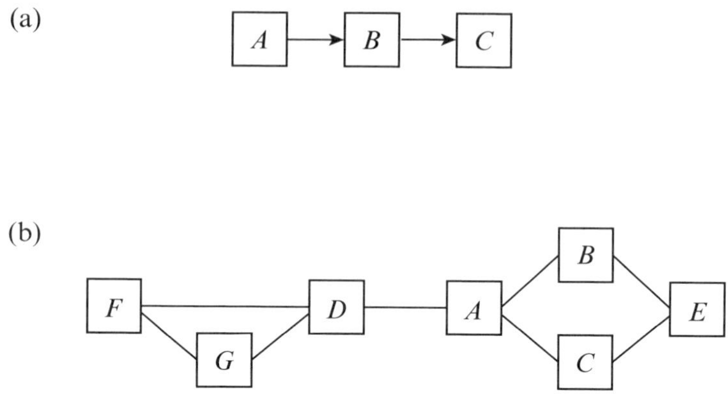

Figure 3.1
Example graphs.

hidden Markov models, influence diagrams, social networks, command-and-control structures, and more. At their cores, these models all have a *graph*: a diagram of nodes and edges that encodes the qualitative relationships (see fig. 3.1 for examples).

From a purely mathematical perspective, the nodes are simply objects, and the edges can be undirected ($A — B$), directed ($A \rightarrow B$), or bidirected ($A \leftrightarrow B$). (In general, italics will be used to denote nodes.) In talking about the graph structure, we often use terminology based on physical relationships. A node is *adjacent* to another one just when there is an edge (of any sort and any direction) between them. For example, B and C are adjacent in figure 3.1a but not in figure 3.1b; A and B are adjacent in both. A *path* between two nodes is a sequence of edges that one can traverse (without regard for edge direction) to get from one node to the other. For example, there is a path from A to C in figure 3.1a, and a path from F to E in figure 3.1b. Actually, there is at least one path between every pair of nodes in figure 3.1b, and so we say that graph is *connected*. For graphs with directed edges, we also use genealogical terminology: for example, in figure 3.1a, A is B's *parent*, B is A's *child*, and so forth. More generally, for any node X, the set of all parents of X, plus the parents of parents of X, plus … , is called the *ancestors* of X. The *descendants* of X are defined similarly.

Of course, we are rarely interested in the graph solely as a mathematical object; rather, we want it to represent something, and so the semantics of the nodes and edges matter. The nodes in a graphical model can correspond to individuals (e.g., in a social network or a command-and-control structure), variables (e.g., in a Bayes net or random Markov field), or something else (e.g., decision nodes in an influence diagram or decision network). The edges can similarly have different meanings, but the edge semantics always involve direct relevance, whether direct causation, a direct communication or social connection, direct probabilistic relevance, or some other sort of direct connection. The repeated word "direct" in the previous sentence is critical: graphical edges do not denote simply that one node matters for another, but rather that one node matters for another *even after we account for all the other nodes in the graph*. In figure 3.1a, for example, *A* is indirectly relevant for *C*, but not directly relevant; its relevance is only through the intermediary of *B*. As this example suggests, direct relevance depends on the other nodes that are included in the graph. To take a contrived example, exposure to the cold virus (probabilistically) causes infection, which (probabilistically) causes symptoms. If we model all three factors, then we have the causal graph *Exposure* → *Infection* → *Symptoms*. If we instead exclude the node *Infection* from our graph, then we have simply *Exposure* → *Symptoms*. In other words, *Exposure* can be either a direct or an indirect cause of *Symptoms* depending on what else we include in the graph. The graph structure can change as we add or remove nodes, even between nodes that are neither added nor removed; these changes follow principled rules that will be discussed in section 4.3.

An important constraint on the overall graph semantics is that the node and edge meanings "fit" appropriately. For example, if the edges are to be understood as causal connections, then the nodes should refer to things that can stand in causal relationships. In the other direction, if the nodes are variables, then the edges should not be, for example, communication relations; what would it mean for an instantiation of an *Exposure* variable to "communicate" (literally, not metaphorically) with an instance of an *Infection* variable? In terms of representation, this node-edge semantic coherence is a local matter: the edges or nodes in a single graph can have different semantics (e.g., causal versus informational edges in influence diagrams), as long as each node-edge-node triple is coherent.[1] Most graphical model types have one or two canonical interpretations, and so we will generally focus on those.

The graph component of a graphical model captures qualitative relevance relations, but it cannot convey quantitative information; nodes are either adjacent or not. For example, a causal graph tells us whether one node causes another, but it cannot convey the strengths of those causal relations. Thus almost all graphical model types have a quantitative component that complements the graph and represents this more precise, often numerical, information. There are many different quantitative components that one can use, including both numerical representations (e.g., joint probability distributions, linear equations) and more categorical representations (e.g., whether the connection is positive or negative, the order of magnitude of the influence). This quantitative component is sometimes provided only implicitly, such as in most social network models.

Each type of quantitative component has a corresponding notion of *independence*: *A* is independent of *B* just when learning about *A* gives no information (in the quantitative component) about *B*. For example, my shirt color and the temperature in Moscow are independent of each other: if you learn that I am wearing a blue shirt, then that provides no information about the current temperature in Russia. Zero correlation is one example of independence:[2] if *A* is uncorrelated with *B*, then information about *A* does not help at all when trying to predict *B*. Alternately, nodes can be *dependent*: learning about *A* does help to predict *B*. For example, the temperature in Pittsburgh and the temperature in Moscow are dependent: learning that it is snowing in Pittsburgh is informative about the likely temperature range in Moscow. Of course, dependence need not be perfect, as we see in this example. Snow in Pittsburgh means that it is winter and so probably colder than the yearly average in Moscow, but we cannot use snow in Pittsburgh to predict the *exact* temperature in Moscow. In general, the function of many standard statistical tests is precisely to help us determine whether two factors are (probably) dependent or independent.[3]

As with relevance, we need to distinguish between direct and indirect in/dependence: two factors can be dependent in isolation, but independent once we learn about other factors in the system. For example, *Symptoms* depend on *Exposure*; learning that I was exposed to a virus is informative about whether I exhibit symptoms. At the same time, however, the two are (arguably) independent once we control for *Infection*: if you already know that I was infected (or not), then learning that I was exposed is no longer helpful in predicting my symptoms. More generally, we say that *A* and *B* are *independent conditional on* C if, given that we already know about *C*'s value, learning about *A*'s value does not help us to predict *B*'s value. Many multivariate statistical tests (e.g., multifactor ANOVAs, tests of significant coefficients in a multivariate linear regression, etc.) are designed and used to determine whether two factors are independent conditional on some other factors.

Graphical models have two distinct components—the graph and the quantitative representation—and those must be connected somehow to yield a single coherent model. The natural coherence constraint is that the graph and the quantitative component should express exactly the same direct relevance or dependence relations. That is, nodes A and B should be directly relevant in the graph if and only if they are directly dependent in the quantitative representation. This constraint is almost always formalized in two separate assumptions that capture the two "directions of fit." In one direction, a so-called *Markov assumption* says that "if two nodes are not adjacent in the graph, then they are independent in the quantitative component (perhaps conditional on some set of other nodes in the graph)." That is, the Markov assumption requires that each direct nonrelevance in the graph have a corresponding (conditional) independence in the quantitative component. In the other direction, we assume that "if two nodes are (conditionally) independent in the quantitative component, then they are not adjacent in the graph." There are many names for this latter assumption (e.g., Minimality, Simplicity, Stability, Faithfulness); I will refer to these as Faithfulness assumptions because that is a now-standard name for one graphical model type used in cognitive science. The exact Markov and Faithfulness assumptions depend on the types of graph and quantitative component in the graphical model, and we explore some instances in sections 3.2 and 3.3. But all graphical models need these two assumptions to maintain full coherence between the two components.[4]

A graphical model in isolation is not particularly useful; one wants to be able to use the representation to predict and explain the world, or to assist with decisions, or to perform many other tasks. Prediction and inference algorithms can be quite local in graphical models precisely because they encode direct relevance relations in the graph. For example, predicting the value of some node requires one to know only the values of "close" (in the graph) nodes. As a result, prediction and inference in a graphical model are usually relatively fast. More importantly, these processes typically scale well as the scope of the graphical model grows: one can (usually) add a large number of nodes to the graphical model without incurring a substantial computational cost in prediction and inference. For example, predictions about node *A* in figure 3.1b depend only on nodes *B*, *C*, and *D*, regardless of how many other nodes we add to the graph (as long as the additional nodes are not adjacent to *A*). This modularity is one key advantage of graphical models and is particularly attractive in thinking about them as models of cognitive representations. Graphical models can be wide-ranging but not suffer computationally when used for prediction and inference, just as our knowledge can be wide-ranging, while we (mostly) attend only to relevant factors.

I indicated earlier that nodes are "just" objects in the graph, but sometimes a node can play a special role as a "switch": as the value of this so-called *context node* changes, the graph for the other variables will change as well. For example, it is normally the case for men that their age is a cause of whether they can grow a beard—the natural graph is *Age* → *Ability to grow a beard*—while these two factors are normally independent in women, and so their graph has no edge between *Age* and *Ability to grow a beard*. We can encode the way that the graph changes depending on one's sex by including a *Sex* node that is a parent of both of these nodes (as shown in Boutilier, Friedman, Goldszmidt, & Koller, 1996; Poole & Zhang, 2003; Zhang & Poole, 1999). The use of context nodes does not increase the representational power of graphical models; mathematically, anything that can be represented with them can also be represented without them. However, their presence can significantly improve both the interpretability (by human eyes) of a graphical model and the computational speed and efficiency of inference in such models. Context nodes will be important in section 5.4.

There are many ways to construct a graphical model. One might simply base it on expert knowledge, for example. More interestingly, we can often learn the graph structure and quantitative parameters from data, even if we have little or no background knowledge. The key to this learning is that essentially all graphical models make predictions about how the world should be. That is, they are almost all *generative models*: representations that can be used to generate "typical" data (according to the model). We can thus find, for any particular data set, the graphical models—graphs plus quantitative components—that could possibly or plausibly have produced data like those. Graphical models give us a language for talking about structures that produce data, and so learning such models from a data set is "just" a matter of finding the structures that yield those particular data. Of course, it is a much trickier matter to develop computationally tractable learning algorithms, which is why scare quotes were used in the previous sentence. Nonetheless, for most of the specific graphical model types discussed in this chapter, efficient and tractable structure learning algorithms of various flavors have been developed and deployed effectively to learn graphical models from data. If there is, for a given data set **D**, a graphical model G that exactly captures it, *and* if both assumptions (Markov and Faithfulness) are satisfied for G, then we will say that G *perfectly represents* **D**.

This section has focused on graphical models as a whole, which has necessitated broad brushstrokes in terms of their features. In practice, one always uses one or another type of graphical model, as well as type-specific restrictions that improve learning, inference, and prediction. We thus turn now to these more specific types of graphical models, with a particular focus on the two model types that will reappear in later chapters.

3.2 Directed Acyclic Graph (DAG) Models

Many relationships in the world are asymmetric, including causal, communication, and hierarchical ones: virus exposure causes symptoms, but symptoms do not cause virus exposure; the general commands the sergeant, but not vice versa; and so forth. These asymmetric relations can be represented with directed edges in the graph component, such as $E \rightarrow S$, $G \rightarrow S$. Moreover, in many of these situations, the full set of relations does not involve a cycle; it is not the case that A has the (asymmetric) relation to B, B has it to C, and so on until we get back to A. For many causal systems, for example, there is no sequence of causes such that one factor causes itself. (One might object that causal cycles such as feedback systems are ubiquitous in nature, but they are only cyclic *through time*; as discussed later in this section, they are acyclic when we explicitly represent time.) Thus one natural type of graphical model uses directed acyclic graphs (DAGs): graphs with (a) only directed edges and (b) no directed cycles: one cannot start from node X and follow a path (that respects the arrow directions) that leads back to X. Figure 3.1a, for example, is a DAG.

Many different types of graphical models are based on DAGs, including Bayesian networks, also known as Bayes nets (Pearl, 2000; Spirtes, Glymour, & Scheines, 2000), (recursive) structural equation models (SEMs) (Bollen,

1989; Kaplan, 2009), and influence diagrams or decision networks (Howard & Matheson, 1981; Shachter, 1986, 1988). In particular, we focus here on DAG-based graphical models in which the nodes correspond to *variables*—factors that take on different values depending on the particular individual or context. For example, *Exposure* is a variable, since it can take the values *Yes* or *No* (or perhaps additional values to encode the intensity of the exposure). In general, any property of individuals has a corresponding variable that ranges over the possible values of that property. Variables can be either *discrete* or *continuous*, depending on whether they have finitely or infinitely many values, respectively.[5] Bayes nets and SEMs differ on precisely this dimension: Bayes nets are for sets of discrete variables, and SEMs are for sets of continuous variables.[6]

Recall that the general Markov assumption says: "If there is no edge in the graph, then the nodes should be (conditionally) independent in the quantitative component." For DAG-based graphical models over variables, we can refine this assumption to say: "Any variable is independent of its nondescendants, conditional on its graphical parents." That is, for any node in the graph, learning about a nondescendant tells us nothing about the variable, given that we already know the values of its immediate parents. Consider, for example, trying to predict the value of *Symptoms* in the DAG shown in figure 3.2. If we know nothing at all, then learning about *Exposure* clearly gives us some information about *Symptoms*, as the latter is "downstream" of the former. However, once we know the value of the parent of *Symptoms* (i.e., *Infection*), then *Exposure* and *Symptoms* are (statistically) independent of each other.

The Faithfulness assumption in DAG-based graphical models can be stated simply as "The only independencies are those implied by the Markov assumption."[7] The two major practical implications of this assumption in DAG-based graphical models are to rule out (i) deterministic systems, though "almost-deterministic" ones (i.e., those with arbitrarily small amounts of noise) are fine; and (ii) exactly counterbalancing pathways. A hypothetical example of the latter possibility can be seen in

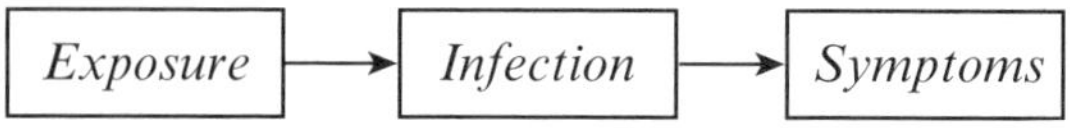

Figure 3.2
Example chain DAG.

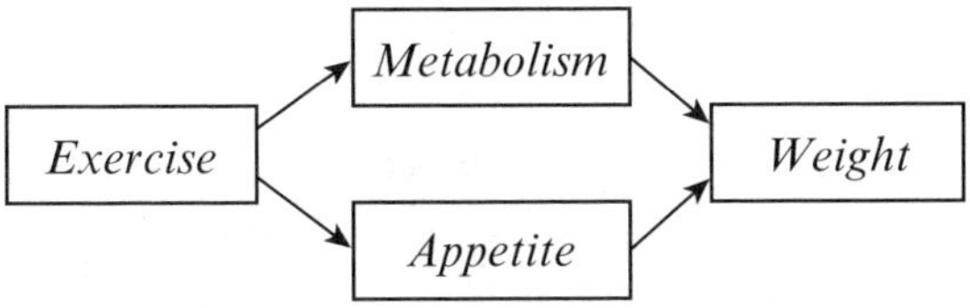

Figure 3.3
Example complex DAG.

figure 3.3. Suppose that *Exercise* increases one's *Metabolism*, which reduces one's *Weight*. At the same time, *Exercise* increases one's *Appetite* (and thus food intake), which increases one's *Weight*. In theory, these two different pathways could *exactly* balance each other, so that variations in *Exercise* were independent of *Weight*. If the causal mechanisms are balanced, then changing one's exercise will not actually matter for one's weight, though they are (in the world) causally connected. In this case, we would have a violation of the Faithfulness assumption, as we have an independence that is not predicted by the Markov assumption.

The Markov and Faithfulness assumptions jointly imply that the quantitative component is modular: we can express every variable as a function of only its graphical parents. That is, we can encode the behavior of the full system simply by encoding how each variable depends on its graphical parents. There is also a purely graphical criterion (called d-separation; see Geiger, Verma, & Pearl, 1989) that one can use to infer the full set of dependencies and independencies in the quantitative component. One can thereby rapidly compute, for any particular variable V, exactly which variables provide information about V given knowledge about any other variables in the graph. The DAG thus enables significant computational savings in both representation and inference, precisely because one can determine, based solely on the graph, exactly which variables are relevant in a wide range of conditions. This modularity also makes it possible to develop computationally efficient algorithms for learning the DAG structure from observational or experimental data (Chickering, 2002; Spirtes et al., 2000). Details about the exact form of this modularity for Bayes nets and SEMs, as well as a precise statement of the d-separation criterion, are provided in section 3.2.1.

One of the most prevalent uses of DAG-based graphical models is to represent causal structures. It is important to realize that nothing in the formalism compels such an interpretation. One can easily use a DAG-based graphical model simply as a representation of the probabilistic or statistical dependencies between variables; in this case, the directions on the arrows arise because of the particular structure of the between-variable independencies and do not necessarily reflect any (nonstatistical) asymmetry in the world. That being said, there are situations in which one can interpret a DAG-based graphical model causally: $C \rightarrow E$ does not simply capture a dependence but additionally means "C causes E." The notion of causation here is a relatively instrumental or pragmatic one: roughly, if one could somehow manipulate C from outside the modeled causal system, then E would (probabilistically) change (Spirtes et al., 2000; Woodward, 2003). A causal interpretation does not necessarily imply any strong metaphysical commitments about the nature of causation, but only a set of commitments about how the system would behave in various hypothetical (and perhaps unrealizable) situations.

When one gives a causal interpretation to a DAG-based graphical model, the assumptions must change accordingly. The causal version of the Markov assumption says: "Any variable is independent of its noneffects conditional on its direct causes." Recall that whether one node is a parent of another can be relative to the other nodes in the graph. Similarly, whether one variable is a direct cause of another can depend on the other variables under consideration; *Exposure* is an indirect cause of *Symptoms* if we include *Infection*, but a direct one if we omit it. The causal Faithfulness assumption simply changes to refer to the causal Markov assumption. Numerous philosophical debates have developed around the causal Markov and causal Faithfulness assumptions, principally whether they hold necessarily or only contingently in the world, and if contingently, whether statistical tests can determine if they obtain in some particular domain (Cartwright, 2002; Glymour, 1999; Hausman & Woodward, 1999, 2004). It is certainly important to be clear about whether one is interpreting a DAG-based model causally, else one can make any number of erroneous inferences about what would happen in response to various actions. At the same time, the causal interpretation is clearly a legitimate one, so we will not delve deeply into the philosophical debates.[8]

Many variations on this core theme have been developed for DAG-based graphical models, as slight modifications are introduced to capture a specific phenomenon. Two such variations are important in thinking about

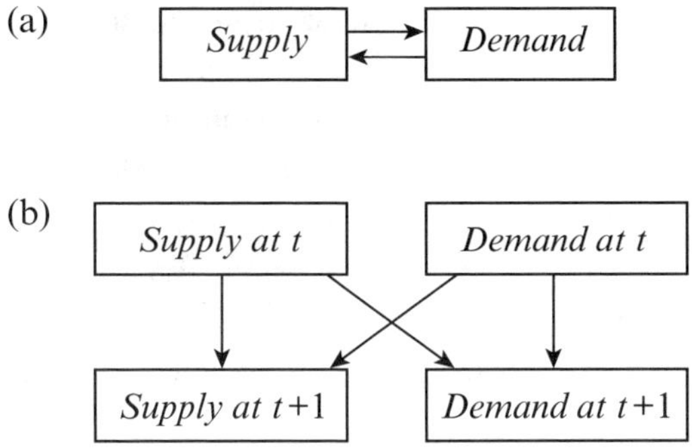

Figure 3.4
(a) Supply-demand cyclic graph; (b) temporally indexed acyclic graph.

cognitive representations. First, one often needs to model processes that unfold in time. Most prominently, many cyclic causal structures involve feedback loops through time and we must adjust the standard DAG-based framework to capture these temporally extended processes. For example, talk of the *Supply–Demand* feedback cycle in figure 3.4a is really shorthand for a more complex dynamical story: the current *Supply* influences *Demand* in the next time period, the current *Demand* influences *Supply* in the next time period, and the current values of both also influence their own values in the next time period. To model such processes, we can add (relative) time indices for the variables—rather than *Supply*, we have *Supply at t*, *Supply at t* + 1, and so forth—to indicate the relative temporal relations and thereby convert the cyclic graph into a DAG, as in figure 3.4b.

Thus, to the extent that causal cycles or feedback loops are temporally extended, we can capture them in DAG-based graphical models. Of course, this move comes at a computational cost, since we are multiplying the number of variables. However, such dynamic models are, in many cases, more useful than working with truly cyclic graphs (Lerner, Moses, Scott, McIlraith, & Koller, 2002).[9]

Second, we often want to incorporate decision possibilities into our graphical model. Influence diagrams or decision networks (names used interchangeably) explicitly include "decision" nodes that have no graphical parents and represent an outside policy maker's decision in this context (Howard & Matheson, 1981; Shachter, 1988). Such models can be used to quickly infer the likely outcomes of various decisions so that one can (hopefully) make a better decision. The key difference from other DAG-based graphical models is that decision nodes in a decision network do not have any "natural" value or probability. These variables are *always* set from outside the system; nothing internal to the graphical model specifies their value. The edges in a decision network thus only characterize what happens once a decision has been made. As a result, the various inference algorithms for DAG-based graphical models must be adjusted somewhat, though all the same inferences are still possible. We will return to decision networks in section 6.3.

3.2.1 Mathematical Details of DAG Models*

This section provides specific mathematical details for DAG-based graphical models in which the nodes are variables. This section presupposes knowledge of probability theory, as well as a basic understanding of statistical notions such as independence and conditioning. For reasons of space, I do not attempt to give an exhaustive introduction to DAG-based graphical models; interested readers are encouraged to consult some of the references mentioned at the beginning of section 3.2. To help with notational simplicity, capitalized letters or words will (generally) refer to variables, and lowercase letters or words refer to values of those variables. Bold text denotes sets of variables or values; italics denote single variables or values.

We focus on DAG-based graphical models over a set of N distinct variables $\mathbf{V} = \{V_1, \ldots , V_N\}$, and so the quantitative component is fully characterized by a joint probability distribution or density, $P(\mathbf{V} = \mathbf{v})$. Recall that the Markov assumption for DAG-based graphical models is that any variable V is independent of its nondescendants conditional on its parents. This assumption implies that we can factor this joint probability distribution into the product of N conditional distributions (densities). Specifically, if $\mathbf{Par_i}$ denotes the set of graphical parents of V_i (and $\mathbf{par_i}$ the values of those variables), then the full joint probability distribution (density) factors into:

$$P(\mathbf{V} = \mathbf{v}) = \prod_{i=1}^{N} P(V_i = v_i \mid \mathbf{Par_i} = \mathbf{par_i}) \tag{3.1}$$

If all variables are discrete, then we have a so-called Bayesian network, and equation (3.1) is the simplest representation of the joint probability distribution. For example, if *Exposure*, *Infection*, and *Symptoms* are all binary variables in figure 3.2, then the joint probability distribution over those three variables is:

$$P(Exposure = e, Infection = i, Symptoms = s) = P(E = e)\, P(I = i \mid E = e)\, P(S = s \mid I = i)$$

Note that the probability that *Symptoms* = *s* does not depend (directly) on *Exposure*; those variables are independent conditional on *Infection*.

If the variables are continuous, then one typically places further constraints on the conditional densities in equation (3.1). Probably the most common restriction is found in linear structural equation models (SEMs): all variables are linear functions of their parents plus Gaussian (i.e., normally distributed) noise. That is, one assumes that every variable can be expressed as:

$$V_i = \sum_{W \in \mathbf{Pa}_i} \alpha_{W,i} W + \epsilon_i$$

where $\alpha_{W,i}$ is the linear coefficient for parent *W*, and ϵ_i is a normally distributed error term. Although this equation is not written as a probability density, it determines a conditional density that is suitable for equation (3.1). Because the variables with no parents still have Gaussian noise terms, the set of equations induces a multivariate Gaussian density over **V**, which allows one to use a wide range of analytically and computationally tractable inference and updating algorithms. In the case of figure 3.2, the resulting set of linear equations is:

$$Exp = \epsilon_{Exp}$$
$$Inf = \alpha_{Exp} Exp + \epsilon_{Inf}$$
$$Symp = \alpha_{Inf} Inf + \epsilon_{Symp}$$

It is important to realize that the restriction to linear equations with Gaussian noise is only one way to further constrain the conditional densities. One could equally well develop a DAG-based graphical model that uses nonlinear equations (Chu & Glymour, 2008; Tillman, Gretton, & Spirtes, 2010) or non-Gaussian noise terms (Shimizu, Hoyer, Hyvärinen, & Kerminen, 2006). In all these cases, the key constraint is that each variable is a function only of its graphical parents, and (usually) independent noise.

The Faithfulness assumption requires that the only independencies be those implied by the Markov assumption. As a result, each variable must depend, at least sometimes, on each of its parents. That is, there cannot be a graphical parent W such that V does not depend on W, regardless of the values of the other parents. In Bayes nets, this implication means that the conditional distribution for V cannot be the same for every value of W (conditional on each set of values for other parents). For SEMs, Faithfulness implies that none of the linear coefficients can be exactly zero. This corresponds to the standard practice when estimating linear models that variables with zero coefficients (or those that are statistically indistinguishable from zero) are removed from the linear equation. The Faithfulness assumption has other implications (e.g., no variable can be perfectly correlated with another one), but this is the key one that will be used later in the book.

Given a particular DAG G, the Markov and Faithfulness assumptions jointly determine a set of independencies (unconditional and conditional) over **V**. That is, there is a purely graphical criterion—d-separation—for whether V_i and V_j are independent conditional on **S** (Geiger et al., 1989). This criterion can thus be used to derive relevance relations from just the graph. To understand d-separation, suppose π is an *undirected path* in DAG G: that is, π is a sequence of r distinct variables $V_{\pi(1)}, \ldots, V_{\pi(r)}$ such that $V_{\pi(i)}$ and $V_{\pi(i+1)}$ are adjacent for all $i < r$, but we do not care about the direction of the edge between $V_{\pi(i)}$ and $V_{\pi(i+1)}$. A node $V_{\pi(i)}$ is a *collider* on π if and only if $V_{\pi(i-1)} \rightarrow V_{\pi(i)} \leftarrow V_{\pi(i+1)}$ on π. For a given conditioning set **S**, define a node X on π to be *blocked* by **S** if and only if either (a) X is in **S** and X is a noncollider or (b) X is a collider and neither X nor any of its descendants are in **S**. We then define a path π to be *active* given **S** if and only if every node on π is not blocked by **S**. And we say that V_i and V_j are *d-connected* given **S** if and only if there is at least one active path between them given **S**. Conversely, V_i and V_j are *d-separated* given **S** if and only if there are no active paths between them given **S**. Finally, one can prove (assuming Markov and Faithfulness): V_i and V_j are independent conditional on **S** if and only if V_i and V_j are d-separated given **S** (Geiger et al., 1989).

As a practical example, consider the exercise case from figure 3.3; for brevity, I simply use the first letters of the variables. Are E and W independent conditional on $\mathbf{S} = \{M, A\}$? There are two paths between E and W: $E \rightarrow M \rightarrow W$ and $E \rightarrow A \rightarrow W$. Both of these paths are blocked by **S**, as the only nonterminal node in each path (M and A, respectively) is a noncollider and also in **S**. Since there are no active paths between E and W given $\{M, A\}$, they are d-separated, and so E is independent of W conditional on $\{M, A\}$. Alternately, are M and A independent given $\mathbf{T} = \{E, W\}$? There are again two undirected paths: $M \leftarrow E \rightarrow A$ and $M \rightarrow W \leftarrow A$. The first path is again blocked, since E is not a collider and is in **T**. The second path, however, is not blocked: W is a collider and is in **T**, so it is active. Thus M and A are d-connected given $\{E, W\}$, and so they are associated conditional on $\{E, W\}$.

This latter result might seem surprising, since we are conditioning on a variable on every path between M and A, and many people believe that (statistical) conditioning can only turn an association into an independence, rather than (as in this case) an independence—M and A are independent conditional on only E—into an association. It is easiest to see how this could occur by thinking about a causal situation. As a simplified example, suppose we have two independent causes of an effect X, where either is sufficient to produce X, and there are no other causes of X. By assumption, the causes are independent, so learning about one (in isolation) tells us nothing about the other. Now suppose that we know that the effect occurred (i.e., we condition on $X = yes$). In this situation, learning about one cause *can* tell us about the other cause: for example, if I learn that one cause is absent, then I know that the other must have occurred, as it is the only remaining explanation for X's occurrence. Thus the two causes are associated conditional on X.

If one has a particular DAG-based graphical model M, including quantitative (parametric) information, then one can straightforwardly infer the probability distribution (density) of different variables given observations of other variables in M. The key to such algorithms is that if X is independent of Y given **S**, then $P(X \mid \mathbf{S}) = P(X \mid Y, \mathbf{S})$. Since (conditional) independence can be computed quickly from the graph using the d-separation criterion, one can determine which variables are relevant for updating the probability distribution and which are irrelevant. In fact, this computational advantage when doing Bayesian updating is what gives Bayesian networks their name, not anything inherently Bayesian about the graphical model itself. The modularity of the graphical model can also be leveraged to develop local, message-passing algorithms for updating given observations: one specifies the value of observed variables, nodes in the graph pass informational "messages" to one another, and the model eventually settles into a state representing the updated joint probability distribution (Pearl, 1988).

If the DAG-based graphical model M can be interpreted causally, then one can also update the joint probability distribution given interventions or manipulations of variables in M. The simplest way to do this is to augment M to a new DAG-based graphical model M^* that explicitly represents the interventions by (i) adding appropriate nodes and edges to the graph to capture the interventions being causes of the "intervenee" variable, and (ii) adjusting the conditional distributions for those latter variables, since the parents of those nodes have changed in M^*. One can then use standard updating techniques in M^* given the "observations" that the interventions are active. A particularly interesting case is a so-called *hard* intervention: one that completely determines the value of a target variable, thereby cutting off the target from its normal causes. When a hard intervention is active on T, the graph in M^* is further adjusted to remove the edges into T from the other parents of T, since they are no longer causes of T. Much of the philosophical literature about causal graphical models has focused on this particular property of hard interventions and the ways in which that property can help or hinder learning and inference (Eberhardt & Scheines, 2007, and references therein). It is important to realize, though, that hard interventions are only one type of intervention; we can also represent soft interventions that influence (from outside the ordinary causal system) a variable's value without completely determining it. In either case, we simply augment the graph to describe the impacts of that intervention and then use standard, noninterventional inference methods on the augmented graph.

Methods for learning DAG structure fall largely into two camps: constraint based or Bayesian/score based. Constraint-based methods try to determine the set of DAGs that imply (by d-separation) exactly the independence and dependence relations that are found in the data. In practice, one cannot test all of the possible conditional independence relations, as there are far too many of them (exponential in the number of variables). Moreover, the statistical power of independence tests decreases as the number of variables in the conditioning set increases, so it is better to base structure learning decisions on independence tests with as small a conditioning set as possible. Various constraint-based learning algorithms incorporate these insights into computationally tractable methods that have been applied in a wide range of domains (Pearl, 1988; Spirtes et al., 2000; Tillman, Danks, & Glymour, 2008). In contrast, Bayesian or score-based methods aim to determine the set of most probable graphs given the observed data. In practice, there are typically too many possible graphs to determine the probability of each, and we are usually more interested in which graphs are most probable, rather than the exact probability of each graph. Thus most score-based learning algorithms examine only a subset of possible graphs, guided by a score that is proportional (by some unknown constant) to the true probability (Chickering, 2002; Heckerman, 1998). Although both types of searches rarely consider all graphs, they provably converge to the true structure as the amount of data grows, if done correctly (as in Chickering, 2002; Spirtes et al., 2000). A third type of causal structure learning algorithm has recently emerged that is specifically designed for linear, non-Gaussian systems and uses independent component analysis (ICA) to determine (when possible) both adjacencies and directions in the DAG (Shimizu et al., 2006), but the details of these algorithms will not be relevant to our use of these graphical models. DAG structure learning algorithms continue to be a major focus of research in machine learning, but we will not use any sophisticated ones in this book.

3.3 Undirected Graph (UG) Models

A different constraint on the space of graphical models is to require that all graphical edges be undirected. Figure 3.1b gives an example of an undirected graph (UG). If we further restrict the nodes to all be variables, then we get a specific type of graphical model with a variety of names, including conditional random fields (CRFs), Markov networks, and the name that I will use, Markov random fields (MRFs) (Lafferty, McCallum, & Pereira, 2001; Li, 2009; McCallum, Freitag, & Pereira, 2000; Sutton & McCallum, 2007). These models are particularly useful for situations in which the dependencies or relevance relations are symmetric. For example, suppose the nodes correspond to the occurrence of disease at a particular spatial location, and the edges denote direct spatial proximity (as in Knorr-Held & Rue, 2002). In this case, the edges ought not be directed, as disease can propagate in either direction, and so a UG is the most appropriate type of graph (see also Waller, Carlin, Xia, & Gelfand, 1997). MRFs have been used successfully in domains such as image processing (Li, 2009), sequence labeling (Lafferty et al., 2001), and speech recognition (Gravier & Sigelle, 1999; McCallum et al., 2000).

Recall that the overarching Markov assumption is "If there is no edge in the graph, then the nodes should not be directly dependent." That is, if there is no edge between A and B in the graph, then there should be some

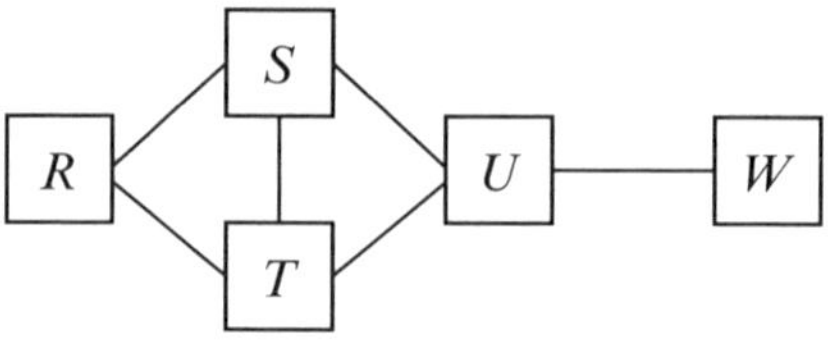

Figure 3.5
Example Markov random field.

set of nodes **S** such that *A* and *B* are independent given that we know the values of **S**. Because the relationships in a UG are symmetric, the natural Markov assumption is thus "Any variable is independent of nonadjacent variables, given the adjacent variables." And as with DAG-based models, we also have a corresponding Faithfulness assumption that says: "The only independencies are those predicted by the Markov assumption." For example, variable *R* in figure 3.5 is independent of variables *U* and *W*, given that we know the values of *S* and *T*. At the same time, *R* is not independent of *S*, regardless of what we learn about the other variables in the system.

Inference in UG-based graphical models is often computationally quite efficient, as the direct relevance relations are straightforwardly represented in the graph. Because the edges are undirected, one can determine relevance between two nodes simply by looking for any path between them without a node whose value is known. A variety of algorithms have been developed for learning UG edge structure from data, particularly for applications such as image processing where we have relatively little background knowledge to substantively constrain the graph structure (Lee, Ganapathi, & Koller, 2007; Taskar, Guestrin, & Koller, 2004). One might wonder whether UG- and DAG-based graphical models can perfectly represent the same data. The short answer is that they cannot, but we return to this issue in section 3.4 when we compare the expressive power of different graphical model types.

Another important class of UG-based graphical models is that of social network models (J. P. Scott, 2000; Wasserman & Faust, 1995). Social networks aim to model the social relationships between a set of individual actors: the nodes denote specific people, and the edges indicate a "direct" social relationship (where the exact nature of the relationship depends on the model). Much of the research on social networks has focused on characterizing various properties of the graph, such as the relative density of connections, the set of "central" individuals, the average path distance between individuals in the graph, and so forth. More recently, research has emerged examining the dynamics of social networks, including the ways in which they change after a disruption (e.g., Butts & Carley, 2007; Lin, Zhao, Ismail, & Carley, 2006). In general, however, social networks tend to be relatively unspecified in their quantitative component: the focus is almost entirely on the connection graph, rather than on the strengths of connections or more fine-grained characterizations of the social relationships. As a result, the predictions and inferences that one can generate with a social network tend to be relatively coarse or high-level (e.g., "all other things being equal, information propagates faster in graph G_1 than in G_2"). Though social networks are also a type of UG-based graphical model, I do not consider them further here, as this book does not focus principally on social relations.

3.3.1 Mathematical Details of UG Models*

I focus in this section on Markov random fields (MRFs), as they are the type of UG-based graphical model that will be used starting in chapter 5. As before, our (undirected) graphical model is over a set of N distinct variables $\mathbf{V} = \{V_1, \ldots, V_N\}$, and so the quantitative component is a joint probability distribution or density, $P(\mathbf{V} = \mathbf{v})$. The Markov assumption holds that any variable is independent of nonadjacent variables, conditional on the adjacent ones. One might have thought that we could use this assumption to factorize the joint distribution (density) in an analogous fashion to equation (3.1) for DAG-based graphical models (except using the set of adjacent variables $\mathbf{Adj}_i$ instead of the graphical parents $\mathbf{Par}_i$). Unfortunately, this will not work for a variety of technical reasons, so we must use a slightly different formulation. There are multiple (possible) Markov assumptions that are only equivalent and only imply the factorization in the next equation if $P(\mathbf{V})$ is positive (Lauritzen, 1996; Moussouris, 1974); that is, the different formulations are equivalent only if $P(\mathbf{V})$ is nonzero for all possible combinations of variable values, though some of those probabilities can be arbitrarily small. Moreover, positivity is required for the Hammersley-Clifford theorem (Hammersley & Clifford, 1971), which provides the foundation for many applications. We thus make the relatively innocuous assumption of positivity in the remainder of this section (though note that positivity, like the Faithfulness assumption, rules out truly deterministic systems).

Define a *clique* $\mathbf{C}$ to be a set of nodes such that every node in $\mathbf{C}$ is adjacent to every other node in $\mathbf{C}$, and define a *maximal clique* to be a clique such that adding any more nodes to it results in a nonclique. As a concrete example, there are three different maximal cliques in the graph in figure 3.5: $\{R, S, T\}$, $\{S, T, U\}$, and $\{U, W\}$. If $\mathbf{G}_1, \ldots, \mathbf{G}_M$ are the maximal cliques, then the joint distribution (density) factors into:

$$P(\mathbf{V} = \mathbf{v}) = \frac{1}{Z}\prod_{i=1}^{M} \psi_i(\mathbf{G}_i = \mathbf{g}_i)$$

where ψ_i is the so-called *clique potential* for clique $\mathbf{G}_i$ (and Z is just a normalization constant that ensures that we actually have a probability distribution). Thus the joint probability distribution (density) for the graph in figure 3.5 factors into:

$$P(R = r, S = s, T = t, U = u, W = w) =$$
$$\frac{1}{Z}\psi_1(R = r, S = s, T = t)\psi_2(S = s, T = t, U = u)\psi_3(U = u, W = w)$$

Clique potentials are simply functions that output a real number for each combination of variable values in the clique, and they are so named because of the use of MRFs in statistical mechanics (where the clique potentials represent the potential energy of a particular configuration). Importantly, clique potentials are *not* necessarily probability distributions: the clique potential for $\mathbf{G}_i$ does not correspond to the marginal distribution over the variables in $\mathbf{G}_i$, nor does it (necessarily) encode the conditional probabilities, nor is it even necessarily individually normalizable. For example, in figure 3.5, $P(R = r, S = s, T = t)$ is not equal to $\psi_1(R = r, S = s, T = t)$; the probabilities of S and T also depend on ψ_2, since the values of S and T are inputs to it. We can thus see that, for a particular $P(\mathbf{V})$, there is not necessarily a unique set of clique potentials, unless we further constrain the functional forms of the clique potentials. If there are no such constraints, then we can, for example, "move probability mass" between potentials ψ_1 and ψ_2 (since both depend on S and T), or between ψ_2 and ψ_3 (since both depend on U), resulting in many different factorizations. In practice, one typically divides the relevant probability mass evenly among the cliques containing a variable V, and so the precise form of the clique potentials depends on the number of cliques containing V.

Gaussian Markov random fields (Rue & Held, 2005) are a special type of MRFs that are used when $P(\mathbf{V})$ is a multivariate Gaussian (i.e., normally distributed). In this case, the UG structure corresponds perfectly with the precision matrix (i.e., the inverse of the covariance matrix for the multivariate Gaussian): there is an edge between X and Y if and only if there is a nonzero entry for X and Y in the precision matrix. The multivariate density for Gaussian MRFs can thus be specified without the need to use clique potentials. Perhaps more importantly, we have a natural way to learn the structure of a Gaussian MRF by statistically estimating the zeros of the precision matrix.

As with DAG-based graphical models, we can use the topological structure of the graph to compute the quantitative in/dependencies, and vice versa. In fact, the relationship is even easier to express in UG-based models, since there are no colliders. A path π between A and B is *blocked by* $\mathbf{S}$ if and only if π contains at least one member of $\mathbf{S}$. For example, in figure 3.5 R and U are blocked by $\{S, T\}$ but are not blocked by S alone. It is straightforward to show that A and B are independent conditional on $\mathbf{S}$ if and only if every path between A and B is blocked by $\mathbf{S}$. That is, two variables are independent conditional on a set if and only if that set blocks every way of getting from one variable to the other. And again, we can use this tight connection between graph topology and quantitative dependence to construct efficient inference and learning algorithms given certain constraints or parametric assumptions (Koller & Friedman, 2009; Rue & Held, 2005). Learning the graph structure in relatively assumption-free settings is much harder: most such methods (e.g., Chen & Welling, 2012) focus on estimating particular models and finding the "zeros" in the model, but this is an area of ongoing machine learning research.

3.4 Expressive Power of Graphical Models

A natural question arises at this point concerning the expressive powers of the different types of graphical models. Recall that we say that a graphical model G perfectly represents some data $\mathbf{D}$ just when G implies (by Markov and Faithfulness) all and only the in/dependencies that are actually found in $\mathbf{D}$. What are the "data spaces" that a DAG-based or UG-based graphical model can perfectly represent? And are those data spaces identical, disjoint, or overlapping? The answers to these questions are complicated but will be important in later chapters when we compare different cognitive theories (expressed as operations on graphical models). In general, the data space that can be perfectly represented by a type of graphical model depends only on the graphs for that type,[10] and so I will largely ignore the quantitative components in this section. Instead we can characterize the expressive powers of different graphical model types solely in terms of topological features of the underlying graphs, though we need several pieces of terminology to express those features.

In a DAG, we say that an *unshielded collider* is any variable T such that (i) $X \rightarrow T \leftarrow Y$, and (ii) X and Y are not adjacent. That is, an unshielded collider in a DAG is any variable with edges directed into it from variables that have no edge between them. For example, in figure 3.6a, T is an unshielded collider. If an edge were present between X and Y in figure 3.6a, however, then T would no longer be unshielded. One can prove: if a DAG-based graphical model with graph G perfectly represents **D**, then there is also a perfectly representing UG-based graphical model if and only if there are no unshielded colliders in G (Pearl, 1988). That is, if the perfectly representing DAG has no unshielded colliders, then there is also a perfectly representing UG; if there is even just a single unshielded collider, then there is no perfectly representing UG. For example, if the graph in figure 3.6a perfectly represents **D**, then there is no UG that can perfectly represent **D**. In contrast, the graph in figure 3.6b has no unshielded colliders, so any data that it perfectly represents can *also* be perfectly represented by a UG; in fact, the corresponding UG is the one shown in figure 3.6c.

We cannot have the same condition for moving from perfectly representing UGs to DAGs, since there are obviously no colliders in a UG. We instead define a *chordal graph* (directed or undirected) to be one in which every path from a node back to itself (ignoring edge directions, if any) has at least one pair of nonsequential (in the path) nodes that are adjacent in the broader graph. For example, the graphs in figures 3.6b and 3.6c are trivially chordal, since there are no paths from a node back to itself. In contrast, figure 3.6d shows a nonchordal graph: in the A—X—T—Y—A path, there is no edge between the nonsequential variables X and Y. Chordality is essentially an "edge density" constraint on the underlying graph. And provably: if a UG-based graphical model with graph G perfectly represents **D**, then there is also a perfectly representing DAG-based graphical model if and only if G is chordal (Pearl, 1988). Thus if the graph in figure 3.6c perfectly represents **D**, then there is a DAG that also perfectly represents **D** (i.e., fig. 3.6b). In

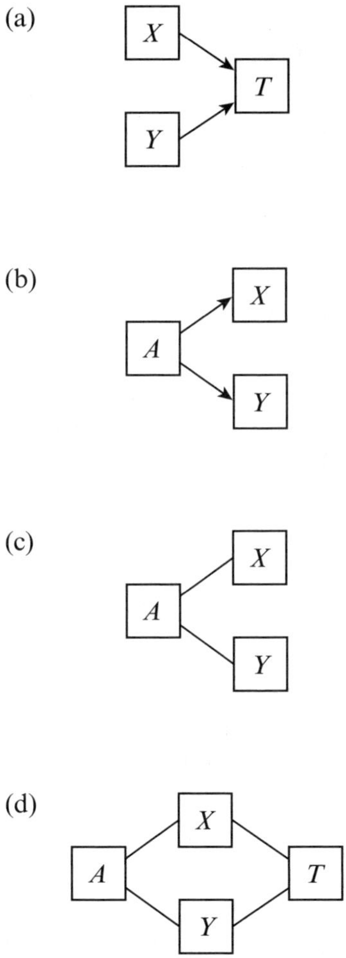

Figure 3.6
Four graphs illustrating colliders and chordality.

contrast, if **D** is perfectly represented by the UG in figure 3.6d, then there is *no* DAG that perfectly represents **D**, since that UG is not chordal.

Unshielded colliders are actually the key to both theorems, as chordal graphs are exactly those in which it is possible to give directions to all the edges so that the resulting graph is both acyclic and has no unshielded colliders. (Notice, for example, that every way of orienting the edges in fig. 3.6d will yield either a cyclic graph or at least one unshielded collider.) Thus it is worth examining unshielded colliders in more detail. Consider the isolated example shown in figure 3.6a.[11] Perhaps the most striking aspect of this graph is that *X* and *Y* are entirely independent of each other, though they are both directly relevant to *T*. Unshielded colliders thus provide the clearest example that dependence is *not* a transitive relation: *X* and *T* are dependent, *T* and *Y* are dependent, but *X* and *Y* are not (unconditionally) dependent. This pattern of in/dependence stands in sharp contrast to the pattern in, for example, figure 3.6b. In that graph, *X* and *A* are dependent, *A* and *Y* are dependent, and also *X* and *Y* are dependent. That is, common effect (fig. 3.6a) and common cause (fig. 3.6b) structures exhibit different patterns of independence, which can be used to help learn edge directions in a DAG (Spirtes et al., 2000). When we turn to UGs, we find that "transitivity of dependence" always holds: if *X* and *Y* are dependent in a UG, as well as *Y* and *Z*, then *X* and *Z* are necessarily also dependent in that UG. Thus we can straightforwardly see why DAGs and UGs have related but not identical expressive power: UGs require dependence transitivity, while DAGs tolerate—and can even require—some violations of it.

DAG- and UG-based graphical models thus overlap in their expressive power: some data can be represented by either type of graphical model, but other data can be represented by only one type. If one is in the overlap region, then it does not matter (from a formal point of view) whether one uses a DAG- or UG-based graphical model; either will suffice. Of course, one may have other reasons to prefer one representation, such as optimized inference algorithms. For example, the widely used hidden Markov models (HMMs) (for overviews see, e.g., Koller & Friedman, 2009; Rabiner, 1989) fall into exactly this overlap: HMMs can be characterized as either a DAG- or a UG-based graphical model. There is no (mathematical) fact of the matter about which is the "right" representation of an HMM. In practice, however, HMMs are often represented as DAGs to simplify the details of various inference and reasoning algorithms.

Since the two model types only overlap, one might instead want to use graphical models whose graphs can have both directed and undirected edges. Such models are able to perfectly represent any data that can be perfectly represented by either a DAG- or a UG-based graphical model, and so provide a measure of unification to those graphical model types. Graphical models with both directed and undirected edges are called *chain graphs* (Andersson, Madigan, & Perlman, 1996; Lauritzen & Richardson, 2002; Lauritzen & Wermuth, 1989; Richardson, 1998); DAG- and UG-based graphical models are simply special cases. Many technical issues about chain graphs are unsolved or unsettled, such as the proper Markov assumption (Andersson et al., 1996) and sensible causal/realist interpretations (Lauritzen & Richardson, 2002). Chain graphs do not play a significant role in this book, however, so we do not need to confront these particular issues. It is worth noting, though, that chain graphs do not merely subsume the DAG- and UG-based graphical model frameworks. Rather, they have strictly greater expressive power than the two frameworks combined: there are data **D** that can be perfectly represented by a chain graph but cannot be perfectly represented by either a DAG- or a UG-based graphical model. For example, any data that are perfectly represented by the graph in figure 3.7 have no perfect representation in a DAG or UG.

Even chain graphs are not universal representers, however. There are data whose independence structure cannot be perfectly represented by a chain graph and so cannot be captured by any DAG- or UG-based graphical model. In fact, many independence structures cannot be perfectly represented by *any* of the standard types of graphical models (Studeny, 1995). Figure 3.8 gives a graphical summary (not to any scale) of the expressive powers of the different types of graphical models.

The presence of white space in figure 3.8 is critical, since it shows that there are limits on the representational capacities of graphical models. The

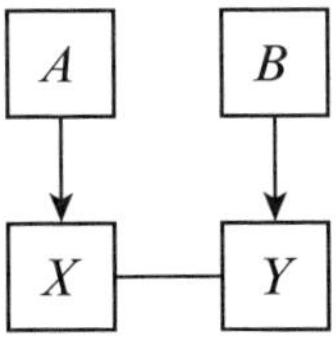

Figure 3.7
Example chain graph.

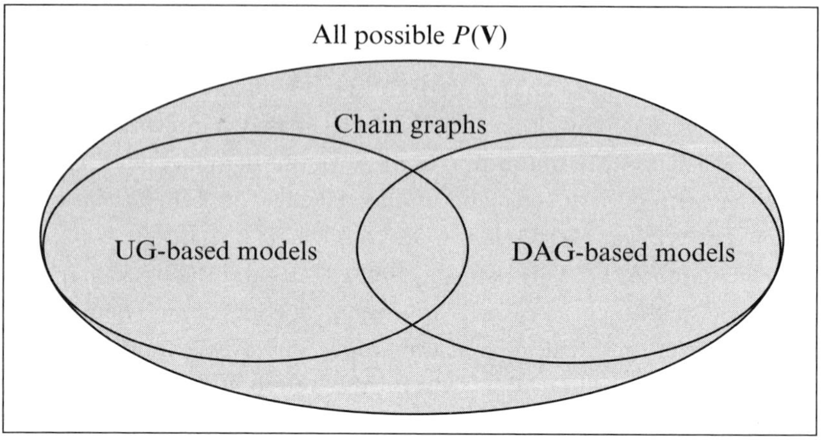

Figure 3.8
Representational power of different graphical model types.

graphical models framework would be relatively uninteresting in cognitive science if it could represent *any* conceivable situation or theory. That is not the case, however: expressing a theory in terms of graphical models imposes significant restrictions and constraints on it; many possible cognitive theories cannot be translated into the graphical models framework.

This chapter has focused on characterizing these different types of graphical models. Now it is time to put them to work as a mathematical framework and language to characterize human cognitive representations. Over the next three chapters, I show how to use graphical models in three different areas of cognition, but we begin with representations of causal structure in the world.

4 Causal Cognition

4.1 A Taxonomy of Causal Cognition

We now have the pieces in place to express particular areas of cognition as operations on cognitive representations structured as graphical models, and to actually understand what that means. We begin in this chapter with causal cognition. Causation is one of the unifying threads of our cognition (Sloman, 2005). We interpret disparate events as parts of a coherent causal structure. We use our causal knowledge to predict future states of the world. Our choices and actions in the world are influenced and guided by our understanding of the causal relations around us. Perhaps most importantly, we understand the difference between causal relationships and those that are only predictive, and our cognition is sensitive to that difference. It has even been suggested that our rich understanding of causal relations is a key feature distinguishing us from other animals (Penn, Holyoak, & Povinelli, 2008). Of course, not all cognition is causal, nor are causal relations the only cognitively relevant ones in the world. But any framework that aims to unify multiple cognitive domains arguably must include causal cognition as a critical element.

Many debates center on the nature of causation (particularly in philosophy), and so we need to be clear about what we mean by "causation." I focus here on causation in our cognition, rather than as an objective, physical relation in the world. Presumably our concept of causation has *some* connection to some metaphysical relation(s) in the world, such as being part of a physically continuous process (Dowe, 2007) or having a difference-making relation toward some factor (Woodward, 2003). However, there is no necessary reason for the content of our concept of causation to be identical with any particular corresponding relation in the world; all that matters is that our concept appropriately tracks some relation(s) in the world that can ground and support the learning, reasoning, and inferences that we do with our causal knowledge (Danks, 2014). Philosophical debates about causation "in the world" are simply beside the point. I will also not focus on people's explicit beliefs about causation, as our explicit beliefs about something can be misleading about the actual content and function of that something. I will instead concentrate on behavior that is based on causal cognition, as that is a better means to learn about the actual notion that plays such a central role in our cognitive lives. Introspection about "what causation seems to be" will not play a role here.

These caveats do not provide much positive guidance about what I mean by causation. The key distinction here is between causation and association (e.g., correlation). If two factors are associated or dependent (to use the term from chap. 3), then they carry information about each other. That is, learning something about one factor tells us something about the other. For example, hair color and job title are associated, at least among academics: full professors are more likely to have gray hair, while assistant professors are more likely to have nongray hair. This association is obviously not perfect—there are full professors with nongray hair and assistant professors who do have gray hair—but there is appropriate information transfer. Moreover, this information transfer, and association more generally, is symmetric: job title can be used to learn (partially) about hair color, and vice versa. At the same time, this association is clearly noncausal, as changes in job title do not directly lead to hair color change, nor is dyeing one's hair an effective strategy to get promoted. The association instead arises because both are functions of one's age and time in the job. In contrast, causal relations are fundamentally asymmetric: causes lead to their effects, but effects do not lead to their causes (at the same moment[1]). If we were to change the state of the cause, then the effect would probabilistically change; in contrast, exogenous changes of the effect do not lead to changes in the cause. For example, flipping the switch leads to the light changing state (probabilistically), but smashing the lightbulb (to force it to be "off") does not affect the light switch at all.

As these examples suggest, it is critical that we cognitively represent the distinction between associations and causal relations: both support predictions based on observations of the world, but only causal relations support predictions when we act on the world (in situations in which our actions are appropriately exogenous). Moreover, our cognitive representations of causal structure should, if they truly represent causation, capture the cause-effect asymmetry. I will thus focus on graphical models with directed edges that represent exactly this asymmetry: $C \rightarrow E$ will mean "C causes E." In addition, since essentially all feedback cycles are temporally extended (and thus acyclic for time-indexed variables), I will focus on acyclic graphs. That is, this chapter will use directed acyclic graph (DAG)-based graphical models. And the key claim of this chapter is that much (though not all) causal cognition can be understood as operations on cognitive representations that are isomorphic to such DAG-based graphical models.

Causal cognition can be broadly divided into causal learning and causal reasoning (Danks, 2009), where causal learning is (roughly) the acquisition of new causal beliefs or changes to existing ones, and causal reasoning is the use of those beliefs in various ways. The distinction is not sharp, as each can depend on the other: causal learning can involve causal reasoning (e.g., learning from predictive failures of prior beliefs), and causal reasoning can involve causal learning (e.g., when reasoning reveals previously unnoticed causal connections). Nonetheless this rough dichotomy is useful, as we can think about learning as changing our representations, and reasoning as using those representations. Causal learning can then be subdivided further into causal inference and causal perception. Causal perception is the relatively immediate perception of causal relations, as when one sees the cue ball *cause* the eight ball to move when it hits the eight ball (Rips, 2011; Scholl & Tremoulet, 2000). Causal inference refers to the process by which we infer causal relations from multiple cases, where causation cannot be directly observed in any particular case (e.g., Cheng, 1997; Danks, 2007a; Gopnik et al., 2004; Holyoak & Cheng, 2011). For example, I can learn that aspirin relieves pain based on repeated instances in which I took aspirin and my pain abated, as well as occasions on which I did not take aspirin and my pain continued.[2] There are both behavioral and neuroscientific grounds for distinguishing between causal perception and causal inference (Blakemore et al., 2001; Roser, Fugelsang, Dunbar, Corballis, & Gazzaniga, 2005; Satpute et al., 2005; Schlottmann & Shanks, 1992). Moreover, this chapter provides theoretical grounds to distinguish them, as I will argue that causal inference can be modeled as operations on graphical models, while causal perception (arguably) cannot.

One obvious lacuna in this taxonomy is so-called learning from description: learning about causal relations in the world from the direct verbal testimony of others (e.g., being told "the third light switch controls the outside lights"). Arguably, much or even most of our causal learning comes from other people's descriptions of the world. I will not explicitly discuss this particular mode of causal learning, however, as there are few experiments and essentially no theories about it. Many important details about causal learning from description are simply unknown. At the same time, I will discuss it implicitly in section 4.3, as many causal reasoning experiments study predictions and inferences generated from causal knowledge acquired through learning from description. Thus, to the extent that the graphical models framework can help us to understand empirical phenomena in causal reasoning, we also have evidence that it provides a good framework for capturing those causal representations. A full account of causal learning from description remains an open research problem, particularly the question of when learners infer the absence of a causal relation (*C* does not cause *E*) from absence of information (the other person simply does not mention whether *C* causes *E*). We clearly make such inferences on a regular basis, and they are critical for us to develop relatively sparse (and thus useful) cognitive representations of causal structure. A range of contextual factors including conversational pragmatics and shared knowledge presumably drives those inferences, however, so a full theory may be a long time coming.

The remainder of the chapter does the positive work of understanding causal inference (sec. 4.2) and causal reasoning (sec. 4.3) as operations on graphical models, and the negative work of arguing that causal perception is unlikely to be captured as a process operating on a graphical model (sec. 4.4). Before beginning, however, a reminder: for some of these cognitive processes, I will show that different, competing cognitive theories can all be captured in the graphical models framework. The intention in this strategy is not to show that we somehow have a universal language that can capture all theories; the graphical models framework is decidedly not that. Rather, the idea is that the cognitive science debates about these theories are about details that do not matter to the cognitive architecture that I am advocating. For example, regardless of whether the correct model of causal inference is the causal power theory, ΔP theory, or some mixture (both discussed in section 4.2), the resulting cognitive representations are arguably structured as a DAG. As a scientific community, we do need to determine the precise DAG parameterization, but resolving that issue is irrelevant to the present claims of my framework. The focus on graphical models permits a certain level of agnosticism about some of the underlying details while showing the "common core" of these various cognitive theories. Moreover, I focus on theories that all have substantial empirical support (at least in some contexts), and so the re-representation of some theory in the graphical models framework thereby provides empirical support for my cognitive architecture.

4.2 Causal Inference

One significant body of psychological research on causal cognition is on causal inference: learning causal structure from a set of cases, none of which explicitly convey causal information. For example, I might observe a group of plants, some of which have been treated with a liquid and some not, and my task is to determine whether the liquid is a fertilizer, poison, or causally irrelevant. This is a particularly challenging problem: I am provided only with statistical information about the correlation between use of the liquid and the plant's health but cannot remain with only these observational associations because, as discussed in section 4.1, associations are not the same as causal relations. I must instead use the observed associations as evidence for (unobserved) causal relations. Historically, this research has been connected closely with the animal learning literature on classical and instrumental conditioning, both to gain inspiration for particular causal learning models and to show how human causal inference differs from animal associative learning. This section shows how to understand this causal inference as operations on and with DAG-based graphical models, and doing so will require going down into the cognitive science details.

In thinking about causal inference, it is helpful to draw a rough distinction between causal *structure* and causal *strength*. Causal structure captures the qualitative causal relations (e.g., "*C* causes *E*"), while causal strength encodes the fine-grained mathematical details of the causal connection (e.g., "*C* is a preventive cause of *E* with strength 0.4"). This is obviously not a bright-line distinction: nonzero causal strength is (arguably) the same as the presence of a causal relation, and we can also have knowledge that falls between these two endpoints in coarseness (e.g., "*C* is a strong generative cause of E"). Nonetheless this distinction can help us to understand theories of causal inference. In particular, many psychological theories of causal inference are fundamentally theories of causal strength estimation: they focus on situations in which the learner confronts only a restricted space of causal structures and must learn causal strengths relative to that background. Causal structure theories have emerged in recent years, though not always in a computationally well-specified form. And most importantly for the purposes of this book, (almost) all of both kinds of theories can be expressed as learning about directed acyclic graphs (Danks, 2007a; Holyoak & Cheng, 2011).

The vast majority of the experimental evidence about causal inference comes from a relatively restricted experimental setting. Participants are told about a focal effect E and a set of potential causes $C_1, \ldots, C_n$, where these are all variables; typically, they are events that either do or do not occur, though some experiments move beyond binary (e.g., "present" or "absent") variables. In other words, participants know the relevant variables, as well as a sorting into causes and effects, whether based on temporal information (since causes cannot occur after their effects), prior knowledge, or some other reason. Participants are also usually warned that "other factors" could produce the effect E. We can capture this possibility by including an always-present, but never-observed, variable B that encapsulates all these background factors. Participants are then asked to learn the causes of E from a sequence of cases. Importantly, causal inference experiments rarely ask participants to determine the full causal structure, including potential causal relations between the C_i's. Of course, causal inference must take such relations into account in some way: if the true causal structure is $C_1 \leftarrow C_2 \rightarrow E$, then C_1 will be associated with E, and we will only learn it is not a cause of E if we condition on C_2. But participants typically do not have to learn explicitly whether, say, C_6 causes C_{17}. Finally, after observing the sequence of cases, participants are asked to give a numeric rating for the causal strength of each potential cause C_i, where different questions are used by different researchers (and where the exact question can matter a great deal, as shown in Collins & Shanks, 2006).

This restricted experimental setting provides a useful starting point for understanding how DAG-based graphical models capture the cognitive representations used in causal inference more generally. Researchers have proposed many different cognitive models to explain human performance

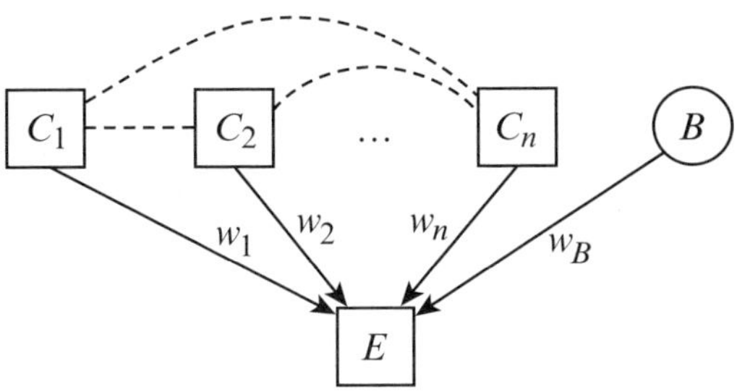

Figure 4.1
Fixed-structure graph for causal inference.

in this setting, and all can be understood as parameter estimation in a fixed-structure DAG-based graphical model (Danks, 2007a). In particular, consider the DAG in figure 4.1, where the dashed edges indicate that there could be edges (in either direction) between each pair of C_i nodes.

We make the parametric assumption that *E* is a function of the values of its causes and, for each cause C_i, a parameter w_i indicating C_i's causal strength. That is, we assume (though just for this setting) that the causes have independent influences, rather than interacting in some more complex way to generate *E*'s value. In many experiments, this assumption clearly holds; more generally, the existence of such parameters is implied by the fact that probe questions ask about "the" causal strength of each potential cause, which suggests that a single number characterizes each causal connection. If this assumption is wrong and there are complex interactions, then Novick and Cheng (2004) show how to capture them in an independent-influence model by introducing new variables to represent the relevant interactions.

The major theories of causal inference (or at least of causal strength learning) all correspond to parameter estimation in this graph; that is, each theory can be understood as people representing the causal structure using the DAG in figure 4.1 and then learning the w_i values for that DAG. (The mathematical details to defend this claim are provided in sec. 4.2.1.) From this perspective, different accounts of causal inference arise because of different assumptions about how the cause-specific strengths interact to produce *E*'s value. That is, all these different theories agree about the underlying cognitive representation of qualitative causal structure: it is the DAG shown in figure 4.1. We get different cognitive models only because the theories posit that people assume different functions for predicting *E* from the observed potential causes. But these differences should not distract us from the underlying *sameness* of the posited cognitive representation of causal structure.

As an example, the well-known Rescorla-Wagner model in animal associative learning (Rescorla & Wagner, 1972) has been proposed as a model of human causal inference (Shanks, 1993, 1995; Shanks & Dickinson, 1987), as has its long-run counterpart (Danks, 2003), the conditional ΔP theory (Cheng & Novick, 1992). This class of cognitive models corresponds to the assumption that the value of *E* (or the probability of *E*, if it is binary) is based on the sum of the w_i strengths of the present causes (Tenenbaum & Griffiths, 2001). In contrast, the causal power theory (Cheng, 1997) and its dynamic implementations (Danks, Griffiths, & Tenenbaum, 2003) are the appropriate parameter estimators when the causal strengths combine as a so-called noisy-OR gate in which the effect occurs just when at least one of the "noisy" causes generates it (Glymour, 1998). A similar characterization can be given for other models of causal inference, including Pearce's (1987) model of configural cue learning, and the pCI or belief adjustment model (Catena, Maldonado, & Candido, 1998; White, 2003a, 2003b). These cognitive models are all quite different, but all share the (perhaps implicit) principle that causal inference is parameter learning in a cognitive representation that is a fixed-structure DAG-based graphical model.

The experimental literature is filled with debates about which cognitive theory is the "right" model of human causal inference; a meta-analysis by Perales and Shanks (2007) actually concluded that *none* fits all the experimental data well (see also Hattori & Oaksford, 2007). This is unsurprising if we think about these models as different functional forms for the same DAG-based graphical model: a single model should fit all the data only if people believe that causes combine to generate the effect value via exactly the same function in every experiment. But if different functions are appropriate in different experiments, then no single parameter estimation model should fit all the data. If, for example, the potential causes and the effect can range over many values and the causes exert independent influences, then the natural functional form is the linear function underlying the Rescorla-Wagner, conditional ΔP, and related models. If we change only the variable ranges so that they can be only present or absent, then the natural functional form is the noisy-OR gate of the causal power theory and its dynamical implementations. Moreover, experimental evidence suggests that people are sensitive to the underlying functional form and change their behavior accordingly (Lucas & Griffiths, 2010). The DAG-based characterization of these cognitive models as parameter estimators thus helps to explain the diversity of results found in the causal inference literature.

Many different theories have also been proposed to explain causal *structure* learning. At a high level, these theories can be classified as either rational or heuristic accounts. In rational accounts of causal structure learning, people are modeled as learning causal structure according to some reliable, correct, principled method, such as a constraint-based algorithm (e.g., Glymour, 2003; Gopnik et al., 2004) or Bayesian inference (e.g., Griffiths & Tenenbaum, 2005; Steyvers, Tenenbaum, Wagenmakers, & Blum, 2003). The various rational accounts differ substantially, but they all agree that people are good at learning causal structure: the core idea behind all these rational models is that people are ultimately learning the "right" thing, though the accounts are essentially all agnostic about how people actually go about learning the right thing. In contrast, heuristic accounts aim to model the cognitive processes by which people learn causal structure. Causal model theory (Waldmann, 1996) proposes that people use a range of factors to settle on a causal structure at the outset of learning, and then they adjust that structure to accommodate inconsistent data (see also Lagnado, Waldmann, Hagmayer, & Sloman, 2007). Other heuristic accounts argue that people focus on learning local aspects of the causal structure such as single links and then assemble this local knowledge into a globally coherent structure (Fernbach & Sloman, 2009; Waldmann, Cheng, Hagmayer, & Blaisdell, 2008; Wellen & Danks, 2012).

Despite this great diversity in accounts of causal structure learning, they all agree that people are trying to learn a DAG. That is, there is great disagreement about the cognitive processes involved in structure learning, but complete agreement across all these different cognitive models that the cognitive representation that is ultimately learned is structured as a DAG-based graphical model. There are, of course, a range of open research questions about human causal structure learning, such as whether some of the heuristic accounts are essentially dynamical implementations of one or another rational account. But the existence of such issues should not obscure the fact that there is unanimity about the representation of causal structure. In this regard, the moral from causal structure learning is the same as for causal strength learning: there are many things that we do not know about this aspect of causal cognition, but it seems that a significant portion of our cognitive representations of causal systems are best understood as a DAG-based graphical model. The next subsection gives the mathematical details to fully explain and justify these claims, and then I turn in section 4.3 to causal reasoning, which arguably provides more direct evidence in favor of DAG-based graphical models as our cognitive representations of (much of our) causal knowledge.

4.2.1 Mapping Causal Inference onto Graphical Models*

All standard causal inference theories assume that the variables come "pre-sorted" into potential causes $C_1, \ldots, C_n$ and a target effect E. The DAG in figure 4.1 provides the graph component of a graphical model (or at least the E-relevant graph) for these theories, and so all that remains is to specify the quantitative component. As noted earlier, we assume that every variable's causal strength can be encoded by a single number; this assumption is easily relaxed (Novick & Cheng, 2004). Thus a fully specified (for E) graphical model requires only that we provide the functional form f and parameters w_i for the following equation:

$$P(E \mid C_1, C_2, \ldots, C_n, B) = f(C_1, w_1, C_2, w_2, \ldots, C_n, w_n, B, w_B) \tag{4.1}$$

Typically, the variables C_i will take on the values 1 or 0 depending on whether they are present or absent, respectively, but that is not assumed here. Causes can be continuous variables that can take on values over a much larger range. This section shows that different cognitive models of causal strength inference are estimators for the w_i parameters in equation (4.1) for different particular functional forms f, where equation (4.1) itself derives from the DAG in figure 4.1.

One set of causal inference theories includes the Rescorla-Wagner model (Rescorla & Wagner, 1972), various dynamical variants of the Rescorla-Wagner model (Tassoni, 1995; Van Hamme & Wasserman, 1994), and the conditional ΔP theory (Cheng & Novick, 1992). The first two types of theories are dynamical theories that characterize case-by-case changes in causal strength beliefs, and the last theory is an asymptotic one that aims to capture people's long-run, stable causal strength beliefs. Provably, the cognitive models based on Rescorla-Wagner converge in the long run[3] (for standard conditions and parameter values) to the conditional ΔP predictions (Danks,

2003), so we can consider these theories as a group. Now suppose that E is a binary variable[4] (either present or absent), and consider, as the functional form f in equation (4.1), the sum of the w_i's weighted by the corresponding cause variables (where present or absent values correspond to 1 or 0, respectively):

$$P(E \mid C_1, C_2, \ldots, C_n, B) = w_B + \sum_{i=1}^{n} C_i w_i \tag{4.2}$$

Provably, the conditional ΔP values are the maximum likelihood estimates of the w_i parameters in equation (4.2) (Tenenbaum & Griffiths, 2001), and so the Rescorla-Wagner-based dynamic models are also case-by-case estimators of those parameters.[5] Thus we can interpret this whole class of theories as maximum likelihood estimators for a DAG-based graphical model in which the quantitative component (for E) is given by equation (4.2).

The weighted sum in equation (4.2) has the odd feature that it can potentially result in a prediction of $P(E = 1)$ that is greater than one, which is of course impossible. If E is a continuous variable (e.g., amount of light, rather than light simply on or off), then predictions greater than one are not necessarily a problem, if we slightly reinterpret equation (4.2) (see note 4). In the case of a binary E, however, such predictions would necessarily be wrong. So consider a different functional form f. Suppose that our causes partition into two disjoint sets—generators $G_1, \ldots, G_m$ (for convenience, let B be G_1) and preventers $R_1, \ldots, R_s$—where E occurs just when at least one generator causes it and no preventer blocks it (where the probabilities of "causing" or "preventing" are given by the corresponding w_i's). That is, we assume that both positive and negative causes have some "capacity" (Cartwright, 1989) to produce or block the effect. For simplicity, we assume that the generators and preventers are all also binary causes.[6] In that case, we get a functional form known as a "noisy-OR/AND" gate:

$$P(E \mid G_1, \ldots, G_m, R_1, \ldots, R_s) = \left(1 - \prod_{i=1}^{m}(1 - G_i w_i)\right) \prod_{j=1}^{s}(1 - R_j w_j) \tag{4.3}$$

One can prove that the maximum likelihood estimates for the w_i and w_j terms in equation (4.3) are provided by the causal power theory (Cheng, 1997), as well as a corresponding dynamic case-by-case updater based on it (Danks et al., 2003). That is, the only difference between the causal-power-centered and Rescorla-Wagner-centered cognitive models is that the former estimate w_i in equation (4.3) while the latter estimate it in (4.2). Despite their disagreements in many quantitative predictions, these different cognitive models are (implicitly) committed to the same cognitive representation of causal structure; they differ only in how those shared pieces combine quantitatively.[7]

Other models of causal strength inference can also be shown to carry out parameter estimation in the DAG shown in figure 4.1. I focus here on just one additional model (though see also Danks, 2007a). In the pCI or belief adjustment model (Catena et al., 1998; White, 2003a, 2003b), the judged causal strength depends on the extent to which the evidence confirms the existence of a causal relationship. More precisely, the proportion of Confirming Instances (pCI) is defined to be the difference between the probability of seeing a case that confirms the causal relation (i.e., C and E either both occurring or both not occurring) and the probability of seeing a disconfirming case. The pCI model has not yet been extended to allow for multiple causes, so we focus on the single-cause situation here. We can also calculate pCI in a purely online manner using a complex update equation (Danks, 2007a). The related belief adjustment model uses pCI as a core but holds that causal strength judgments are not a function of the full sequence of cases. Those judgments are instead a weighted average of (i) the previous judgment and (ii) the cases seen since the last judgment. In practice, it is often unclear what constitutes a "judgment" outside the lab. In addition, many in-laboratory experiments use only a single judgment at the end of learning, and so the belief adjustment model collapses to the pCI model. We thus focus on just pCI.

To understand pCI as graphical model parameter estimation, we first focus on the case in which $P(C) = P(\neg C) = 0.5$. In this special case (and for a single cause), pCI is actually identical with ΔP, and so we can use equation (4.2) as the functional form for the graphical model parameter estimation. However, pCI and ΔP diverge if $P(C) \neq 0.5$. In fact, we can prove that there is *no* functional form for which pCI is the maximum likelihood graphical model parameter estimate (in the fig. 4.1 DAG) when $P(C) \neq 0.5$ (Danks, 2007a). Specifically, if $P(C) \neq 0.5$, then (i) if C and E are statistically independent, then pCI $\neq 0$; and (ii) if C and E are statistically associated, then there are cases in which pCI $= 0$. The single-cause version of the graphical model in figure 4.1 requires, however, that $w_C = 0$ if and only if C and E are statistically independent. Thus there is no way of getting w_C to track pCI when $P(C) \neq 0.5$. This might be interpreted as a failing of the graphical models framework, but it actually points toward a deep problem with pCI. Essentially every theory of causation holds that causation and association go hand in hand in this specific experimental setting (single cause, no possibility of confounding, and no other oddities). Since $P(C) = 0.5$ is arguably the special case condition, we thus see that pCI makes the clearly false prediction that people should be mistaken in almost all their *qualitative* causal judgments.

We turn now to theories of causal structure learning. The rational theories hold that people are using some principled algorithm that is provably reliable at structure learning. In all cases, those theories are explicitly derived from machine learning algorithms for extracting DAG-based graphical model structure from observational and interventional data (Chickering, 2002; Heckerman, 1998; Spirtes, Glymour, & Scheines, 2000). It is nonetheless helpful to see how those algorithms must be modified to accommodate human behavior. Constraint-based human causal inference algorithms (Glymour, 2003; Gopnik et al., 2004) determine the set of causal structures that imply exactly the observed statistical in/dependencies. In practice, humans appear to be able to learn causal structures from relatively small sample sizes, so those in/dependencies cannot be determined using standard statistical tests but must instead be computed by overweighting the observed cases (Gopnik et al., 2004) or using some other method for judging independence, such as Bayesian statistics (Danks, 2004). Bayesian human causal inference algorithms (Griffiths & Tenenbaum, 2005; Steyvers et al., 2003) seek to find the DAG-based graphical model that is most probable given the data (see also the discussion of Bayesianism in sec. 8.2.2). These algorithms work well with small sample sizes but can be computationally complex and thus typically incorporate either various approximations (Griffiths & Tenenbaum, 2005) or restrictions on the space of possible graphs that must be examined (Steyvers et al., 2003).

Heuristic theories of human causal structure learning make no claims to asymptotic reliability; in fact, many of them hold that people's causal learning is not even governed by statistical information. The important thing for our present purposes, however, is that all these theories are expressed in terms of learning the structure of a DAG-based graphical model. The specific heuristics differ across theories, but the underlying representation does not. For example, causal model theory accounts of structure learning hold that people use easily discoverable features of the situation to choose a preliminary causal structure, and then they revise that structure only as necessary to accommodate surprising data (Lagnado et al., 2007; Waldmann, 1996). For example, suppose there are two potential causes C and D, and the first case that I see is C, $\neg D$, and E. The co-occurrence of C and E, coupled with the absence of D, suggests the causal structure $C \rightarrow E$ with no edges involving D. Thus I might believe that particular causal structure until I see some problematic or potentially disconfirming evidence (e.g., a case with $\neg C$, D, and E). Regardless of how the initial causal structure is determined or subsequently changed, however, these algorithms always assume that the relevant representation is a DAG-based graphical model. A different type of heuristic algorithm attempts to construct a global causal structure from local information. That is, these algorithms suppose that people do not try to learn a full causal structure in one fell swoop but rather construct it from smaller pieces. Those subgraphs can be learned from many different sources with varying or context-sensitive reliability, including temporal and intervention information about single edges (Fernbach & Sloman, 2009), associations within particular clusters of variables (Wellen & Danks, 2012), or simple unconditional co-occurrence information (Meder, Gerstenberg, Hagmayer, & Waldmann, 2010). Again, though, all these algorithms explicitly understand causal structure learning as people trying to learn the graphical component of a DAG-based graphical model. Causal structure and parameter learning cognitive models can thus universally be understood as people acquiring cognitive representations that are structured as DAG-based graphical models.

4.3 Causal Reasoning

Learning causal structures in the world is only one part of causal cognition; we also need some way to use the results of that learning. The most obvious form of causal reasoning is when we predict or infer something about the state of the world based on our understanding of the causal structure, perhaps coupled with some observations. For example, I infer that the light switch in my office is in the up position because I know that the switch controls the lights and I observe that the lights are currently on. This type of reasoning is easily performed using graphical models; as noted in chapter 3, graphical models were developed in part to optimize exactly this type of inference. The central challenge in any inference is almost always determining what is relevant to the question at hand, and graphical models (by design and construction) encode exactly these relevance relations. Because of this compact encoding of relevance, inference and prediction can occur through information "flowing" (metaphorically, of course) along the edges in the graph, where there are many different practical implementations of this high-level idea. (Technical details about inference using graphical models are provided in sec. 4.3.1.) Of course, the fact that prediction and inference can easily be done with graphical models does not imply that *people* actually operate this way. The descriptive question is whether people make inferences and predictions about their world using causal knowledge in a way that conforms (at least roughly) to inference on DAG-based graphical models.

Suppose that I know something about the causal structure of the world; perhaps I know that C causes M and M causes E (i.e., $C \rightarrow M \rightarrow E$), and I additionally know something about the degree or strength of the causal connections. If I then learn something about the state of one part of the world, what inferences do I draw about other parts of the world? For example, if I learn that C actually occurred, I might conclude that E probably also concluded. Rottman & Hastie (2014) performed an exhaustive survey of almost all published (at that time) experiments on this type of causal reasoning. They found experiments testing an extremely wide range of different causal structures and information sets and aimed to determine whether standard normative inference algorithms, applied to DAG-based graphical models, can provide a good fit to the quantitative data collected in those experiments. It is important to recognize that their survey speaks only indirectly to issues of cognitive representations; they are principally concerned with the reasoning algorithms or processes that people use, rather than directly assessing whether our cognitive representations are structured (approximately) like graphical models. Nonetheless, to the extent that people behave normatively, we have indirect evidence that our cognitive representations are (probably) structured like a DAG-based graphical model.

Rottman and Hastie conclude that, in general, people largely exhibit normative causal reasoning; that is, our causal reasoning appears to be based on DAG-based graphical models. Their survey noted, however, two important, systematic deviations in people's behavior. First, people seem to systematically underuse parametric information; for example, they do not properly take into account information about the base rate at which some event occurs. Alternately, if $C \rightarrow M \rightarrow E$, then people typically underestimate the impact of C's presence on E's occurrence. This general finding of relative conservativeness in inference (more generally, underuse of information) fits with a much broader pattern of results that extends outside causal reasoning: people frequently fail to fully use all available quantitative information when making inferences about their world. There are multiple plausible explanations for this general pattern of findings. For example, perhaps people rely on prior knowledge from outside the lab rather than on the evidence actually provided. Alternately, inference might occur through an anchor-and-adjust process with insufficient adjustments. More generally, this puzzle is the topic of active research in cognitive science. Importantly, however, it does not necessarily give us reason to think that our causal knowledge is not structured like a graphical model. This systematic deviation suggests that people use nonnormative reasoning algorithms or processes, which could equally well be applied to DAG-based graphical models or not. In fact, many of the alternative, nonnormative reasoning algorithms that have actually been proposed in the psychological literature operate on graphical models. That is, this particular deviation does not provide evidence against the view being proposed in this book. Instead it offers evidence only against the idea that people always use normative reasoning processes on those graphical models, rather than sometimes using more psychologically plausible, but also more heuristic, procedures.

The second deviation from normative behavior is not so easily handled, since it (seemingly) directly implies that our cognitive representations have a different structure. Recall that graphical models must satisfy a Markov assumption that says (roughly) that if two nodes are not adjacent, then they are not informationally relevant to each other (perhaps after conditioning on other nodes). In the causal structure $C \rightarrow M \rightarrow E$, for example, C is not informationally relevant to E once we know (with certainty) the value of M. To make it concrete: once I know that I am infected with a particular strain of the influenza virus (M), learning that I was exposed (C) no longer helps to predict my symptoms (E). The Markov assumption is an absolutely fundamental part of the graphical models framework, as it enables the model to encode ir/relevance. Graphical models are only useful as models of relevance relations—informational, causal, or other—if they can compactly encode which elements are not important for one another, and that depends on the Markov assumption. If people do not seem to follow the Markov assumption, then we seem to have a direct disconfirmation of a core principle underlying the graphical models approach. And it does appear that people systematically violate the Markov assumption: in cases like this example, their predictions about *E* change depending on whether they learn that someone has both *C* and *M*, versus learning only that someone has *M*. That is, information about *M* does not fully block the relevance of *C* on *E*. Most of the research on these seeming violations of the Markov assumption has taken place in the context of causal-structure-based categories, and so I will fully discuss this issue in the next chapter (on concepts).[8] The key point now is that I will argue in section 5.3 that there are multiple natural explanations for people's behavior that are completely consistent with the relevant representations being structured as a DAG-based graphical model. Given the substantial evidence in *favor* of the graphical models approach, much more definitive evidence is required about seeming violations of the Markov assumption before we abandon the graphical models framework.

None of the causal reasoning discussed so far in this section, though, is actually distinctively *causal*: one could make all the same inferences—whether exactly normatively correct or systematically deviating in certain ways—with a noncausal representation.[9] As noted earlier, causal representations enable us to make predictions and reason about interventions or actions that come from outside the causal system. One type of reasoning about interventions is action selection: given a causal structure and a desired outcome, which variable or node should be the target of my action? People's behavior on this problem largely conforms to the DAG-based graphical model predictions; people correctly use their causal knowledge to choose actions that will largely be efficacious at obtaining some desired outcome (Hagmayer & Meder, 2013; Meder et al., 2010; Nichols & Danks, 2007; Sloman & Hagmayer, 2006). I will return to discuss this point in greater detail in chapter 6, since this causal reasoning naturally serves our decision making.

A more restricted type of causal reasoning about interventions is determining the likelihood of various outcomes given that I perform an action on the causal structure, rather than simply observing some part of the causal structure. There is clearly a difference between action and observation: if I observe that the lights are off, then I can make an inference about the state of the light switch; if I break the lights, then no such inference is warranted. More generally, psychological experiments have focused on cases in which an action is a so-called hard intervention that breaks all the other causal connections into that particular variable. For example, when I break the lights, I also sever the *Switch* → *Lights* causal connection, which yields a graph in which there is no edge (and thus no relevance relation) between *Switch* and *Lights*. According to this modified graph, I cannot make any inferences about *Switch* given information about *Lights* (and vice versa). Moreover, people appear to be highly sensitive to this distinction: they know, for example, that the observation of an effect supports inferences about the cause, while an intervention on it does not (Sloman & Lagnado, 2005; Waldmann & Hagmayer, 2005). People are appropriately sensitive even in more complex structures: given the causal structure $E_1 \leftarrow C \rightarrow E_2$, they realize that an observation of E_1 is informative about E_2, but an intervention on it is not. Some evidence even suggests that the observation/intervention distinction is important in causal reasoning by nonhuman animals (Blaisdell, Sawa, Leising, & Waldmann, 2006; Leising, Wong, Waldmann, & Blaisdell, 2008).

The general moral of this research is that the different ways that people use information from observations versus interventions in their causal reasoning can be modeled as different operations on the same underlying cognitive representations, structured as DAG-based graphical models. Our causal reasoning does seem to be "truly causal," in the sense that it recognizes and respects the differential impact of interventions from outside the causal structure. Having said that, one might object that this conclusion is too quick: if the causal structures were learned from data that included interventions, then people could have learned (in a noncausal way) that the relevance relations vary across contexts, such as the "intervene on effect" versus "observe effect" contexts. This worry turns out to be misplaced, however: Waldmann and Hagmayer (2005) and others have shown that people make the normatively correct (i.e., as predicted by graphical models) postintervention inferences even when causal structures are learned from purely observational data. This is a particularly striking finding, since people are making (correct) inferences that differ from any data that they have ever seen. The causal knowledge that we get from causal inference really does seem to be structured as (something like) a graphical model, regardless of whether the learning data came from observations, interventions, or a mixture.

I have focused so far on our qualitative causal reasoning about interventions and observations: do people realize that actions or interventions can break causal connections? One could additionally ask about people's *quantitative* postintervention causal reasoning, and here the story is trickier. The numeric estimates that people provide when engaged in postintervention causal reasoning often do not precisely conform to the normative predictions, which might appear problematic for my graphical-models-based cognitive architecture. Recall, however, that an intervention (at least in these psychological experiments) is essentially a graph modification operation that takes an initial causal structure and removes the edges into any node that is the target of an intervention. Postintervention causal reasoning can thus be understood as a two-step process: (i) transform the causal graph, and (ii) do "standard" causal reasoning on the modified graph. I argued earlier that step (ii) seems to involve processes or algorithms that are not (strictly speaking) normatively correct, though they still operate on DAG-based graphical models. The key question is thus not whether people's behavior is normatively correct when reasoning about postintervention causal systems but whether that behavior looks like this type of two-step process. The answer appears to be yes: the systematic deviations that people make in their quantitative postintervention causal reasoning are exactly the behavior that we would expect if they were doing post*observation* causal reasoning (with its two characteristic types of deviation) on an appropriately altered graph. Thus the quantitative deviations in postintervention causal reasoning seem to arise for exactly the same reasons as—and in an important sense are identical with—those deviations in postobservation causal reasoning.

A very different type of causal reasoning occurs when people reason about the causes in some particular case. In particular, we frequently encounter a situation and need to use our causal knowledge to determine which potential causes were actual causes. That is, given that some event occurred (and given our background causal knowledge), what caused the event? Our causal knowledge about general types of situations is clearly connected with what we know or infer in a particular situation. Part of the reason that I infer that aspirin stopped my headache this morning is because I know that aspirin generally stops headaches. And observations of particular instances are part of the reason that I learned the general structure. At the same time, reasoning in a particular case must take into account the specific details of that situation, and so is at least a more complicated type of graphical model inference.

Historically, much of the research on causal judgment in specific cases has focused on reasoning in social situations and, in particular, the challenge of determining whether someone's actions are caused by the environment/situation or by the individual's persistent personality traits. People's behavior can vary widely across different circumstances, and predicting future behavior requires separating out the influences of situation from those of the person's stable personality (Mischel & Shoda, 1995). A substantial empirical literature examines people's judgments in these types of cases, but there are two reasons why it is unclear whether graphical models can help with this literature. First, we (as researchers) often have substantial ambiguity about what causal knowledge subserves much social cognition and inference, and so we do not know what is potentially represented as a graphical model. For example, general folk theories of behavior exhibit significant cultural variations that seem to lead to differences in (social) causal attribution (Norenzayan, Choi, & Nisbett, 2002), but we do not actually know the precise structure of those background folk theories. In particular, we do not know whether those theories can be captured in a graphical model, and if so, whether our behavior can be modeled as inferences on that model. Second, and more importantly, social causal attribution is closely bound up with many factors besides just causation: judgments of blame, responsibility, praise, legal culpability, and more all factor into our social judgments. As such, it is not always clear what morals can be drawn about general causal attribution from findings about distinctively social causal attribution.[10] Even if these causal judgments start as causal inference in a graphical model, they are clearly subject to many other influences that have not yet been put into the graphical models framework.

At the same time, some of these theories of causal attribution have been stated in more general terms that extend beyond social situations, even if they were originally inspired by problems in social psychology. Historically, such models have tended to focus on the importance of correlation: for any particular case, the most likely causes of some event E are those factors that most strongly covary with E (e.g., Kelley, 1973). Such accounts can straightforwardly be captured in the graphical-models-based framework if we think that causal attribution is simply a matter of inferring which causes were likely present, given an observation of the effect. That is, these accounts propose that causal attribution is no different (in kind) from the observational inference that we just showed could be understood as (nonnormative, psychologically plausible) operations on causal knowledge structured as a graphical model.

General causal attribution is not, however, so simple, precisely because our causal knowledge is often richer than the simple model used in these correlation-based accounts. In particular, we often have information about causal mechanisms.[11] For example, we may know details about a particular causal connection, such as when it is (and is not) likely to be active, the steps by which the cause at the start of the mechanism leads to the effect at the end, and so forth. Moreover, this additional causal knowledge makes a difference: if two potential causes have the same correlation with the effect, then people disproportionately select the factor about which they have more mechanism information as "the" cause (Ahn & Bailenson, 1996; Ahn, Kalish, Medin, & Gelman, 1995). As a concrete example, suppose a car accident occurs when the road was icy, and also the driver took a medication that (somehow) causes one to be more likely to have a car accident. Furthermore, suppose that the correlation between the medication and a car accident is equal to that between icy roads and a car accident. In this example, people will be much more likely to select the icy road as "the" cause, at least partly because they know a mechanism by which road conditions can lead to a car accident, while that type of mechanism information is missing for the medication. This finding is relatively unsurprising, since the mechanism information helps us to have more confidence, for example, that this situation is one in which the mechanism could have been active, whereas knowledge of the correlation supports no such claims.[12] The relevant question here is whether this finding can be explained in terms of operations on a DAG-based graphical model.

To answer this question, we need to understand better what is involved in the "mechanism" information in these experiments. In practice, the focus has been on information about how some causal factor brings about the effect. For example, an icy road leads to a car accident because the wheels slip and the driver loses control over the vehicle. As this example shows, this type of mechanism information is largely about intervening variables on the causal pathway: instead of *Ice* → *Accident*, we have *Ice* → *Slipping* → *Loss of control* → *Accident*. That is, people tend to select factors as "the" cause when they know about the mediating factors along the causal pathway. The relationship between mediating variables and the overall causal relation is easily captured in the graphical models framework (through the notion of marginalization; see sec. 4.3.1 for the technical details). And we can use this technical machinery to explain and justify the overall preference: if people make reasonable inferences from the stories that they are told, then they should (justifiably) think it is more likely that the factor with a known mechanism is the actual cause.

One final way of investigating causal reasoning is simply to look at the way that we use causal talk in our everyday language. Rather than presenting people with novel situations or sequences of cases, we could instead try to determine the meanings of causal terms in natural language. For example, one could ask about the content of the terms "cause" and "enable" such that people readily utter sentences such as "the spark caused the fire, but the oxygen in the room enabled it," with the implied contrast between "cause" and "enable." In general, this type of everyday language turns out to be (arguably) best explained in terms of "force dynamics" (Talmy, 1988; Wolff, 2007; Wolff & Song, 2003). More specifically, this account says that people think about the world in terms of forces that, like those in naive physics, have direction and magnitude.[13] When I raise my coffee mug, for example, the force of gravity pulls the mug downward, and the force produced by my arm directs it upward. When the force from my arm exceeds that from gravity, the mug moves toward my mouth, and most people would say that my arm *caused* the mug to move *despite* gravity. If the force of gravity is stronger than my muscles, however, then people say that gravity *caused* the mug to stay still *despite* my arm. More generally, the force dynamics model provides semantic content for many different causal verbs in terms of patterns of relative directions and magnitudes of the relevant forces (Talmy, 1988; Wolff, 2007; Wolff & Song, 2003).

The force dynamics model is frequently expressed using arrows to represent forces, but the account is very different from the graphical-models-based approach advocated in this book. The edges in the graph part of a graphical model represent only qualitative relations of direct relevance. In contrast, the arrows in a force dynamics model encode *quantitative* information about the direction and magnitude of the force. Both types of accounts use arrows, but they mean very different things by those arrows, and so the force dynamics model appears to represent a serious challenge to the graphical-models-based view. They are, however, potentially more compatible than initially appears, as they seem to be based on different sets of "causal representational simples" (for a similar point, see Gerstenberg, Goodman, Lagnado, & Tenenbaum, 2012).

Most of the work supporting the force dynamics model has looked at causal language in the manipulation and use of physical objects, or cases for which physical object manipulation provides a natural analogy. This type of causal reasoning is almost certainly based on causal knowledge derived from causal perception. In contrast, reasoning about the effect of aspirin on my headache does not seem to be based in analogies with the manipulation of physical objects but rather depends on causal knowledge from causal inference. I will argue in section 4.4 that, in contrast with representations from causal inference, the products of causal perception are likely *not* well modeled using graphical models. Thus causal terms in everyday language may be grounded in two different representational bases, depending on the particular problem, domain, or knowledge source (perception versus inference). Of course, this assumes that the semantics of everyday causal language about knowledge gained from causal inference can be captured using graphical models. To my knowledge, this is essentially an open problem, though it seems likely given the other evidence reported in this section.

4.3.1 Causal Reasoning as Graphical Model Reasoning*

Causal reasoning experiments that ask for judgments about the likelihood of different events are essentially just asking for conditional probability judgments; in fact, the experimental probes sometimes ask exactly that question. In these situations, the normative response is to give the actual conditional probability. As a running example, suppose that the causal structure is $C \rightarrow M \rightarrow E$. This structure implies that the joint probability distribution factors into $P(C = c, M = m, E = e) = P(C = c)\ P(M = m \mid C = c)\ P(E = e \mid M = m)$. For simplicity, we can assume that all three variables are binary valued. Now, suppose that we want to infer the likelihood that E is present given that C is present; that is, we want to compute $P(E = 1 \mid C = 1)$. Given the Markov factorization of the joint probability distribution, this conditional probability can straightforwardly be computed as $P(E = 1 \mid M = 1)P(M = 1 \mid C = 1) + P(E = 1 \mid M = 0)P(M = 0 \mid C = 1)$. More generally, there are easy algorithms for translating any conditional probability into this type of "sum of products" of terms in the Markov factorization. There are also various distributed methods for carrying out this inference, such as message-passing algorithms (Pearl, 1988). In a message-passing algorithm, the nodes "talk" to one another along the edges; essentially nodes "know" their own probability distribution, and they "tell" their neighbors whenever their own estimate changes. These algorithms are typically quite fast and relatively low computation and thus appear to be psychologically plausible. Message-passing algorithms have even been suggested as neurally plausible models for these kinds of inferences (Lee & Mumford, 2003).

The systematic review by Rottman and Hastie (2014) told us that people do not always provide the normatively correct response; normatively correct message-passing algorithms capture much of human behavior but cannot be fully descriptively accurate, at least at the cognitive level. As a reminder, I focus here on the relative underweighting of information in causal reasoning and postpone (until chap. 5) a discussion of the claim that people violate the Markov assumption. We currently have no well-specified causal reasoning algorithms that can fully account for the experimental data, but several plausible options immediately suggest themselves. One natural proposal is that inference proceeds through message passing in which the messages simply do not have the normatively correct impact on the receiving node's "self-distribution." This proposal is underspecified, however, as no account is provided for when and why the messages fail to have the correct impact. People do sometimes engage in normatively correct causal reasoning (multiple examples are discussed in Rottman & Hastie, 2014), and so any message-passing algorithm that simply discounts messages across the board will fail to capture the empirical data.

A very different type of reasoning algorithm is based on "sampling" our causal knowledge. Almost all graphical models are also generative models that can be used to produce a simulated or imaginary data set. We first generate values for the exogenous (i.e., parentless) variables by sampling from their unconditional probabilities; note that $P(X)$ is a term in the Markov factorization for any exogenous X, so this is easy. Given values for the exogenous variables, it is straightforward to probabilistically determine the values of their children, and then their children's children, and so forth. At each step, the probabilistic "choice" is simply a sample from a conditional distribution term in the Markov factorization, and so this procedure is fast and easy. At the end, we have a data set of imaginary but fully specified cases that mirrors (up to sampling variability) the joint distribution in the quantitative component of the graphical model. One method for determining $P(E = 1 \mid C = 1)$ would thus be to generate an imaginary data set in which every "individual" has $C = 1$, and then just compute the frequency (in that data set) of $P(E = 1)$. Introspectively, the data set generation seems easy: just imagine a bunch of individuals with C and then let the causal structure "flow" forward until you have an idea about how many have E. The output of this type of "reasoning as sampling" algorithm (Vul, Goodman, Griffiths, & Tenenbaum, 2009; see also Denison, Bonawitz, Gopnik, & Griffiths, 2013) will converge to the normatively correct answer as the size of the imaginary data set grows, but it can give decidedly nonnormative responses if one generates very small, or even just single-data-point, data sets (Vul, Goodman, Griffiths, & Tenenbaum, 2009). It is an open theoretical and empirical question whether this type of reasoning algorithm can account for the nonnormative behavior found in causal reasoning from observations, but it is a promising alternative to "simple" underweighting that can also explain a number of nonnormative behaviors in other areas of cognition. More importantly, these two proposals together show that we have little reason to conclude that DAG-based graphical models are an insufficient representation for causal reasoning, as there are reasoning algorithms that (likely) can predict people's nonnormative behavior.

Now consider trying to reason causally about the impact of an action or intervention. The experimental literature has focused almost exclusively on "hard" interventions that break all other arrows into (but not those out of) the target of the intervention whenever the intervention is active. When one performs a hard intervention or action, a highly predictable change occurs in the graph component of the graphical model, and thus a predictable corresponding change in the Markov factorization of the joint probability distribution.[14] For example, suppose we intervene to force $M = 1$. In this case, the $C \rightarrow M$ edge is removed from the graph in our running example because C no longer matters for M, but the $M \rightarrow E$ edge is left intact. The resulting joint probability distribution factors as $P(C = c, M = m, E = e) = P(C = c)\ P(M = m)\ P(E = e \mid M = m)$, where $P(M = 1) = 1$. The important point here is that the result of the intervention operation is just another well-specified graphical model. Thus postintervention causal reasoning is formally identical with postobservation causal reasoning, but with a (potentially) modified graph. All the arguments and observations from the previous discussion thus apply equally to postintervention causal reasoning. In particular, we have a set of possible reasoning algorithms that can explain people's nonnormative behavior (again, leaving possible violations of the Markov assumption to sec. 5.3) as inferences in a DAG-based graphical model.

Now consider the causal reasoning problem of determining "the" cause in some particular case. Because we have a specific case, we have definite values for (most of) the variables, and so this causal reasoning problem is not obviously a conditional probability judgment problem, and we cannot straightforwardly use the algorithms and observations from the preceding paragraphs. Judgments about "the" cause arise precisely because we recognize that a cause variable can be present without *actually* causing the effect. For example, suppose a drunk driver is completely stopped at a light and someone else runs into him. There are clearly versions of this scenario in which the driver's being drunk was causally irrelevant to the accident, though being drunk is, in general, a cause of car accidents.[15] One natural way to capture this in DAG-based graphical models is to add an unobserved variable *CP* for each separate causal "pathway" that indicates whether that particular pathway was active on this particular occasion.[16] In the case of the drunk driver, the standard causal pathway from *Drunk* to *Accident* is not active, though both *Drunk* and *Accident* have the value *Yes*. There are serious questions about exactly how to individuate causal pathways, but various proposals aim to solve this problem (e.g., Hausman & Woodward, 2004), and the distinction is often clear in practice. Given such an individuation, the challenge of determining "the" cause becomes the problem of determining which causal pathway (with the cause present) was most likely active.

To give a concrete example (and to see how the mathematics work), suppose that we have the causal structure $C_1 \rightarrow E \leftarrow C_2$, where (i) C_1 and C_2 influence E along separate causal pathways; (ii) C_1, C_2, and E all actually occur; and (iii) the conditional probabilities for E are $P(E = 1 \mid C_1 = 1, C_2 = 1) = 0.875$; $P(E = 1 \mid C_1 = 1, C_2 = 0) = 0.75$; $P(E = 1 \mid C_1 = 0, C_2 = 1) = 0.5$; and $P(E = 1 \mid C_1 = 0, C_2 = 0) = 0$. (These conditional probabilities correspond to a noisy-OR structure (see sec. 4.2.1) with $w_1 = 0.75$ and $w_2 = 0.5$.) If we augment the DAG-based graphical model to include the *CP* variables, then we get the graph in figure 4.2, and the conditional probability of E changes to be a deterministic function in which E occurs if and only if both C_1 and CP_1 are present, or both C_2 and CP_2 are present.

To fully specify the graphical model, we must also provide the unconditional probabilities of CP_1 and CP_2, but those are simply the probabilities

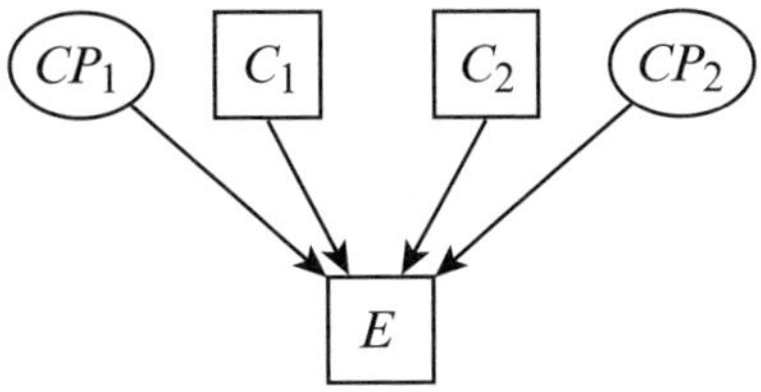

Figure 4.2
Causal graph augmented with causal pathway (mechanism) variables.

of E given that only the corresponding cause variable is present; that is, they are 0.75 and 0.5, respectively. Given this augmented graphical model, one can determine "the" cause by computing the relative probabilities that each CP variable is present, given that C_1, C_2, and E all actually occur. In this particular case, it is straightforward to compute that $P(CP_1 = 1 \mid C_1 = C_2 = E = 1) > P(CP_2 = 1 \mid C_1 = C_2 = E = 1)$, and so people should judge C_1 to be more likely to be "the" cause. More generally, this approach predicts that judgments about which factor is the cause (given multiple options) should be in relative proportion to their reliability to bring about the effect (i.e., the likelihood that their causal pathway is active); in unpublished experiments with David Rose and Edouard Machery, we found people exhibiting exactly this behavior.

Now, consider what it means to know the existence of a mechanism. In the relevant experiments, this information is invariably knowledge about the intervening variables by which some cause can bring about the effect. For example, I know that the switch causes the lights by controlling the flow of electricity in the wires; instead of just *Switch* → *Lights*, I know that it is *Switch* → *Electricity in wires* → *Lights*. There may be other information that we would want to call mechanism knowledge (Machamer et al., 2000), but these causal reasoning experiments focus on this type of knowledge. One nice feature of graphical models is that we can straightforwardly use them to model the inclusion or exclusion of mediating variables (Richardson, 2003; Richardson & Spirtes, 2002). In particular, if one marginalizes out (i.e., ignores) an intermediate variable in some causal chain—for example, M in the causal structure $C \rightarrow M \rightarrow E$—then the resulting graphical model simply has a direct edge from the cause to the effect: $C \rightarrow E$. Technically, these procedures require the use of acyclic directed *mixed* graphs (ADMGs) rather than standard DAGs, since a variable being ignored might be a common cause of multiple variables in the graph (which produces a bidirected edge "↔" in the graph). None of the experimental cases involve cases like these, though, and so marginalization yields DAGs.

We can combine these two ideas—the model of judgments of "the" cause and mechanism information as knowledge of intervening variables—to understand the causal reasoning results showing a preference for factors for which we know the causal mechanism. More specifically, suppose we know the causal structure $C_M \rightarrow E \leftarrow C_C$ and we have mechanism information for $C_M \rightarrow E$ but not $C_C \rightarrow E$. Since we do not have mechanism information for C_C, we need to introduce a variable CP_{CC} indicating whether that causal pathway is active. In contrast, we can change $C_M \rightarrow E$ into $C_M \rightarrow M \rightarrow E$, reflecting our mechanism knowledge. Moreover, this mechanism information means that we do *not* need to add a CP_{CM} variable to the graph, since the C_M pathway being active *just is* M being present. Instead we need to add a variable CP_M indicating whether the $M \rightarrow E$ pathway is active. That is, the full graph is not the simple common effect model from the beginning of the paragraph but rather the more complicated graph shown in figure 4.3.

Now consider the experimental setting in which we know that C_M, C_C, and E all are present, and the correlation between C_M and E is the same as the correlation between C_C and E. To identify "the" cause, we must determine which causal pathway variable has higher probability. Importantly, however, CP_{CC} is compared not with CP_{CM} but with CP_M. The matching of correlations implies that $P(CP_{CM} \mid C_M, C_C, E) = P(CP_{CC} \mid C_M, C_C, E)$. At the same time, it is simple to prove that $P(CP_M \mid M, C_C, E) > P(CP_{CM} \mid C_M, C_C, E)$, assuming that the mechanism is generative. Thus the variable with mechanism

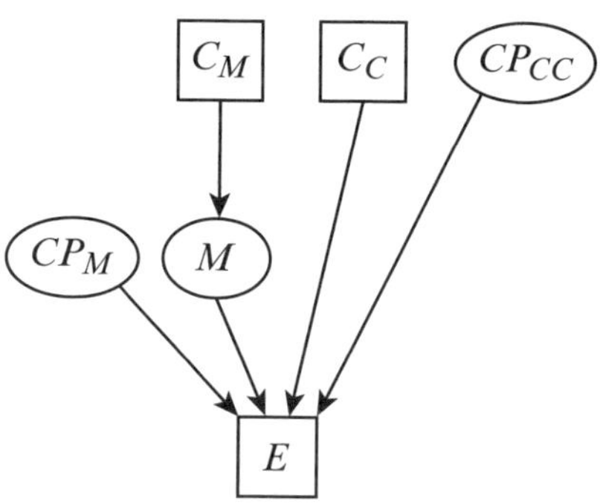

Figure 4.3
Expanded graph with mechanism information.

information should be chosen as "the" cause just when we know (or believe) that *M* occurred. In all the standard psychological experiments, either the mechanism variable is explicitly known to occur, or nothing at all is mentioned about it. In the latter case (and given that all these mechanisms are relatively reliable and well-known), a natural inference is that absence of mention implies nothing unusual or abnormal; that is, participants can very naturally infer that *M* is present. And putting these pieces together, we see that there is a normative explanation of the preference for choosing as "the" cause exactly those variables about which we have mechanism information.

I have focused here on a computational explanation for this preference, since it makes the most direct case for the graphical models framework. Other types of reasoning could also potentially explain this preference, and these alternatives are equally consistent with cognitive representations of causal structure being DAG-based graphical models, though they do not depend quite so centrally on it. For example, Hitchcock and Knobe (2009) have argued that people choose as "the" cause exactly those variables that are better targets for future interventions. Many different types of mechanism information can inform our intervention decisions, including the actions or form that those interventions take. Hence variables about which we have mechanism information will be better targets for intervention. This explanation depends, however, on people actually having the preference that Hitchcock and Knobe suggest ("the" cause should be something suitable for intervention), and there is reason to question that empirical claim (Sytsma, Livengood, & Rose, 2012). More importantly, this explanation differs at the level of processing algorithm, not representations. Hitchcock and Knobe's idea can easily be translated into the graphical models framework, and so it provides no reason to think that the preference—variables with mechanism information are more preferred as "the" cause—poses any challenge to the view expressed here. In contrast, one particular kind of causal cognition *does* pose such a threat, as we see in the next section.

4.4 Causal Perception

Any exploration of causal cognition would be incomplete without some discussion of causal perception. The canonical example of causal perception is the so-called launching effect, investigated extensively by Michotte (1946). The launching effect is essentially an abstract version of a moving billiard ball hitting a stationary one. Picture a square at rest in the middle of a screen, and then another square moving toward it from offscreen. When the moving square makes contact with the stationary square, the moving one stops, and the stationary one begins moving offscreen. In cases such as these, people almost universally declare that they saw the first square *cause* the second one to move. The perception of this sequence is not simply as a set of motions but rather as an event that involves a rich (in some sense) causal connection. Moreover, this causal perception is quite sensitive to spatiotemporal characteristics of the sequence; a spatial gap between the blocks or a temporal mismatch (the motionless block moving either too early or too late) can destroy the phenomenological experience of causation (Michotte, 1946; Schlottmann & Anderson, 1993). Causal perception extends beyond just the simple launching effect. People also directly perceive other types of physical causal relations such as pulling, shattering, or exploding (Michotte, 1946; White & Milne, 1997, 1999). Causal perception even extends into the social and psychological domain, as some motion sequences lead to the direct perception of personality traits: for example, if one sees a square move erratically across a screen with a triangle smoothly following it, then one often thinks that the square is scared and the triangle is chasing it (Csibra, Gergely, Biro, Koos, & Brockbank, 1999; Gergely, Nadasdy, Csibra, & Biro, 1995; Heider & Simmel, 1944).

The launching effect reliably emerges around six months of age, followed by more complex, sophisticated types of causal perception (including social causal perception) over the following six months (Csibra et al., 1999; Leslie, 1982; Oakes & Cohen, 1990). Causal perception does not seem to be subject to top-down cognitive influences (Blakemore et al., 2001), which has led some authors to suggest that causal perception might be a modular process (Scholl & Tremoulet, 2000), though the evidence on that specific point is mixed (Schlottmann, 2000). Causal perception exhibits many interesting context effects: whether an ambiguous stimulus is perceived causally depends on other events that occur around that time, as well as our attentional focus and other factors (H. Choi & Scholl, 2004, 2006; Gao, Newman, & Scholl, 2009; Scholl & Nakayama, 2002). Causal perception also does not occur in a vacuum, as it is connected with other aspects of cognition such as our knowledge of forces and haptic information (White,

2009, 2012) or our perception of the spatial locations of various objects (Scholl & Nakayama, 2004). Rips (2011) and Scholl and Tremoulet (2000) provide recent reviews of empirical phenomena related to causal perception (see also Danks, 2009). But most important for our present purposes, both neuropsychological and behavioral evidence seem to demonstrate that causal perception and causal inference are cognitively distinct processes (Roser et al., 2005; Schlottmann & Shanks, 1992). As a result, we cannot simply transfer the graphical-models-based analyses from previous sections to causal perception.

In fact, I argue in the remainder of this section that we have good reasons to think that a graphical-models-based analysis of causal perception is unlikely to be forthcoming. It is difficult to draw definitive conclusions about the possibility of a model of causal perception based on graphical models, as there are currently no well-specified formal or computational models of causal perception in *any* framework, so we have no standard against which to judge proposals. However, there are important ways in which the graphical models framework does not seem to "fit the phenomena" of causal perception appropriately. In particular, causal perception depends on fine-grained spatiotemporal details about the objects in question. In contrast, graphical models have principally been (successfully) applied to relatively *dis*continuous phenomena, either discrete-time causal structures (e.g., DAG-based time series models in econometrics) or causal relations between spatially distinct spatial regions (e.g., UG-based models of disease spread in epidemiology). One idea would be to integrate these two types of models into a single causal structure of motion and collisions in the world, where causal perception is some type of inference using that model. Although this seems initially promising, there are many challenges to making it work.

To see some of the difficulties, consider a natural way to try to use graphical models to capture just the launching effect. We start with a large spatial grid in which each location corresponds to a graphical node (with node value denoting whether an object is present at that location). We also assume that time is suitably discretized into a sequence of distinct timesteps. We can then represent movement by using two sets of nodes—one for time t and one for time t+1—where there is an edge from node A in the t-graph to node B in the t+1-graph just in case it is possible for an object to move from A to B in one timestep. This graph is insufficient, however, as it cannot properly represent the acceleration of an object. To capture those features, we need to include at least three timesteps in our graph: edges from t to t+1 indicate movement with a given velocity, while edges from t to t+2 provide information about the acceleration (so that we can predict where the object should be in the next timestep). Given these edges, we can parameterize the graph to encode folk beliefs about the behavior of objects (e.g., an object in motion tends to stay in motion, except when friction slows it down). Finally, to capture the idea of a collision, we need to adjust the parameterization so that an object O at node A that is not moving[17] at t begins to move at t+1 when an object M occupies an adjacent node at t, and M would (if not for O) occupy node A at t+1.

This complicated graphical model *might* capture the launching effect, though it cannot yet handle, for example, the possibility of objects that are large enough to be distributed across multiple spatial nodes. More importantly, though, this graphical model falls far short of modeling causal *perception*: it includes no role for, among other things, the influences of context, attentional grouping, spatiotemporal timing, or mass and force information. And matters get even trickier when we consider more complex types of causal perception, such as exploding (where the cause does not necessarily touch the effect objects) or social causal perception (where fine details about the long-term movement patterns are often relevant). It simply does not appear promising to model causal perception as inference over some causal "motion" graph.

One diagnosis for these difficulties is that they arise from the identification of graphical nodes with spatial locations; perhaps it would work better to use an "object-oriented" model in which the nodes correspond to properties of the blocks themselves. That is, one might consider a graphical model in which the nodes are, say, the spatial locations, velocities, and accelerations of block A, block B, and so forth. One could then build distinct graphical models such as M_{launch}, $M_{explode}$, or M_{chase} corresponding to different ways that the position, velocity, and acceleration of each block can be caused by its own previous state, as well as the states of the other blocks (depending on their location and movement). One would also need a "something else" model that encodes movement patterns that do not fit any causal perception pattern.[18] Once we have this assortment of models, causal perception becomes a matter of model choice: given some perceptual input, one determines which model is the most likely to have produced that particular observation.

There does seem to be something right about the idea of causal perception involving some sort of model choice. Analyses of causal perception in terms of schema activation (or related ideas, such as selecting an intuitive physics model) share this intuition that causal perception involves selection of one possibility from among a larger set (Gerstenberg et al., 2012; Scholl & Nakayama, 2002; White, 2009). The problem, however, is that graphical models do not appear to be the right way to express those different possibilities. First, one cost of using object-oriented graphical models is that we need to have different models depending on the number of objects in the scene. Various computational techniques can handle this problem using plate notation (Koller & Friedman, 2009), but the need for this change already calls into question whether graphical models are an appropriate modeling framework. Second, even if we fix the number of objects, all the different graphical models will be structurally identical. The explanatory work is done entirely by the parameterizations, and those parametric differences will typically be quite subtle and complex. As a result, any insight is unlikely to be due to the graphical models aspect of the framework but rather will arise from something like the fact that these are generative models (Gerstenberg et al., 2012). Third, the previously mentioned context effects depend in part on the fact that causal structures can encompass multiple objects. We thus need to augment all these perceptual models with various possible causal structures over the different objects, thereby further complicating the model choice problem in important ways.

I should reiterate here that I have no definitive proof that causal perception can *not* be fruitfully explained using the graphical models framework. In fact, something "graphical" might very well turn out to be critical, given the importance of force information to causal perception (White, 2009; Wolff, 2007) and the frequently used graphical representation of force dynamics. These graphs are not, however, the same as the graphical models that I employ in this book. As noted earlier, the arrows in a directed acyclic graph are quite different from the arrows in a vector diagram; as just one example, the length of an edge in a DAG is meaningless, whereas the length of an arrow in a vector diagram communicates critical information about the magnitude of the force. We must be careful not to take evidence in favor of vector force diagrams to be evidence in favor of DAG-based graphical models of causal structure of the sort that we discussed earlier. It might be possible to unify the two types of graphs in some way (see also Danks, 2009); in section 10.1 I briefly revisit the challenge of spatiotemporally continuous phenomena for graphical models. In the meantime, we should recognize the possibility that some key cognitive phenomena might not naturally be understood as inference on cognitive representations structured as graphical models.

4.5 Conclusion

Causal cognition as a subject is wide-ranging, and instances of it can be found throughout cognition more generally. It is thus critical that any attempt to unify the mind have a serious engagement with causal learning and reasoning. As I have shown throughout this chapter, we can straightforwardly understand large aspects of our causal cognition as operations on graphical models, specifically DAG-based ones. At the same time, causal cognition was a relatively easy target, as it is arguably the area of cognitive science in which graphical models have already been most widely used and adopted. DAG-based graphical models were originally motivated and developed in part to capture causal relations (Spirtes et al., 2000), so it is perhaps unsurprising that we can use them to unify much of causal cognition (at least to the extent that we think that our cognition tracks or mirrors the world around us). A decidedly more challenging task is showing that graphical models are useful for other types of cognition, so we turn now to the many types of cognition involving concepts.

5 Concepts, Categories, and Inference

5.1 Concepts as Fundamental Building Blocks

The previous chapter showed how to use graphical models to capture our cognitive representations of causal structure, and the operations we perform in causal learning and reasoning. As I noted there, however, causal cognition was arguably an easy target, as one of the principal uses of graphical models over the past twenty years has been to model causal structures in the world. If our cognitive representations track the world to any significant degree, then we should expect that much of our knowledge about causal structures should be structured approximately as a DAG-based graphical model. A far more challenging task is to show that other cognitive representations can usefully be understood as graphical models. In this chapter, I attempt to do just that for concepts.

Concepts are used throughout our cognition to carve up the world ("that's a cat, while that's a dog"), make inferences about new individuals or objects ("that plant has red berries, so they are probably tasty"), organize our knowledge about diverse sets ("cats and whales are very different, but they are both mammals"), and perform many other functions. It is natural to think of them as the foundational elements or building blocks for almost any cognitive representation (Murphy, 2004). For example, the causal structures discussed in the previous chapter were partly built out of concepts: when I believe "flipping the switch causes the light to turn on," I am using many different concepts, including SWITCH, LIGHT, FLIP, and so forth. (For convenience, I will use SMALL CAPS to indicate concepts.) This chapter focuses on how to use graphical models to understand these basic building blocks. The overall thesis of this book—large pieces of our cognition can be unified by understanding them as different operations on shared cognitive representations that are structured (approximately as) graphical models—would clearly not be believable if concepts could not be incorporated, since they are a, perhaps *the*, key aspect of our cognitive representations. This chapter is thus essential, as it provides the grounding (in graphical models) of one of the core constituents of cognition. At the same time, this chapter is but one piece in a broader picture, and so it will at times paint with a broad brush: some distinctions will be blurred (e.g., between a concept and a category), and not every facet of concepts qua knowledge structure will be explored.[1] I will instead focus on showing how many of the key cognitive operations involving concepts—feature inference, categorization, hierarchical inference, and more—can be understood as operations on graphical models.

There is a massive array of different models of concepts. In this chapter, I focus on three major ones—exemplar, prototype, and (one type of) theory theory accounts—all of which have corresponding computational versions. There are certainly many other theories about concepts, some of which are computationally well specified (e.g., Love, Medin, & Gureckis, 2004), and others that are stated in less mathematical terms (e.g., Barsalou, 1999). My goal in this chapter is not completeness about theories of concepts, as that would require at least a full book on its own, as others have shown (e.g., Murphy, 2004; Pothos & Wills, 2011). Instead I aim to demonstrate that (i) three of the "biggest names" in theories of concepts can be understood as describing particular types of graphical models; (ii) many cognitive processes involving concepts can be understood as operations using these graphical models; and (iii) the graphical models framework can help us to make sense of experimental results, and also some of the ways in which concepts can be related to one another. In the remainder of this section, I outline the conceptual foundations of these three theories of concepts. Sections 5.2 through 5.4 then show qualitatively how goals (i) through (iii) can be met using the graphical models framework, and section 5.5 provides the relevant mathematical details.

One major theory of concepts holds that they are sets of exemplars—salient, previously observed members of the category (Kruschke, 1992; Lamberts, 1998, 2000; Medin & Schaffer, 1978; Nosofsky, 1984, 1986, 1991; Nosofsky & Palmeri, 1997; Nosofsky & Zaki, 2002; Zaki, Nosofsky, Stanton, & Cohen, 2003); Logan (2004) provides a good overview of exemplar-based theories of concepts. The underlying intuition for these theories is that each concept is defined by a set of "canonical cases" that were previously observed to be a member of the relevant category. For example, the concept Tiger would be represented by my previous observations of tigers, or at least the salient observations. This set of exemplars provides an implicit encoding of the relevant information about the concept, including its key properties, representative instances, and relations with other concepts. For example, properties that are possessed by every exemplar will tend to be critical for categorization judgments. Importantly, exemplar-based theories require only that the relevant or salient features of the category exemplars be encoded. The theories are not committed to the computationally implausible claim that I remember every feature of every tiger that I have ever seen; rather, I encode just the features that I learn or believe to be important for the category. Exemplar-based theories of concepts are particularly good at explaining our ability to recognize unusual members of a category and also provide a basis for multiple cognitively plausible theories of concept learning.

A second major theory is that concepts are defined by some prototypical case (Minda & Smith, 2001, 2002; Posner & Keele, 1968; Reed, 1972). A prototype-based concept is similar in many ways to an exemplar-based one with only one exemplar, except that the prototypical instance need not have been observed. In fact, the prototypical instance can have features that cannot occur in the real world. For example, every actual bird either can fly or cannot; the prototypical instance for the concept Bird, in contrast, could have some intermediate value to indicate that only some individuals in the population of birds actually fly. In general, the precise interpretation of the prototype is usually ambiguous between two interpretations. In some settings, the prototype is supposed to represent the stereotypical instance of the category (e.g., the stereotypical bird is 95 percent of a "flyer"), where that case clearly need not occur in the world. On other occasions, the prototypical instance encodes summary information about the observed cases (e.g., 95 percent of birds fly). These two different interpretations typically do not conflict, though they are obviously conceptually distinct: the stereotypical instance need not have features that exactly match the observed statistics. Thankfully, this ambiguity will not be an issue for us. Prototype-based theories of concepts are particularly good at explaining phenomena such as our ability to rapidly identify stereotypical instances of a category, even when we have never before seen that particular instance.

A third major class of models of concepts is the so-called theory theory, which holds that concepts are either small (quasi-scientific) theories or key terms in such a theory (Carey, 1985; Gopnik, 1988; Gopnik & Meltzoff, 1997). That is, concepts are determined by the roles that they play in our broader knowledge structures, rather than being solely driven in a bottom-up fashion by the observations that we make. There are many different ways of understanding a "theory," and so the theory theory is better understood as a very large set of distinct accounts of concepts. Moreover, many of these accounts have not been clearly specified but rather have relied on relatively qualitative explications. One well-specified version that has been heavily tested is causal model theory (Oppenheimer, Tenenbaum, & Krynski, 2013; Rehder, 2003a, 2003b; Rehder & Hastie, 2004; Rehder & Kim, 2006), which focuses on causal structures as the key type of theory. More precisely, causal model theory holds that some categories are determined by identity of underlying causal structure. That is, individual members of a category are bound together by having the same underlying causal structure, at least for the relevant observed features. For example, any animal with the appropriate causal structure would be classified as a TIGER, even if it had no observable features in common with "normal" tigers. Causal structures support counterfactuals, and so even though an animal might not look like a tiger at this moment, the key question is whether the cognizer believes that the animal *would have been* a "normal" tiger in various counterfactual situations. Causal model theory is particularly well suited to explaining our ability to reason about complex counterfactuals involving members of a category, as well as why the statistical frequency of a property (within a category) is often a poor guide to the property's importance in reasoning about the category.

As noted earlier, these three types of theories cover many of, though certainly not all, the proposed accounts of concepts. At the same time, all three of these theory types can fruitfully be understood within the framework of graphical models. The next section shows qualitatively how this representation can be done. Section 5.3 then shows how various cognitive processes involving single concepts (e.g., feature inference) can be understood as operations on those graphical models. Section 5.3 also shows how to understand categorization (i.e., between-concept competition) in the graphical models framework. Section 5.4 then examines the various between-concept relationships that can obtain, such as one concept being superordinate to another. The mathematical details for all the qualitative claims in sections 5.2 through 5.4 are provided in section 5.5. As in chapter 4, much of the work of this chapter is to show that different extant cognitive theories can be captured in the graphical models framework, so I will not dwell on many of the important empirical disputes about concepts. Throughout, it is important to bear in mind the overarching theme of this book: we can fruitfully understand disparate types of cognitive activity as different processes operating on a shared store of cognitive representations, expressed as graphical models. The following sections aim to show that this thesis holds for basic cognitive operations involving concepts.

5.2 Concepts, Probability Distributions, and Graphical Models

Probability distributions have long been used to provide precise content for different qualitative concept types. More precisely, we first assume that, for each concept *C*, there is some (possibly quite large) collection of features and properties that are relevant to *C*. For example, the concept Dog presumably involves properties such as barking, typically having four legs, and so forth. These features can all be straightforwardly understood as variables that could take on different values; the property of barking might be treated as the variable *Barks* with possible values "yes" or "no." This set of variables **F** (again, possibly quite large) is exactly the sort of thing over which we can define a probability distribution. And the qualitative intuitions underlying the concept types can then be understood in terms of constraints on acceptable probability distributions, where any particular concept *C* is represented by a specific probability distribution over the relevant features. For example, a set of exemplars (implicitly) determines a probability distribution, so we can represent (aspects of) the concept with that distribution. It is important to recognize that "represented by" is not the same as "identical with." In particular, we can use probability distributions in this way without being committed to the implausible claim that concepts are *nothing more* than those distributions; rather, the idea is to use probability distributions to make precise some of the qualitative ideas underlying each concept type. For convenience, I will denote the probability distribution for a particular concept by $P_C(\mathbf{F})$, but all the mathematical details will be confined to section 5.5.

Several different theories of concepts (and categorization; see sec. 5.3) have previously been understood directly in terms of constraints on the possible probability distributions for particular concepts of that type (Ashby & Alfonso-Reese, 1995; Ashby & Maddox, 1993; Myung, 1994; Rosseel, 2002). In contrast, my core thesis requires that I translate these theories of concepts into constraints on graphical models (and their accompanying probability distributions); since not every probability distribution has a perfect graphical model representation (recall sec. 3.4), my task goes further than that previous work. The translation of concepts into graphical models is trivial in the case of causal model theory, as it is already stated in the language of causal DAG-based models. More precisely, causal model theory is defined as the theory that concepts are determined by shared causal structure, where that causal structure is expressed as a DAG-based graphical model, just as we saw causal structure represented in chapter 4. As a result, causal model theory concepts are already required to use only probability distributions $P_C(\mathbf{F})$ that satisfy the causal Markov and Faithfulness assumptions for a DAG encoding that causal structure.

The translation into graphical models and accompanying probability distributions is less straightforward for exemplar- and prototype-based models, as they have not previously been expressed in the graphical models framework. In general, the intuition behind exemplar-based concepts is that the connection between an individual X and a concept C should be based on the similarity between X and each of the exemplars of C. If X is very similar to most of the exemplars, then it is probably a C; if it is quite different from most of the exemplars, then it is probably not a C. There are many different quantitative versions of exemplar-based models, where the best-known one is Nosofsky's (1986) generalized context model (GCM). All these different quantitative models formalize the intuition that similarity is the basis of categorization by defining the "fit" of X into concept C to be the (weighted) average similarity between X and each exemplar of C.[2] Different methods of assessing similarity lead to different cognitive theories, though we find shared features across theories: for example, things are always more similar to themselves than anything else. Each precise notion of "fit" or "average similarity" determines a probability distribution for the concept C, where $P_C(\mathbf{F})$ is maximal for the instances that best fit C, and the probability decreases proportionally as the fit worsens. That is, the

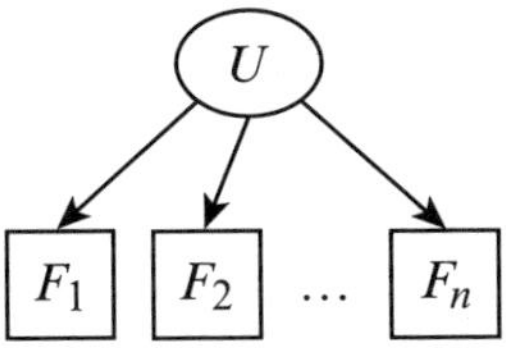

Figure 5.1
Graphical model for exemplar-based concepts over **F**.

probability distribution for an exemplar-based concept tracks the similarity function that is determined by the set of underlying exemplars.

At the same time, consider the graphical model shown in figure 5.1, where U is unobserved. In this graphical model, each observed variable/feature F_i depends directly on only the unobserved cause, rather than on any of the other observed variables/features. In machine learning contexts, this type of DAG is frequently labeled a naive Bayes model (Mitchell, 1997), but there is nothing inherently Bayesian about the DAG. It is simply a representation of the structures in which every pair of observed features is associated, but those associations are entirely due to an unobserved common cause.

It turns out that there is a tight connection between the DAG in figure 5.1 and exemplar-based concepts. In particular, suppose **EC** is the set of $P_C(\mathbf{F})$ for exemplar-based concepts; that is, **EC** is the set of probability distributions that correspond to some exemplar-based concept. Also, suppose $\mathbf{GM}_{\mathbf{EC}}$ is the set of probability distributions that satisfy the Markov and Faithfulness assumptions for the DAG in figure 5.1; that is, $\mathbf{GM}_{\mathbf{EC}}$ is the set of probability distributions that can be perfectly represented by the figure 5.1 DAG. We can then prove (see theorems 5.1 and 5.2 in sec. 5.5) that $\mathbf{EC} = \mathbf{GM}_{\mathbf{EC}}$. In other words, there is a direct translation in both directions between (the mathematical statement of) any exemplar-based concept and a graphical model with the figure 5.1 DAG (under mild assumptions). In fact, theorems 5.1 and 5.2 provide a recipe for both directions: given precise numbers for one side, one can immediately derive the appropriate numbers for the other side.

Now consider prototype-based concepts. Concepts involving only the set of variables/features **F** are essentially always mathematically characterized as "exemplar-based concepts with only one exemplar." The fit of any

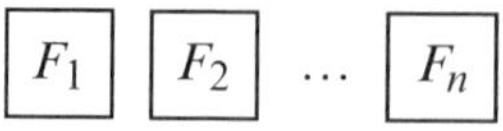

Figure 5.2
Graphical model for prototype-based concepts over **F**.

particular individual X is therefore just the similarity to the prototypical instance, and that function determines a corresponding probability distribution. Of course, the learning algorithms for prototype-based concepts are quite different from those for exemplar-based concepts, since exemplars must actually have been observed, while prototypes need not. However, the mathematics for the resulting concepts are essentially the same when the prototype is defined over only **F**. We can define **PC1** to be the set of probability distributions for prototype-based concepts involving only **F**.

On the graphical models side, consider the graph in figure 5.2. This is a so-called empty graph: there are no edges between any of the nodes. Empty graphs can be considered as either DAGs or UGs, so we can regard the resulting graphical model in multiple ways, including as a causal Bayes net (DAG) or Markov random field (UG). Let $\mathbf{GM}_{\mathrm{PC1}}$ be the set of probability distributions that satisfy the Markov and Faithfulness assumptions for the empty graph in figure 5.2; that is, $\mathbf{GM}_{\mathrm{PC1}}$ are the probability distributions that can be perfectly represented by the figure 5.2 graph. We can then prove (see theorems 5.3 and 5.4 in sec. 5.5) that $\mathbf{PC1} = \mathbf{GM}_{\mathrm{PC1}}$. In other words, the probability distributions for prototype-based concepts (involving only **F**) are exactly those that can be perfectly represented by the graph in figure 5.2.

Prototype-based concepts involving only **F** can capture the idea that prototypes should be the "stereotypical" case, but they are arguably unable to satisfy the intuition that the prototypical instance should encode (in some sense) the previously observed cases. In particular, any summary of the observed data needs to be able to represent patterns over multiple features. A simple way to encode these patterns is through the use of second-order features: features whose value is entirely determined by the values of two variables/features in **F** (Gluck & Bower, 1988; Rehder, 2003a, 2003b). For example, flying with wings is important for the concept Bird; birds are not just animals that fly and have wings but rather fly with those wings. In this case, we can define a second-order variable *Winged Flyer* that takes the value "yes" just when both *Flies* and *Wings* are "yes." This particular second-order feature is based on the logical operation of AND; other natural ways of defining second-order features could use logical OR, or the joint similarity of multiple features/variables in **F**, or many other functions. More generally, a growing body of experimental evidence suggests that interactions among features must somehow be modeled, at least for some concepts (Gluck & Bower, 1988; Murphy, 1993; Neumann, 1974; Rehder, 2003a, 2003b; Wattenmaker, Dewey, Murphy, & Medin, 1986).

If we have second-order features, then the fit of an individual *X* is not the similarity to the prototypical instance over just **F** but rather the similarity based on **F** *plus* the second-order features. We have additional dimensions that matter for similarity. As a result, when the second-order features are nontrivial, we can get quite different similarities for particular individuals, and thus a much larger set of possible probability distributions. Let **PC2** be the set of probability distributions for prototype-based concepts with second-order features. On the graphical models side, we can let $\mathbf{GM}_{PC2}$ be the set of probability distributions that satisfy the Markov and Faithfulness assumptions for a UG-based graphical model (plus some minor quantitative assumptions). We can then prove (see theorems 5.5 and 5.6 in sec. 5.5) that $\mathbf{PC2} = \mathbf{GM}_{PC2}$; that is, the probability distributions for prototype-based concepts with second-order features are the same as the distributions for UG-based graphical models (with minor constraints). Moreover, we have a recipe for translating between prototype-based concepts and graphical models: given precise numbers for one, we can derive the numbers for the other. In particular, the edges in the graph correspond exactly to the second-order features. We can even extend the mathematical derivations in section 5.5 to allow for third- or higher-order variables/features, though such features are rarely used in cognitive models.

This result provides us with a clear characterization of the expressive power of second-order features within prototype-based concepts and, more generally, of the amount that they add to the expressive power of models of concepts. Substantial experimental evidence demonstrates that psychological models of concepts must have some way of representing important connections between features, and second-order features have been a popular way to model these connections in prototype-based concepts (though see Rehder, 2003a). At the same time, the precise content and value added by second-order features have not always been clear.[3] Prototype-based concepts with second-order features are much more expressive than those without them, suggesting that models of such concepts should receive more attention than has traditionally occurred.

These various translations into the framework of graphical models provide a novel method for analyzing the conditions in which the cognitive theories of concepts are, or are not, distinguishable from one another. More precisely, because the different models of concepts—exemplar, prototype, and causal model based—correspond to different sets of graphical model structures, we can use known results about the expressive power of those graphical models to understand when the different psychological models make distinct behavioral predictions.

For example, if U in figure 5.1 has more than one value, then (assuming Markov and Faithfulness) any pair of features that are adjacent to U will be associated with each other regardless of what else we know. The only graphical models over only **F** that can express this fact (assuming Markov and Faithfulness) are those that have an edge between every pair of U-adjacent (in fig. 5.1) features. Since prototype-based concepts without second-order features correspond to empty graphs, we can thus immediately conclude that no (interesting) exemplar-based concept can possibly be represented as a prototype-based concept without second-order features. At the same time, exemplar-based concept models are unable to perfectly represent any causal-model-based concept that is not a complete graph, or any prototype-based concept with second-order features for only some pairs of features.[4]

These translations can also help us to understand the relationship between causal-model-based concepts and prototype-based ones with second-order features. In section 3.4, we explored the relative expressive powers of DAG-based and UG-based graphical models and found that they overlap: some probability distributions can only be represented by a DAG, others only by a UG, and some by both. Specifically, if the representing DAG has an unshielded collider (e.g., $X \rightarrow Y \leftarrow Z$, where X and Z are not adjacent) or the representing UG is nonchordal (e.g., a diamond), then the other type of graphical model can *not* represent that distribution. Otherwise one can represent the probability distribution with either type of graphical model.

With these results in mind, consider two conditions from Rehder (2003a). In the common cause condition, participants are taught a causal-model-based concept whose underlying causal structure is $A \leftarrow B \rightarrow C$. This DAG has no unshielded colliders, and so any probability distribution for it can also be represented by the UG $A — B — C$. If participants actually learned the underlying causal structure, then we should therefore expect identical model fits for a causal-model-based concept and a prototype-based concept with second-order features, since each can fit the corresponding probability distribution equally well. This is exactly what Rehder (2003a) found (see Rehder's table 5 on p. 729). On the other hand, consider the common effect condition in which participants learned a causal-model-based category with causal structure $X \rightarrow Y \leftarrow Z$. This DAG has an unshielded collider, so no UG can perfectly represent the probability distribution. As a result, prototype-based concepts, even with second-order features, should not provide a good model of human behavior with this concept (again, assuming people learned the intended causal structure). The model fits again bear this out: causal-model-based concepts fit human responses significantly better. We thus have a principled explanation for why the psychological models had the same fit to data in one condition but a quite different fit to data in another. With these benefits in mind, we turn now to the question of how to model cognitive processing with either single or multiple concepts in light of all these translations of the different types of concepts into the graphical models framework.

5.3 Reasoning with Concepts

Much of our reasoning about and with concepts involves only a single concept. For example, I might know that my friend has a dog, and so wonder whether it is likely to bark. To answer this question, I only need to have the concept Dog; I do not need to know anything about any other animals. Alternately, I might wonder which properties of a concept are "important," in some sense of that word; again, I can presumably determine this without knowing (much) about other concepts.[5] These different cognitive operations have in common that I know that some individual falls under concept C, and I then want to make various inferences about that individual's features. A natural issue, therefore, is how such inferences are possible in the graphical-model-based understanding of these different theories of concepts.

The basic challenge of so-called feature inference is to determine the likely features or properties of some individual, given that I know that the individual falls under some concept C, and where I might also know some other properties of the individual. The example from the previous paragraph of inferring whether a dog likely barks is exactly such a case. This type of inference is essentially asking for a conditional probability: what is the probability that this individual barks, given that this individual is a dog? Using the notation of the previous section, the challenge is to determine $P_C(F \mid G, H, \ldots)$ for features $F, G, H, \ldots$ in **F**.[6] Graphical models were originally developed partly to optimize the computation of such conditional probabilities, and so this type of inference is completely straightforward if our concepts are structured approximately as graphical models. Many different algorithms can efficiently compute conditional probabilities in a graphical model, but the exact details do not matter here. The relevant point is that any analysis of feature inference as computing conditional probabilities can easily be translated into the framework of graphical models, now that we have in hand the translations of the different types of concepts into that same framework.

For example, consider the task in experiment 1 of Rehder and Burnett (2005). They taught people a concept by explaining the causal structure underlying members of that category. They then provided a member of that category along with information about its values for three of the four properties. Participants had to determine the likelihood that the individual had some fourth property. As a concrete example, participants might learn that Lake Victoria shrimp (an imaginary species) have the causal structure given in figure 5.3.

A particular Lake Victoria shrimp is then chosen at random, and the participants are told, say, that it has (a) high levels of ACh neurotransmitter, (b) rapid flight response, and (c) accelerated sleep cycle. The target question of interest is: how likely is it that this particular shrimp has high body weight? Rehder and Burnett (2005) show that people's inferences

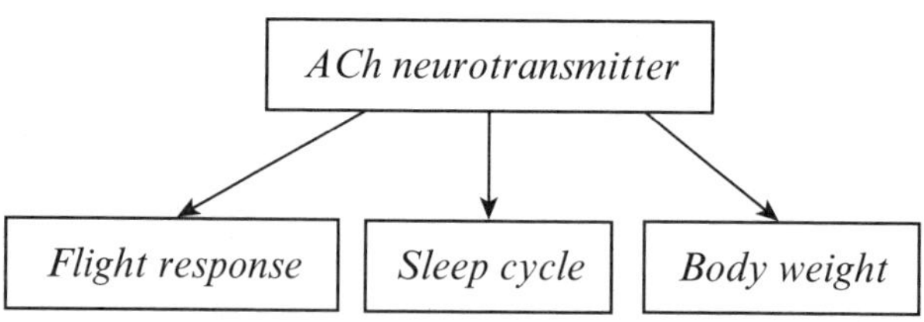

Figure 5.3
Causal structure for Lake Victoria shrimp.

track the conditional probabilities dictated by the concept (at least mostly; see the next paragraph). In fact, many experimental studies have demonstrated that feature inferences track conditional probabilities, where those conditional probabilities are determined by whatever concept people have inferred, whether exemplar, prototype, or causal model based (Johansen & Kruschke, 2005; Rehder & Burnett, 2005; Yamauchi & Markman, 1998, 2000). The mapping from feature inference to conditional probability inference in a graphical model seems to be empirically well supported.

People, however, do exhibit one notable divergence from this generalization: they systematically use information about features that ought (probabilistically) not to matter for the feature inference task. This behavior is sometimes described as a "violation of the Markov assumption" (Rehder & Burnett, 2005; Rottman & Hastie, 2014) and was previously mentioned in section 4.3.[7] I argue here that this description is actually incorrect. First, we need to understand the empirical phenomenon. In chapter 3, we saw that the Markov assumption essentially tells us about (ir)relevance: nodes that are not adjacent in the graph are informationally independent conditional on some set of other nodes in the graph. If we apply the Markov assumption to figure 5.3, for example, we get the prediction that *Sleep cycle* should be independent of *Flight response* given *ACh neurotransmitter*. That is, once we know the value for *ACh neurotransmitter*, learning about *Sleep cycle* does not provide us with any additional information about the value of *Flight response*. This is not, however, what people do. Rehder and Burnett (2005) present experimental evidence that predictions about *Flight response* depend partly on the value of *Sleep cycle*, even when *ACh neurotransmitter* is known. Moreover, this general finding has since been replicated multiple times (Mayrhofer, Goodman, Waldmann, & Tenenbaum, 2008; Mayrhofer, Hagmayer, & Waldmann, 2010; Walsh & Sloman, 2007); Rottman and Hastie (2014) review the different relevant experiments. We thus seem to have a stark disconfirmation of the idea that these cognitive representations are structured as graphical models: even when people are explicitly taught a causal-model-based category using a graph, they seemingly do not make inferences according to it.

This conclusion is, however, too hasty, as there are at least two natural explanations for this behavior. First, causal connections are frequently tied together in various ways: the operation of one biological pathway often depends on the proper functioning of other biological pathways, or both

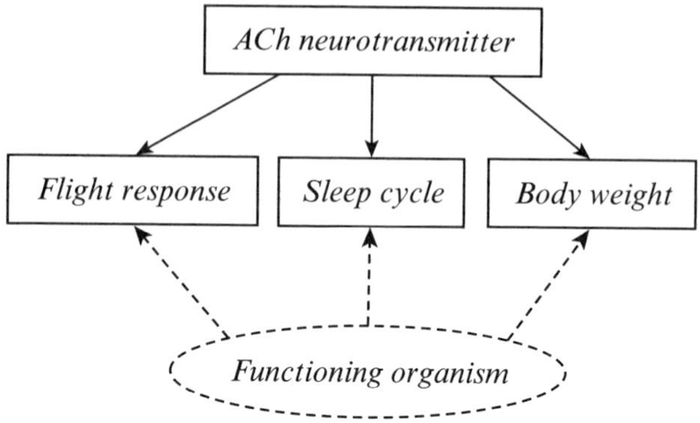

Figure 5.4
Alternative causal structure for Lake Victoria shrimp.

can depend on the overall functioning of the organism. If pathway functioning is correlated in this way, then apparent violations of the Markov assumption are actually the normatively correct inferences (Mayrhofer et al., 2008). At the extreme, inferences about shared mechanisms should almost certainly not obey the Markov assumption, and those are exactly the conditions in which people seem to be the most "non-Markov" (Park & Sloman, 2013). That is, what appears to be a normative violation or error may actually be exactly the right inference. For example, plausible domain knowledge suggests that the proper causal structure for Lake Victoria shrimp is not the one in figure 5.3 but rather something like the graph in figure 5.4. And in figure 5.4, the effects of the common cause are *not* independent of one another given just the observed common cause feature, and so people's behavior is entirely consistent with their cognitive representations being structured as graphical models.

A second plausible explanation for these apparent violations of the Markov assumption is that participants believe that there is some possibility of error in identifying the species of the novel individual. If there is even a small chance of misidentification, then (for almost any alternative) the observations of the different effects are informative, even given knowledge of the common cause *ACh neurotransmitter*, about the likelihood that this is *really* a Lake Victoria shrimp. That is, learning that the individual has, say, both a rapid flight response and an accelerated sleep cycle makes it quite certain that it is really a Lake Victoria shrimp rather than some other kind of shrimp. And changes in the likelihood of really being a Lake Victoria shrimp should influence judgments about the various factors, so we have a second explanation of the apparent violations of the Markov assumption. Moreover, these two explanations do not compete; both could be correct. Of course, it is also possible that both of these possible explanations could be shown to be empirically false; perhaps people are not thinking about these cases in these ways. In the absence of such a demonstration, however, these experimental results do not, despite much of the rhetoric surrounding them, yet present a problem for a graphical-models-focused account of cognitive representations.

Returning to feature inference in general, multiple experiments have also examined whether people learn different concepts depending on whether they are taught by repeatedly categorizing instances or by repeatedly doing feature inference (Chin-Parker & Ross, 2002, 2004; Markman & Ross, 2003; Yamauchi & Markman, 1998). In other words, do we learn something different about a concept when we do feature inference, rather than simply being provided with many instances of the concept? A consistent finding in these studies is that people do learn differently in these two conditions (Markman & Ross, 2003; Yamauchi & Markman, 1998). This result is not predicted by many standard accounts of concept learning, as the category label appears to be "just another feature," and so the two modes of learning should be essentially the same (Anderson, 1991b). In the graphical models account, however, this finding is unsurprising: learning a category or concept requires learning an entire graphical model (including probability distribution); learning to infer features requires only learning the part of the graphical model that involves that feature. We thus have a natural explanation for why, in many cases, these two types of learning result in different understandings of the concept.

A different mode of reasoning about individual concepts is determining which features are the most important, in some sense of that word. Multiple studies have shown that causally "earlier" features contribute more to judgments about a concept than do causally "later" ones (Ahn, Kim, Lassaline, & Dennis, 2000; Rehder & Kim, 2006, 2010; Sloman, Love, & Ahn, 1998). For example, if concept C is given by the underlying causal structure $X \rightarrow Y \rightarrow Z$, then when all else is held equal about the features (e.g., salience, etc.), X will be judged by multiple measures to be more important than Y or Z for the concept C. One model of this so-called causal status effect is that features with more and stronger causal dependents—direct and indirect effects—are simply more important (Sloman et al., 1998). In contrast, Rehder and colleagues have argued over multiple studies (Rehder, 2006; Rehder & Kim, 2006, 2010) that the disproportionate impact of causally earlier features is entirely normative and arises because those factors typically have a larger impact on the various probabilities used in reasoning about and with concepts. That is, people weight earlier factors more because they really do matter more (normatively). For example, suppose I am doing feature inference, and I want to decide whether a novel instance of C has the feature Y (where $X \rightarrow Y \rightarrow Z$, as before). In this case, it turns out that (for most quantitative components for that graph) learning whether X obtains will lead to a larger change in my estimate of $P(Y)$ than learning whether Z. The key point for this chapter is that the causal status effect can straightforwardly be explained by causal-model-based concepts, which was one of the three concept types that I showed (in the previous section) corresponds to cognitive representations based on graphical models.

Of course, not all reasoning with concepts is about individual concepts; we sometimes need to work with sets of them. For example, another key function of concepts is grouping: when I determine that multiple animals in my house fall under the concept CAT, I thereby group them together as similar in certain respects. This cognitive operation necessarily involves *multiple* concepts: grouping is valuable precisely because some individuals are not in the group, and so different inferences are possible depending on the group. More generally, groups are determined at least in part by what they are not, and thus by the alternative possibilities for some individual. In experimental settings, this categorization behavior is studied directly by (i) teaching a set of distinct concepts to the participant, (ii) presenting a novel instance, and (iii) seeing how it is categorized. Categorization in many natural settings is a probabilistic phenomenon: the same case can be classified, by the same individual, sometimes as an A and sometimes as a B, particularly if the test case is ambiguous in various ways. Models of categorization behavior must allow for this possibility.

An enormous variety of categorization models have been proposed; many of the computationally well-specified ones are discussed in Pothos and Wills (2011). I focus here on categorization models for exemplar-, prototype-, and causal-model-based concepts. In practice, these categorization models are essentially all constructed as two-step models: given a novel instance, the categorizer (i) computes the similarity or fit between the novel instance and each possible category and then (ii) uses these similarities to make a choice. The similarities in step (i) are exactly the ones that we discussed in section 5.2, and that determine the probability distributions for concepts. By a wide margin, the most common choice rule for integrating similarity scores in step (ii) is the Shepard–Luce rule (Luce, 1963; Shepard, 1957), which is discussed in more mathematical detail in section 5.5. This choice rule basically just converts the similarities into probabilities (possibly weighted by "salience" or base rates) and then uses the resulting probability distribution (over the possible concepts) to categorize the novel instance.

In the graphical models framework, the problem of categorization is essentially one of model choice: given a set of possible graphical models and some new individual, what is the likelihood that each graphical model could have produced that individual? The optimal or normative way to answer this question is to compute $P(C_i \mid \mathbf{X})$ for each concept C_i—the probability of each concept given the individual **X**. We can use Bayes' theorem to express these conditional probabilities in different terms, but the precise mathematical details are not important (though see sec. 5.5). The key is that one part of the result depends on $P(\mathbf{X} \mid C_i)$—the probability of seeing an individual like **X** given that we know that it is a C_i. As we saw in section 5.2, this is just $P_C(\mathbf{F})$; that is, one part of the normative graphical model choice is exactly what is computed in step (i) of the two-step psychological categorization models. Moreover, the remaining parts of the graphical model choice turn out to be exactly what is calculated in the Shepard–Luce rule used in step (ii). That is, categorization using these types of concepts just is optimal classification using graphical models, and vice versa.[8] More generally, this translation into the graphical models framework provides a measure of unification to disparate categorization theories by showing how they differ only in the graphs that underlie their probability distributions. We can thus talk sensibly about categorization decisions involving concepts of different types; for example, the cognitive agent might need to decide whether some novel individual falls under exemplar-based concept *E* or prototype-based concept *P*. Such situations fall outside the scope of standard categorization models, since the concepts are of different types, but are easy to model if our cognitive representations (of concepts) are understood as graphical models.

5.4 Building Webs

Categorization involves concepts competing with one another. However, many interesting between-concept relations do not involve competition. For example, the same individual can fall under both the ANIMAL and DOG concepts. One standard view is that many concepts are arranged hierarchically, though any particular concept or individual can participate in multiple hierarchies. More specifically, many groups of concepts have a "basic level" concept that is most natural, typical, and so on, and the other concepts are either superordinate or subordinate to that basic level (Rosch, 1973; Rosch, Mervis, Gray, Johnson, & Boyes-Braem, 1976). DOG is a subordinate category of ANIMAL, since any individual that falls under DOG also falls under ANIMAL (though not vice versa); alternately, we can say that ANIMAL is a superordinate category of DOG. An extensive literature examines these conceptual hierarchies, much of which has focused on the characteristics that determine the basic level for a particular group of concepts (Johnson & Mervis, 1997; Markman & Wisniewski, 1997; Murphy & Lassaline, 1997; Rosch et al., 1976). Some experiments suggest that people might not always understand these multiconcept structures as strict, exceptionless hierarchies (Sloman, 1998), but diverse evidence also suggests that many of our concepts are structured at least approximately hierarchically.

Such quasi hierarchies are easily captured in the graphical models framework if we make an additional move. Each concept can (mathematically) be represented as a graphical model, but we are concerned here with inferences between *multiple* concepts, so we need some way to bring these diverse single-concept graphical models into the same structure. The basic idea is to introduce new nodes that indicate whether an individual falls under one or another *concept*, and then have those new nodes be the graphical parents of the features that matter for each of those concepts. This idea is perhaps easiest to explain with an example, so consider the concepts DOG and CAT with graphical models G_D and G_C for them, involving features $\mathbf{F}_D$ and $\mathbf{F}_C$. Figure 5.5 gives incredibly simple toy examples.

We can now build a single graphical model G that has nodes for all of $\mathbf{F}_D$ and $\mathbf{F}_C$, as well as a new node A that is a graphical parent of all of them, as in figure 5.6. (For ease of comparison with fig. 5.5, nodes from just $\mathbf{F}_C$ are in dashed boxes, the node from just $\mathbf{F}_D$ is in a dotted box, and nodes from both are in solid boxes.) A can take on two values {*Cat*, *Dog*} and

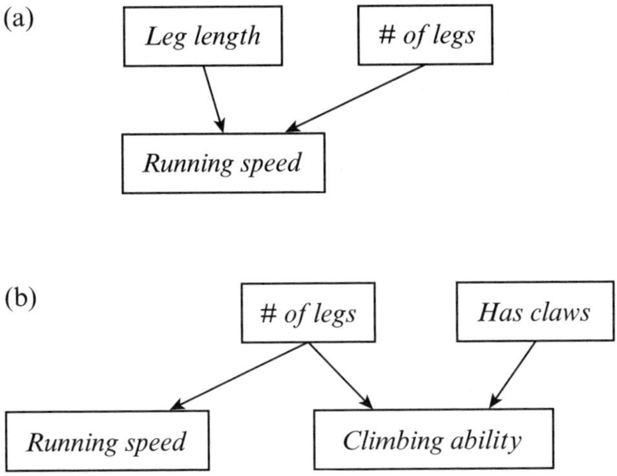

Figure 5.5
Toy example graphs for (a) DOG and (b) CAT.

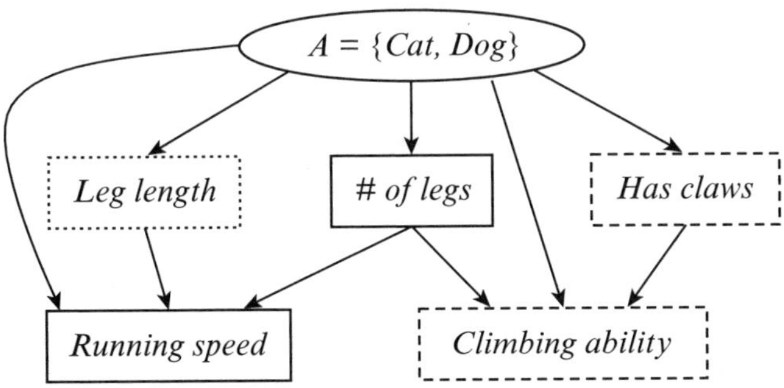

Figure 5.6
Multiple-concept graphical model.

functions as a "context node" (Boutilier et al., 1996), switching the edges over features depending on its value. When $A = Cat$, for example, the edge between *Has claws* and *Climbing ability* is active, but the one between *Leg length* and *Running speed* is not. These mutually exclusive concepts can thus be incorporated into a single graphical model by introducing a variable that (a) ranges over those concepts and (b) changes the feature probabilities and connections appropriately depending on its value.[9]

If we incorporate enough different values for A, then this node (with the rest of the graphical model) arguably becomes the concept of MAMMAL, since it encodes the relevant hierarchical information that every mammal—every individual with a value for MAMMAL—is a dog, or cat, or human, or other appropriate species (i.e., has that species as the *Mammal* variable value). Moreover, since this new node is "just" another node in the graphical model, we can repeat this process to introduce, for example, a variable corresponding to ANIMAL. Features that are distinctive of MAMMAL (i.e., shared by all mammals, but not necessarily all animals) can then be direct graphical children of ANIMAL, thereby encoding the fact that the value of MAMMAL (dog versus cat versus ...) does not matter directly for those features. By iterating this process, we can build a much larger, richer graphical model that can account for diverse between-concept relations, since the edge between ANIMAL and the node corresponding to MAMMAL can itself be probabilistic in various ways (see also Danks, 2007b).

This rich graphical model can be used to help make sense of the literature on inductive reasoning involving concepts. Suppose, for example, that you are told that cats have chemical *X* in their bloodstream, and you want to decide whether whales also have chemical *X*. This is a single-premise inductive inference, as the conclusion ("whales have chemical *X*") is evaluated on the basis of only one premise ("cats have chemical *X*"). The standard finding here is that, for both children and adults, induction goes up with increases in either the typicality of the premise category or the premise-conclusion similarity (Gelman, 1988; Gelman & O'Reilly, 1988; Heit, 2000; Osherson, Smith, Wilkie, Lopez, & Shafir, 1990). In the graphical models framework, learning the premise amounts to adding a node and edge to the existing graphical model; for example, "cats have chemical *X*" implies that we should add a "chemical *X*" node and connect it appropriately. Crucially, however, there are multiple places where we could add the edge, corresponding to whether the property "attaches" to CAT, MAMMAL, ANIMAL, or some other concept. Once the proper graphical parent is determined, the reasoner must then determine the appropriate parameters to use in the quantitative component of the (new) graphical model.[10] In general, we can think about typicality effects as arising because features of "typical" categories (e.g., DOG is typical of ANIMAL) are more likely to be due to the feature *actually* arising from the superordinate category; similarity effects arise because the concepts are closer in the full graphical model, and so it is easier (in some sense) to attach the feature to the conclusion concept.[11]

Alternately, you could be provided with multiple premises—for example, also the information that "mice have chemical *X*"—before evaluating the putative conclusion. The key empirical finding here is a diversity effect (Osherson et al., 1990): the induction becomes stronger as the diversity of concepts in the premises increases. For example, the inference to "whales have chemical *X*" is stronger from premises about mice and cats, compared to the cat premise coupled with one about dogs. Again, this effect is straightforwardly modeled in the graphical models framework, as the increased diversity makes it more probable that the new feature actually attaches to the node corresponding to a superordinate category. It is important in all this modeling, however, to ensure that we have the appropriate graphical model, as substantial empirical evidence indicates that the same concept can appear in multiple hierarchies, such as DOG being in both a taxonomic hierarchy as subordinate to MAMMAL, and also in a food-based hierarchy as subordinate to OMNIVORE (Heit & Rubinstein, 1994; Ross & Murphy, 1999; Shafto & Coley, 2003). A significant open question is how the appropriate graphical model is actually selected.

5.5 Putting Together the (Mathematical) Pieces*

The previous sections made a number of bold claims about concepts that were supported by translating them into graphical models and then using that representation to make sense of many cognitive operations using concepts. The goal of this section is to provide the mathematical statements and justifications for those claims. In particular, section 5.5.1 shows precisely how to translate between the three concept types and the graphical models framework. Section 5.5.2 then shows how to translate the various cognitive processes into that same framework. This section is substantially more formal and technical than the mathematical sections of chapter 4, precisely because theories of concepts have largely not been expressed using graphical models, while many of the theories of causal cognition are quite explicitly stated in that language. I thus have to provide more machinery (which the reader may unfortunately have to work harder to understand) to connect cognitive representations of concepts with graphical models, but the payoff is arguably larger as a result. Throughout this section, I assume that an individual can be defined by an m-dimensional feature vector $<F_1, \ldots , F_m>$, where the features (i.e., variables) are either all continuous valued or all discrete valued. For ease of presentation, I assume that discrete-valued features are binary valued; this assumption is solely for rhetorical purposes, as discrete-valued features with more than two values can be represented by sets of binary features (Love et al., 2004). Particular individuals will be denoted by **X**, where X_i denotes the value of feature F_i for **X**.

5.5.1 Concepts as Probability Distributions*

The first task is to show how to translate, for each of the concept types, between the similarity or fit functions for that concept type and graphical-model-based probability distributions. If we denote the similarity function for a concept C by $S_C(\mathbf{X})$, then this amounts to proving that $S_C(\mathbf{X}) \propto P_G(\mathbf{X})$ for every S_C for a concept type and P_G for a graphical model type. The relationship is only one of proportionality because the range of values for the similarity functions need not be restricted to [0,1], while probabilities are restricted in that way. It is easy—in fact, trivial—to establish this proportionality/equivalence for causal-model-based concepts. The standard cognitive theory based on those concepts says that the fit of an instance **X** to concept C is simply the probability that **X** would be generated by the causal Bayesian network corresponding to C. That is, the psychological theory is explicitly defined as $S_{CM}(\mathbf{X}) = P_{BN}(\mathbf{X})$, where S_{CM} is a similarity function for a possible causal-model-based concept, and P_{BN} is a probability distribution that satisfies the Markov and Faithfulness assumptions for some DAG-based graphical model (typically a Bayes net). Causal-model-based concepts are essentially already defined in terms of graphical-model-based probability distributions, and so no additional mathematical work is required.

Matters are not so simple for exemplar- and prototype-based concepts, as we first need to specify the cognitive theories. Similarity functions for these theories all start with similarity between two different individuals—either an exemplar and **X** or the prototype and **X**. There is a relative standard definition of the plausible, cognitively sensible similarity functions between two different individuals:

Definition: *Sim*(**X**, **Y**) is a *proper similarity function* if and only if:

(a) $Sim(\mathbf{X},\mathbf{Y}) = \prod_{i=1}^{m} Sim(X_i, Y_i)$

(b) for all i, $Sim(X_i, Y_i) = s_i(|X_i - Y_i|)$, where $s_i(\epsilon)$ is positive and a strict maximum at $s_i(0)$.

(c) $\int_0^\infty s_i(\epsilon)d\epsilon < \infty$

Condition (a) is a decomposability constraint that the overall similarity be the product of the similarities along each feature dimension. Condition (b) constrains each feature-specific similarity to be a function (always greater than zero) of only the relative difference between the two feature values, rather than the absolute feature values. In addition, any particular feature value must be more similar to itself than to any other value. Finally, condition (c) ensures that the feature-specific similarity function behaves "nicely" as the distance varies. Overall this is an extremely general definition of a similarity function: *Sim* need not be a distance metric, it need not be monotonically decreasing as ϵ increases, and so forth. More importantly, every extant psychological model expressed in terms of similarity conforms to this definition (see also Ashby & Alfonso-Reese, 1995).

For exemplar-based concepts, overall similarity is "weighted similarity to the exemplars," and so an *exemplar similarity function* is defined to be

$$S_E(\mathbf{X}) = \sum_{k=1}^{e} W_k Sim(\mathbf{X},\mathbf{E}^k)$$

where $\mathbf{E}^k$ is the k-th exemplar, W_k is the exemplar weight, and $Sim(\mathbf{X}, \mathbf{E}^k)$ is some proper similarity function. Prototype-based concepts are essentially just exemplar-based concepts with a single exemplar; if there are r second-order features (defined in the next paragraph), then the prototype, individuals, and proper similarity function are all defined in terms of m+r-dimensional feature vectors.[12] We thus define a *prototype similarity function* to be $S_P(\mathbf{X}) = Sim(\mathbf{X}, \mathbf{R})$, where $\mathbf{R}$ is the fixed concept prototype, and $Sim(\mathbf{X}, \mathbf{R})$ is a proper similarity function. For convenience, I will use $S_{P1}(\mathbf{X})$ to pick out prototype similarity functions involving only first-order features, and $S_{P2}(\mathbf{X})$ for functions that involve at least one second-order feature.

All that remains on the similarity function side is to define the space of possible second-order features for $S_{P2}(\mathbf{X})$. It is notationally simpler to define second-order features in terms of the component features' distances from their prototypical values, rather than their particular values. We thus let $\delta_i = |R_i - X_i|$ and define a *second-order feature* to be any deterministic function $h_k(\delta_i, \delta_j)$. This definition does not assume that the second-order feature is symmetric in the two arguments, and is generally weak; the key constraint is simply that the second-order feature is a function of the two "distances from prototype," rather than the absolute feature values. Moreover, this characterization clearly covers all the intuitively natural cases, including logical OR and AND for binary features, and joint Euclidean distance from the prototype for continuous features. To ensure that we use only second-order features that are actually meaningful, we further require that the similarity function for the second-order feature not be expressible as the product of similarities over the first-order features. More precisely, if F_k is a second-order feature for F_i and F_j, then there cannot be $f(\epsilon)$, $g(\epsilon)$ such that $s_k(|h_k(X_i, X_j) - h_k(Y_i, Y_j)|) = f(\epsilon_i)\, g(\epsilon_j)$ for measure one of (ϵ_i, ϵ_j). If we could decompose s_k in this way, then there would be no need to include the second-order feature; all the work could already be done by the first-order features. We thus have a complete specification of the similarity functions for exemplar- and prototype-based concepts, regardless of whether there are second-order features.

We now turn to graphical models and probability distributions. Define an *edge-deletion transform of* G to be any graph G^* with the same nodes as G, but where the edges in G^* are a (not necessarily proper) subset of the edges in G. In other words, G^* is just G with zero or more edges removed from it. Given an additional variable U with u distinct values, we define $P_E(\mathbf{X} \cup U)$ to be the class of probability distributions and densities that satisfy the following conditions:

(a) $P_E(\mathbf{X} \cup U)$ satisfies the Markov and Faithfulness assumptions for some edge-deletion transform of the graph in figure 5.1.

(b) For all values j of U, there is an m-dimensional point R^j such that, for all i, $P(X_i \mid U = j) = f_{ij}(|R_i^j - X_i|)$, where f_{ij} is a strict maximum at $f_{ij}(0)$.

(c) For all $k > 1$, there is a Q_{ik} such that $P(X_i \mid U = k) = P(X_i + Q_{ik} \mid U = 1)$ for all X_i.

Condition (a) is obviously the most important one for the overall thesis of this book, as it connects the set of distributions P_E with graphical models. Condition (b) simply says that each U-conditional distribution has a point of maximal probability for each u and is symmetric around that point. Condition (c) requires that, for each feature F_i, the different U-conditional distributions are identical up to translation of the maximal point. We can now prove the following theorems (for readability, all proofs are provided in the appendix):

Theorem 5.1: For all $S_E(\mathbf{X})$, there exists a P_E such that $S_E(\mathbf{X}) \propto P_E(\mathbf{X} \cup U)$, where U has e many values (and measure zero of the P_E's violate Faithfulness[13]).

Theorem 5.2: For all $P_E(\mathbf{X} \cup U)$, there exists an S_E such that $S_E(\mathbf{X}) \propto P_E(\mathbf{X} \cup U)$, where S_E has u exemplars.

That is, we can translate any S_E into a P_E and vice versa; similarity functions for exemplar-based concepts are the same (mathematically) as suitably symmetric probability distributions that satisfy Markov and Faithfulness for the figure 5.1 DAG. Moreover, the proofs of these two theorems provide an explicit construction algorithm for transforming models of one type into models of the other type; I later use this translation with the generalized context model (GCM).

We can further restrict P_E by requiring that U have only a single value; denote that set of probability distributions by $P_{P1}(\mathbf{X})$. Since U is a constant, there is no need to include it in the distribution, and it is necessarily independent of all other variables. The graph for every distribution in P_{P1} must therefore be the empty graph, which can be considered as either a DAG or a UG. It is straightforward to prove:

Theorem 5.3: For all $S_{P1}(\mathbf{X})$, there exists a P_{P1} such that $S_{P1}(\mathbf{X}) \propto P_{P1}(\mathbf{X})$.

Theorem 5.4: For all $P_{P1}(\mathbf{X})$, there exists an S_{P1} such that $S_{P1}(\mathbf{X}) \propto P_{P1}(\mathbf{X})$.

In other words, we can use the construction algorithms in the proofs to translate similarity functions with no second-order features into probability distributions that satisfy the Markov and Faithfulness assumptions for the empty graph.

Finally, we can expand P_{P1} to include all distributions that satisfy the Markov and faithfulness assumptions for a UG over $\mathbf{F}$, rather than the empty graph. Recall from chapter 3 that a probability distribution for a UG is decomposed into a product of clique potentials—functions $g_D(\mathbf{X})$ that depend only on the values of variables in the (maximal) clique $\mathbf{D}$. We can additionally impose a factorization constraint on the clique potentials to keep the probability distribution from getting too complex: $g_D(\mathbf{X}) = \prod_{i,j \in \mathbf{D}} f_{\mathbf{D},ij}(X_i, X_j)$. This constraint requires that each clique potential be expressible as the product of functions that depend only on pairs of variables in the clique. It is trivially satisfied for cliques of size two, though it is a nontrivial constraint for cliques of size three or more. Even in those cases, though, the constraint is still relatively weak, since no restrictions are placed directly on the $f_{D,ij}$ functions beyond their product matching g_D. Denote the probability distributions that satisfy this constraint (and Markov and Faithfulness for a UG with at least one edge) by $P_{P2}(\mathbf{X})$. We can then prove:

Theorem 5.5: For all $S_{P2}(\mathbf{X})$, there exists a P_{P2} such that $S_{P2}(\mathbf{X}) \propto P_{P2}(\mathbf{X})$, where there is an edge in the P_{P2} UG for each second-order feature in S_{P2} (and measure zero of the P_{P2}'s violate Faithfulness).

Theorem 5.6: For all $P_{P2}(\mathbf{X})$, there exists an S_{P2} such that $S_{P2}(\mathbf{X}) \propto P_{P2}(\mathbf{X})$, where S_{P2} has a second-order feature for each edge in the P_{P2} UG.

In other words, just as with exemplar- and (first-order) prototype-based concepts, we can translate between similarity functions for (second-order) prototype-based concepts and graphical-models-based probability distributions, where UGs (rather than DAGs or the empty graph) provide the relevant graphical models in this case.

The preceding results are all in terms of extremely high-level similarity functions. In practice, cognitive models that use these types of concepts do not function at such a high level of generality. To see how these results could be used in particular cognitive models, consider the well-known GCM (Nosofsky, 1986) that is the base similarity function for many exemplar- and prototype-based cognitive models; a similar example could easily be provided for the more complex case of S_{P2}. Similarity between $\mathbf{X}$ and $\mathbf{Y}$ in the GCM is defined as $S_{GCM}(\mathbf{X},\mathbf{Y}) = e^{-c \times dist(\mathbf{X},\mathbf{Y})^{\gamma}}$, where c is a global weighting parameter and $dist(\mathbf{X}, \mathbf{Y})$ is the weighted (by the salience of F_i) distance between $\mathbf{X}$ and $\mathbf{Y}$: $dist(\mathbf{X},\mathbf{Y}) = \left(\sum_{i=1}^{m} \alpha_i |X_i - Y_i|^d \right)^{1/d}$. The S_{GCM} function factors as required for a proper similarity function only if $\gamma = d$ (Ashby & Alfonso-Reese, 1995), so we focus on $\gamma = d = 1$ and $\gamma = d = 2$. In those cases, $s_i(|X_i - Y_i|) = e^{-(c\alpha_i/m)|X_i - Y_i|^d}$ for $d = 1, 2$, which clearly satisfies all the relevant properties for a feature-specific similarity function.

We can now provide a "bridge principle" that yields GCM-specific corollaries to theorems 5.1 through 5.4:[14] $S(\mathbf{X})$ is GCM based if and only if, for all i, j, $P(X_i \mid U = j)$ is either a double Laplace ($d = 1$) or Gaussian ($d = 2$) distribution with mean μ_{ij} and variance σ_i^2. In other words, GCM-based similarity functions correspond to probability distributions in which all U-conditional distributions (or unconditional distributions for members of

Table 5.1
Parameters for *U*-conditional Gaussians for example GCM

	$U = 1$	$U = 2$
$P(X_1 \mid U = ...)$	1.0 (1.42)	0.0 (1.42)
$P(X_2 \mid U = ...)$	1.0 (5.93)	0.0 (5.93)
$P(X_3 \mid U = ...)$	1.0 (3.43)	0.0 (3.43)

P_{P1}) are members of the same distribution family, and for each feature, the corresponding *U*-conditional distribution has the same variance for all values of *U*, though the means of that conditional distribution can vary (since the means are the corresponding exemplar feature values).

For example, suppose we have a GCM category with three continuous features for two equally weighted exemplars: <1.0; 1.0; 1.0> and <0.0; 0.0; 0.0>, and the following (randomly chosen) GCM parameters: $d = \gamma = 2$; $c = 2.3$; $\alpha_1 = 0.46$; $\alpha_2 = 0.11$; and $\alpha_3 = 0.19$. The graphical model version of this exemplar-based category includes *U* with two values and all the edges in figure 5.1. Because the exemplars are weighted equally, we have $P(U = 1) = P(U = 2) = 0.5$. Because $d = 2$, all the *U*-conditional distributions are Gaussian, and their means (variances[15]) are given in table 5.1.

The theorems presented in this section are not only theoretically useful in unifying various concept types but also practically useful, since they provide explicit translation methods, not just representation theorems.

5.5.2 Feature Inference, Categorization, and Conceptual Hierarchies*

Given that concepts are represented as graphical-model-based probability distributions, it is straightforward to capture the standard cognitive operations involving concepts. Feature inference is essentially the problem of computing $P_C(F_i \mid K(\mathbf{F}))$, where $K(\mathbf{F})$ denotes information (possibly empty) about the other feature values. That is, feature inference involves determining the probability of one variable conditional on values of other variables. Graphical models were partly developed exactly to speed these computations, and we have many well-known and well-studied algorithms for inferring conditional probabilities for arbitrary graphical models (Bishop, 2006; Pearl, 1988). In addition, as explained in section 5.3, apparent violations of the Markov assumption in these inferences (whether for causal-model-based or other concepts) are naturally and easily explained through the introduction of an unobserved variable that indicates, for example, that the mechanisms underlying the causal structure are functional. The introduction of such a variable is a straightforward matter, given that we have the graphical-model-based representation of the joint probability distribution; Mayrhofer et al. (2008) provide one natural way to do it.

Categorization is similarly straightforward given that our cognitive representations are structured like graphical models. In practice, categorization models are almost always two-step: one first computes a similarity score for each concept and then chooses (probabilistically) the concept using the Shepard-Luce rule (Luce, 1963; Shepard, 1957):

$$P(\text{choose } C \mid \mathbf{X}) = \frac{\beta_C S_C(\mathbf{X})}{\sum_{Q \in \mathbf{Q}} \beta_Q S_Q(\mathbf{X})}$$

where $\mathbf{Q}$ denotes the set of possible concepts and β_Q is the response bias for category Q. The previous section showed that similarity functions $S_C(\mathbf{X})$ correspond to probability distributions $P_C(\mathbf{X})$. Response biases are typically understood to be the "default" response rate for the category, which is essentially the concept base rate $P(C)$. Now, consider the Bayes' theorem expression of $P(C_i \mid \mathbf{X})$:

$$P(C_i \mid \mathbf{X}) = \frac{P(\mathbf{X} \mid C_i)P(C_i)}{P(\mathbf{X})}$$

Since $P_C(\mathbf{X}) = P(\mathbf{X} \mid C)$, we can immediately see that the expressions for $P(\text{choose } C \mid \mathbf{X})$ from the Shepard-Luce rule and $P(C \mid \mathbf{X})$ from Bayes' theorem are identical; that is, $P(\text{choose } C \mid \mathbf{X}) = P(C \mid \mathbf{X})$. It is thus immediately the case that two-step categorization models all correspond to optimal categorization for graphical models corresponding to that type of concept.[16]

Now consider the matters of conceptual hierarchies and inductive inference discussed in section 5.4; the modeling here will be more qualitative, as there are relatively few precise computational models of these processes. The key to modeling conceptual hierarchies is the use of context nodes whose values range over mutually exclusive categories, such as CAT versus DOG versus MOUSE (Boutilier et al., 1996; Poole & Zhang, 2003; Zhang & Poole, 1999). Importantly, these nodes are *parametrically* special, not structurally so; they are distinctive because of the quantitative relationships that they have with their children (typically acting as a "switch" for between-children edges), rather than being marked in any qualitative or structural way. It thus suffices to show how to introduce these context nodes. Given a set of graphical models $G_1, \ldots, G_m$ (over nodes $\mathbf{N}_1, \ldots, \mathbf{N}_m$) corresponding to mutually exclusive concepts, let G be a graphical model over $\mathbf{N} = \mathbf{N}_1 \cup \ldots \cup \mathbf{N}_m \cup \{C\}$, where C is a novel variable with m values. For all $X, Y \in \mathbf{N}$, if $X \rightarrow Y$ in some G_i, then include $X \rightarrow Y$ in G. Also, for all $X \in \mathbf{N}$, include $C \rightarrow X$ in G. Finally, the quantitative component of G is chosen so that $P_G(\mathbf{N}_i \mid C = i) = P_i(\mathbf{N}_i)$. That is, if $C = i$, then the relevant variables $\mathbf{N}_i$ have the probability distribution that they had in G_i. This obviously underdetermines P_G, since it does not specify the probability of variables in $\mathbf{N} \setminus \mathbf{N}_i$ when $C = i$, but there are many natural ways to fill in these blanks. And, of course, we can iterate this process if there is another graphical model H for mutually exclusive concepts $H_1, \ldots, H_k$, but where G and H are mutually exclusive (e.g., ANIMAL versus PLANT). At the same time, note that the graphical model M for a concept can participate in *multiple* hierarchies by starting with distinct sets of mutually exclusive concepts.

A graphical model G with one or more context nodes can be used for single- and multiple-premise inductive inference. Suppose our inductive inference involves premise concepts $B_1, \ldots, B_n$ and conclusion concept C. Let J be the "lowest" context node such that C and each B_i are each values either of J or of a context node descendant of J. All inductive inference consists of (i) adding a node to the graph G for the novel feature F, (ii) making F the child of J,[17] and (iii) specifying the (possibly qualitative) parametric information. Steps (i) and (ii) are clearly unproblematic; the interesting work happens in step (iii), as we must specify parametric information for F conditional on $J = C$. The natural model is that we consider two factors: (a) the F-relevant information in concepts (i.e., alternate values of the context node) that are similar to C (i.e., concepts A such that $P(\mathbf{N} \mid J = A)$ is similar to $P(\mathbf{N} \mid J = C)$); and (b) whether parametric information about *non-F* features of the Bs are shared by other concepts, including C (i.e., whether $P(\mathbf{N} \mid J = B)$ is predictive of $P(\mathbf{N} \mid J = A)$ for arbitrary A). But this process immediately yields the similarity and typicality effects for single-premise inductions. And the diversity effect for multiple-premise inductions arises both because different sets of Bs can lead to using different context nodes J, and because the information available for factors (a) and (b) can change as we vary the typicality and similarity of the premise concepts. Finally, I note as an aside that this formal model can also potentially explain some of the non-monotonicity phenomena observed by Osherson et al. (1990), though that aspect has not yet been worked out carefully.

5.6 Conclusion

Concepts are a foundational aspect of our cognition, and so they are unsurprisingly perhaps the most-studied type of cognitive representation. The results in this chapter show that many aspects of concepts can be captured in the same graphical models framework that can capture our causal knowledge (chap. 4). We thus have a unification of the cognitive representations for these two domains of cognition, though different cognitive processes are applied to that common representational store. Of course, learning and inference are relatively useless without some connection to decision and action, and so we now turn to understanding human decision making using the framework of graphical models.

6 Decision Making via Graphical Models

6.1 Roles for Causal Knowledge in Decision Making

The previous two chapters focused on using graphical models to represent our causal and conceptual knowledge. Those cognitive representations are, however, essentially impotent on their own; they are only useful if they are connected in some way with decision-making processes that can (intelligently) use them. The first section of this chapter aims to show that causal knowledge—represented as a DAG-based graphical model—plays a key role in much of our decision making. In particular, causal knowledge can guide us to attend to the proper factors and enable us to better predict the outcomes of our own actions. One type of decision making can thus be understood as operations on graphical models. Graphical models are not restricted, however, to serving as input to standard decision-making algorithms. In section 6.2, I describe two novel decision-making algorithms that are inspired and shaped partly by the advantageous features of their graphical model input. These novel algorithms still show only that graphical models can be an input to our decision making. I thus turn in section 6.3 to model the decision-making process itself as operations on decision networks (also called influence diagrams), a generalization of the DAG-based graphical models used in previous chapters. But first we look at the "easy" case: causal knowledge (structured as a DAG-based graphical model) provides a basis for intelligent decision making.

One important challenge in judgment and decision making is determining which factors should be the focus of one's attention; that is, my decision making requires that I pay attention to possibly relevant factors, rather than the definitely irrelevant ones. Many accounts of human decision making assume that this information search problem has already been solved, as they assume that relevant features of the decision situation are provided as input. We can instead determine the relevant factors dynamically using causal knowledge, particularly if it is structured as a graphical model. In particular, suppose that my decision depends on some factor *T* that I do not know and thus need to predict. In that case, I should presumably focus on *T*'s direct causes and direct effects. This intuition has been explored extensively in the context of the "Take the Best" (TTB) heuristic for binary forced choices (Gigerenzer, 2000; Gigerenzer & Goldstein, 1996), and so we need a brief digression to explain TTB. It is important to recognize, however, that what matters is how causal knowledge can, in general, support information search in decision situations; the focus on TTB is a purely contingent matter. In particular, I will not discuss whether TTB is empirically correct, since we are principally interested in a functional role of causal knowledge (in information search) for decision contexts.

Consider making a choice between two options relative to some criterion, such as which washing machine is better or which city is larger. The basic idea of TTB is that people sequentially consider different cues—properties or features of the options—until they find a cue for which the options have different values (e.g., positive versus negative versus unknown), and then people choose the one with the "better" cue value. To take a simple example, suppose one is trying to decide which of two American cities is larger. One feature of American cities (that is related to size) is whether they have a professional (American) football team; TTB says (again, roughly) that if one city has a professional football team (positive cue value) but the other does not (negative cue value), then one should choose the city with a team as larger. Alternately, I might be trying to purchase a washing machine and decide between two options based solely on which is cheaper, or which has the longer warranty. Many papers provide empirical evidence that people behave roughly as predicted by TTB, though the precise empirical scope of TTB is a complicated matter (Broder, 2000; Gigerenzer, 2000; Gigerenzer & Goldstein, 1996; Goldstein & Gigerenzer, 1999; Newell & Shanks, 2003).

At the same time, it is somewhat puzzling that people would use TTB, as this strategy appears to be highly suboptimal. In TTB, decisions ultimately rest on only a single cue; it is, to use the jargon, noncompensatory: no amount of information in other cues can compensate for the single, critical difference. Thus, for example, one might judge Pittsburgh to be larger than Los Angeles, since Pittsburgh has a professional American football team and Los Angeles does not, despite the numerous other cue differences telling us that Los Angeles is much larger. Perhaps surprisingly, however, the suboptimality of TTB is only apparent, not actual. In practice, TTB frequently produces close-to-optimal performance on various tasks (Chater, Oaksford, Nakisa, & Redington, 2003; Gigerenzer, Czerlinski, & Martignon, 1999; Hogarth & Karelaia, 2006; Martignon & Hoffrage, 1999), principally because cues are *not* considered in a random order. Rather, TTB assumes that people consider the different cues in order of their cue *validity*: the probability that a cue provides an accurate decision, given that it discriminates between the options at all. TTB works well precisely (and only) because the order in which people consider cues tracks their likelihood of giving the right answer (Newell & Shanks, 2003). This assumption that cues are considered in order of their validity is relatively innocuous in experimental settings, as participants are often told the cue validities (or are assumed to know them from life experience). In the real world, however, it is unclear how people identify possibly relevant cues, how they learn the appropriate validities, or whether they consider the cues in the proper order even if they have somehow learned the validities.

Causal knowledge potentially provides a solution to this problem of knowing what factors matter for a decision (Garcia-Retamero & Hoffrage, 2006; Garcia-Retamero, Wallin, & Dieckmann, 2007). In particular, causes and effects of the decision-relevant attribute T are more likely to be valid cues for T (Garcia-Retamero & Hoffrage, 2006). For example, having a professional American football team is an effect of a city's size, as a large population base is one cause of whether sufficient financial and political support exists for a team. Conversely, being a state capital is plausibly a cause of a city's size, as the presence of the state government causes there to be more jobs (all else being equal) and so more people. One might thus expect that both being a state capital and having a professional American football team would have significant, nonzero cue validities for city population, as they in fact do. On the other hand, the length of a city's name is not plausibly a cause or effect of the city's size, so we should expect that its validity would be essentially zero.

We thus seem to have a potential solution to the problem of the source of cue validity orderings and values: we use our causal knowledge to identify direct causes and effects and then compute cue validities for them (Garcia-Retamero & Hoffrage, 2006). We previously saw (in chap. 4) that our causal knowledge seems to be structured as DAG-based graphical models. The identification problem is easily solved using such a graphical model, as the direct causes and effects are simply the factors that are (graphically) adjacent to *T*. And cue validities can easily be computed from the parametric information contained in the graphical model,[1] so we can order the cues correctly. Moreover, experiments have found that people perform substantially better on these types of binary forced-choice problems when they can use their causal knowledge, compared to having to estimate cue validities from observations (Garcia-Retamero et al., 2007); observed cue validity information is sometimes employed but requires some pretraining (Garcia-Retamero, Muller, Cantena, & Maldonado, 2009). It thus seems that TTB in real-world situations is plausibly an operation on a DAG-based graphical model. More generally, causal knowledge can provide the necessary structure for successful information search in decision situations.

We now turn to examining a role for causal knowledge in the actual decision-making process, not just as an attentional focusing mechanism. An almost-ubiquitous schema for cognitive models of decision making is that people (i) have a set of possible actions; (ii) consider for each action the various probabilistic outcomes of that action; and (iii) choose the action that has the best (probabilistic) value. There are, of course, many ways of instantiating this schema and many processing variants. However, this basic schema—evaluate the possible outcomes of different actions and choose the "best"—underlies almost all psychological models of choice (and most normative ones). One issue for any model of decision making is explaining step (ii): how does the decision maker determine the probabilistic outcomes of an action? One cannot simply compute (naive) probabilities conditional on the state resulting from the action, since those do not distinguish between causes and effects. For example, the probability of being over fifty conditional on having gray hair is *not* the same as the probability that I will be over fifty if I dye my hair gray. Actions on *T* presumably (though see sec. 6.3) only lead to probabilistic changes in *T*'s effects, not *T*'s causes, and so, to ensure correct predictions in step (ii), we need to know which associated factors are causes and which are effects (Joyce, 1999; Lewis, 1981).

The graphical-models-based approach can easily make sense of this critical distinction if I understand my decisions or actions as interventions that override (or "break") the normal causal structure. As we have seen several times earlier in the book, interventions on *T* break the edges into *T*, but not the ones out of *T* (Pearl, 2000; Spirtes, Glymour, & Scheines, 2000), and this behavior exactly satisfies the requirement from the previous paragraph.[2] This complication did not arise when discussing TTB, since the decisions in that process are based on causal structure but do not change it. Both causes and effects can provide valuable cues for TTB, since both carry information. In contrast, actually acting in the world requires that we distinguish (correctly) between causes and effects in both learning and reasoning.

Thus, to the extent that people actually understand their choices as interventions, causal knowledge (represented as a DAG-based graphical model) can satisfy a critical role in decision making by providing the resources to solve step (ii). Substantial empirical evidence now shows that people do think about their own actions in this way. For example, if people believe that *C* causes *E*, then they conclude that an action on *E* will make no difference to *C*, while actions on *C* will be a good means to bring about *E* (Hagmayer & Sloman, 2009; Sloman & Hagmayer, 2006; Waldmann & Hagmayer, 2005). In addition, quantitative aspects of the causal knowledge matter: stronger causes are more likely to be chosen when people are trying to bring about some effect (Nichols & Danks, 2007). Of course, one might wonder whether the causal *knowledge* is really being used for decision making, rather than people relying on habits or implicit learning. It is surely the case that some "decisions" actually arise from habit and so might not be based on causal knowledge. Just as surely, not all decisions are habitual; many decisions are based on conscious deliberation, whether that reasoning occurs spontaneously (e.g., in novel situations) or in response to a prompt. Moreover, when people deliberate on their decision, then they make different, and better, choices than when simply responding immediately or automatically (Mangold & Hagmayer, 2011). This result suggests that many decisions are actually based on reasoning about the system. Finally, changes in one's beliefs about the causal structure lead to corresponding changes in decisions that cannot be explained simply on the basis of observed associations (Hagmayer & Meder, 2013). We thus have multiple threads of evidence that people's decision making frequently uses their distinctively causal knowledge to predict outcomes of interventions or actions. More importantly for me, this causal knowledge is best understood in terms of DAG-based graphical models; that is, decision making arguably depends (often) on exactly the shared representational store that underlies cognition about causation and concepts.

6.2 Novel Decision-Making Algorithms

The previous section focused on ways in which traditional, empirically supported decision-making algorithms can be understood as operations on cognitive representations of causal knowledge (structured as DAG-based graphical models). The graphical models framework can also suggest some novel ways to approach decision making, and I explore the computational aspects of two proposals here. Unfortunately, no empirical tests have occurred for either proposal, so we cannot determine whether either is descriptively correct. I thus focus more on the ways that novel decision-making theories can arise if cognitive representations are (approximately) graphical models.

The first novel approach starts with the observation that standard decision-making algorithms assume that people calculate, perhaps implicitly, the (probabilistic) outcomes of their actions to make a choice. In situations with complex causal structures, however, these computations can be quite complex, so we might hope to avoid them by using a suitable heuristic. Meder, Gerstenberg, Hagmayer, and Waldmann (2010) propose an Intervention-Finder heuristic: in trying to bring about some *E*, people consider each of the possible causes of *E* (identified by statistical or other cues) and simply choose the option *C* that maximizes the observed (not causal) conditional probability of *E* given *C*, $P(E \mid C)$. That is, their heuristic uses causal knowledge to narrow the scope of deliberation to just the potential causes (rather than effects) but does not use that knowledge for the probability calculations. In particular, the Intervention-Finder heuristic does not attempt to account for common causes or other reasons why $P(E \mid C)$ might be large; it simply uses the observed conditional probability as a "good estimate" of what (probabilistically) would happen if one acted on *C*. Unsurprisingly, this heuristic works best when the different possible causes are not highly associated with one another; surprisingly, it performed close to optimally in a large-scale simulation study (Meder et al., 2010). Although the Intervention-Finder heuristic ignores causally important information, it turned out (in that simulation study) that the information being ignored did not usually make a difference as to which action was selected: the additional causal knowledge typically changed the value estimates of the actions, but not the overall rank order of them. This heuristic thus shows one way in which causal knowledge (structured as a DAG-based graphical model) can suggest a novel decision-making algorithm that is normatively incorrect (since it does not actually try to determine the outcome probabilities) but nonetheless successful. Unfortunately no empirical studies have yet explored whether the Intervention-Finder heuristic is actually used by people, though the theoretical possibility is intriguing.

A somewhat more radical novel decision-making model emerges when we reflect on the assumption (of the standard decision-making schema) that the decision maker is presented with a set of actions to consider. More than fifty years ago, Duncan Luce (1959, pp. 3–4) wrote:

> There seems to have been an implicit assumption [in decision models] that no difficulty is encountered in deciding among what it is that an organism makes its choices. Actually, in practice, it is extremely difficult to know. ... All of our choice theories—including this one—begin with the assumption that we have a mathematically well-defined set, the elements of which can be identified with the choice alternatives. How these sets come to be defined for organisms, how they may or may not change with experience, how to detect such changes, etc., are questions that have received but little illumination so far.

The situation arguably has not improved substantially since the publication of Luce's book. In response, one could flip the definition of a decision problem from being "action based" to "goal based": that is, a decision problem can potentially be characterized by a desired outcome state, rather than a set of possible actions. Goal-defined decision problems are surely not the only type that we face, but they seem to constitute a large set of everyday choices.

Given that we have only a desired outcome state and not a set of actions, we can use our causal knowledge—structured as a DAG-based graphical model—to dynamically construct possible choices. At a high level, the decision maker starts with the target variable T and considers actions on its direct causes (according to her causal knowledge), given observations of the factors adjacent to T. That is, the decision maker first considers only those factors that her causal knowledge deems to be immediately relevant to T. If one of those actions is acceptable,[3] then the decision maker performs that action. If no actions are acceptable, then the decision maker moves her scope "out" one step on the basis of her causal knowledge: rather than considering actions that affect the direct causes (i.e., parents) of T, she considers actions that change the causes of the causes (i.e., grandparents) of T. And if none of *those* is acceptable, then she iterates back yet another step.

The process continues until the decision maker either finds an acceptable action or decides to stop for other reasons, whether boredom, frustration, or other demands on her cognitive resources. This method thus naturally constructs an appropriate set of possible actions, and so we seem to have the beginnings of a response to Luce's challenge.

Moreover, this algorithm can be extended in intriguing ways. Dynamic information gathering can be incorporated immediately, since, for any action *A*, the most relevant other factors that need to be considered are alternative causes of *A*'s descendants. That is, if I am considering an action on node *A*, I can easily use my causal graph to determine the other variables that might interact with my action to produce good or bad effects. A small adjustment to the algorithm thus yields a dynamic attentional focusing mechanism. Alternately, a challenge for decision making is recognizing and accounting for side effects of our choices. Such side effects can readily be determined for each action because the algorithm does not use a fixed variable set, though this additional computation does have some cost. Finally, planning behavior can be modeled by evaluating multiple actions rather than simply single ones, though that extension is still only hypothetical.

At any particular moment in the decision process, this method looks quite similar to the standard decision-making schema: the decision maker is considering the (probabilistic) impacts of a potential action to decide whether it is worth doing. Overall, however, there are several crucial differences. Perhaps most importantly, this decision method is fundamentally dynamic in scope, and so one's information-gathering and "action possibility" space are constantly changing. The decision maker never evaluates all possible actions but instead evaluates, and either accepts or rejects, each choice individually. The set of possible actions changes throughout the course of deliberation, as do the variables that are relevant for value judgments. Decision making thus shifts from the standard model of a process in which the decision maker is selecting from a menu of options to one in which the decision maker can dynamically explore and construct the very possibility set being evaluated. As a result, "choose the optimal action" cannot possibly be a decision criterion, since the decision maker will not necessarily ever know what constitutes "optimal." In many cases, the decision maker will be in a state of uncertainty about whether a better option potentially lurks over the horizon if she would consider just one more action. Roughly speaking, the agent can safely stop looking for better options only if there is a "dominant" cause that is more efficacious than combinations of other changes and cannot reliably be brought about through indirect means.[4] There must inevitably be a satisficing aspect to many of the decisions made by this process: the eventual decision is selected because it is judged to be "good enough," not because it is known to be optimal (though it might be).

Despite these limitations, simulation tests that I conducted with Stephen Fancsali revealed that (a fully precise version of) this algorithm performs close to optimally using significantly fewer computations. For these simulations, we used a version of this algorithm that regards an action as "acceptable" if its value—operationalized as expected value—exceeds some threshold τ; obviously, much more sophisticated versions are possible. We used two additional simplifications in these simulations: (i) when actions have costs, they depend only on the variable, not the value to which it is set; and (ii) the target T being in the desired state is worth one unit of value, and all other results are worth zero. These assumptions mean that the value of an action is always less than or equal to one and can be negative (if the action is costly but unlikely to produce the desired state). We tested the algorithm on a large number of different causal structures under a wide range of parameter settings. I group together causal structures with the same number of variables (denoted by V), as this is a major driver of computational challenges. We otherwise simply average over performance for each graph size; the graphs in figures 6.1 through 6.3 provide mean performance for roughly 100,000 (V = 4), 300,000 (V = 6, 8, 10), or 10,000 (V = 15) graphs. Note that these results are for random graphs and parameterizations. There are obviously specific graphs on which this algorithm does quite poorly; I give an example later in this section when discussing empirical tests of this algorithm. One open question is what causal belief structures are "typical," and whether this algorithm performs particularly well on those graphs.

A first question is whether this algorithm typically finds the optimal action. Figure 6.1 plots the fraction of times that the algorithm selected the optimal action (vertical axis) against τ, the value threshold for "acceptability" (horizontal axis). Unsurprisingly, the probability of choosing the optimal action increases as τ does; if one is choosier about the action, then one is more likely to wait until the truly optimal action is found. More interestingly, the mean match rate only exceeds 95 percent for $\tau = 0.8$. For small

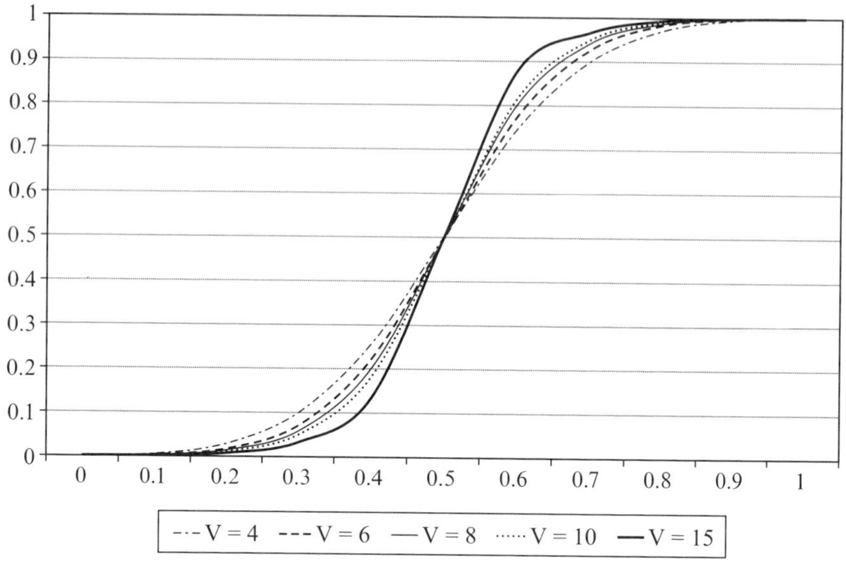

Figure 6.1
Match rate as a function of value threshold.

value thresholds—that is, if the algorithm is not particularly "choosy"—the algorithm rarely selects the optimal action.

An immediate follow-up question to this first analysis is: How good are the actions that *are* selected? Although the algorithm rarely selects the optimal action, is it choosing ones that are nonetheless reasonably good? Figure 6.2 shows the expected loss as a function of τ; recall that the values of all choices are between zero and one (since their values must be less than or equal to one, and the algorithm can always choose to do nothing and receive at least zero units of value). Unsurprisingly, the mean loss decreases as τ increases: if one is more stringent about what one will accept, then one should ultimately make a better choice. More surprisingly, the algorithm performs quite well with only small losses in (absolute) expected value for small values of τ. Even in the extreme case of $\tau = 0$ (i.e., accept the first considered action with a positive expected value), the algorithm performed reasonably well. At the upper end, the mean expected value loss for $\tau = 0.6$ was less than 0.01. This latter result is particularly notable given that the algorithm only chooses the optimal action 80 percent of the time when $\tau = 0.6$.

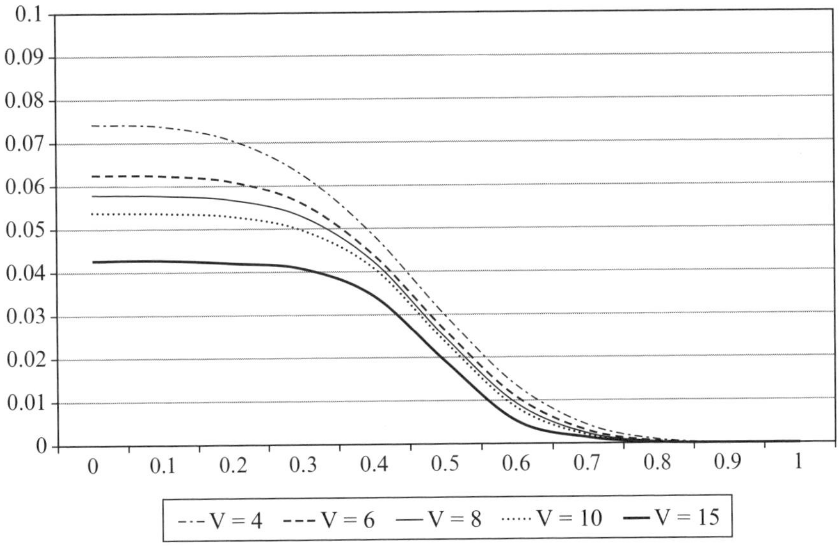

Figure 6.2
Expected loss as a function of value threshold.

Part of the cognitive plausibility of this algorithm is that it appears to be computationally much simpler. To confirm this idea, we compared the number of actions checked by the algorithm (including the "null" action of doing nothing) and the number of actions that were checked in finding the optimal choice. Figure 6.3 shows the former divided by the latter as a function of τ, so smaller numbers indicate that the present algorithm considered fewer possible actions. Note that this measure ignores memory and other costs involved in information search when trying to find the optimal choice. A value of 1.0 indicates that optimal search and this algorithm evaluated the same number of actions; in these simulations, that point generally occurred around $\tau = 0.6$. One might be surprised to see numbers greater than 1.0. These are possible because the present algorithm collects information only gradually and thus rechecks the null action ("do nothing") after each new observation, while the optimal search algorithm checks it only once.

The key to these simulations is to consider figures 6.1 through 6.3 together, as they show the following two points: for small values of τ, this algorithm is computationally much simpler (10–30 percent of the computational cost) and achieves close-to-optimal performance; for large values

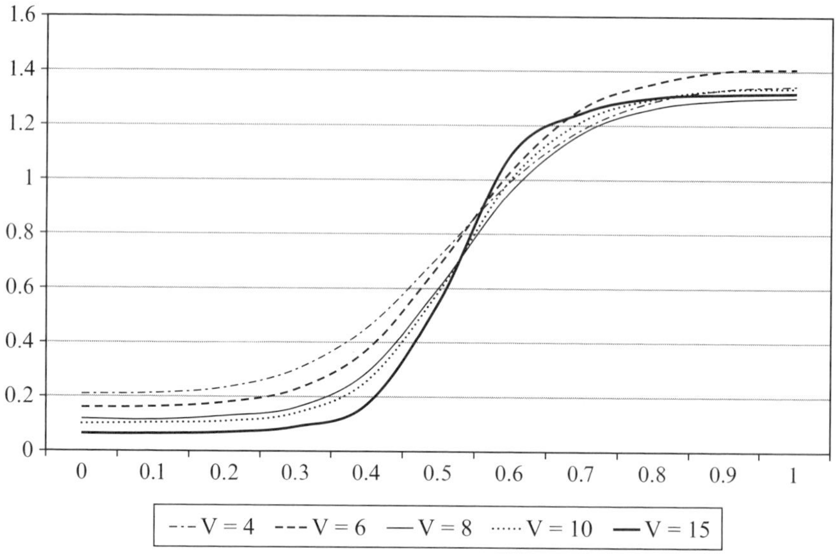

Figure 6.3
Fraction of actions checked relative to optimal algorithm.

of τ, the algorithm is only slightly more complicated and successfully finds the optimal choice. Perhaps most importantly, as V gets larger, the computational advantage increases, and the expected value loss decreases. Given that people's causal knowledge presumably ranges over thousands of variables (or more), it is important that the performance trends of this algorithm are headed in the correct direction. Moreover, these changes as V increases are unsurprising, as this algorithm is explicitly designed to first check the options that are most likely to be best, while the optimal algorithm must check every conceivable option. By exploiting the relevance relations encoded in the causal knowledge graphical model, this algorithm exhibits a performance profile that fits the decision maker's needs and can usefully and sensibly be tuned as appropriate.

Of course, these simulations do not tell us that people's decision making actually uses something like this algorithm. I thus close this section by considering three ways to empirically test the algorithm. The real keys here, though, are not the particular experiments but (a) the way that the graphical models framework inspires a novel decision-making algorithm, and (b) that these experiments would arguably not be conducted without thinking

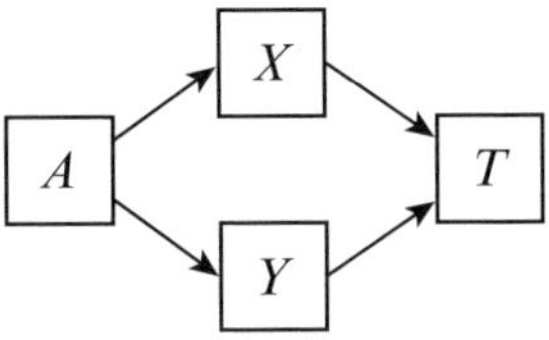

Figure 6.4
Structure to test decision-making algorithm.

about decision making through a graphical model lens. The first experiment looks at people's information acquisition patterns when confronted with a novel choice problem. Specifically, this proposed algorithm predicts that people will seek out information about direct causes before indirect causes. This prediction can be tested straightforwardly by teaching people a novel causal structure and then introducing a cost to information retrieval (e.g., forcing people to move a mouse over an on-screen box to learn a variable value). We can then investigate the patterns of information search that people exhibit.

A second experiment focuses on the dynamic "satisficing" aspect of the algorithm. More specifically, suppose that people learn, either from experience or from description, the causal structure in figure 6.4. This graphical model can have natural causal strength parameters that imply that *A* is a more efficacious action than either *X* or *Y* alone. For example, suppose *X* and *Y* are both relatively weak causes of *T*, but *A* is a strong cause of both of them. In this case, acting on *A* makes *T* more likely than an action on *X* or *Y* alone, precisely because there are two causal pathways from *A* to *T*. The present algorithm predicts, however, that people should sometimes act suboptimally in cases such as these. That is, there should be conditions in which people will choose to do either *X* or *Y* rather than *A*, such as when there is time pressure or when the stakes are very low (and so people might be willing to perform actions even when they are not obviously close to optimal).

A third experiment is similar but instead uses the causal structure in figure 6.5, where we additionally assume that *X* is a deterministic effect of *A*—*X* occurs if and only if *A* does—and that *Y* is relatively ineffective. Because *X* is a deterministic effect of *A*, actions on *A* and *X* result in exactly the same probability of *T*. If actions on *A* and *X* have the same cost, then almost all models of decision making predict that people should choose

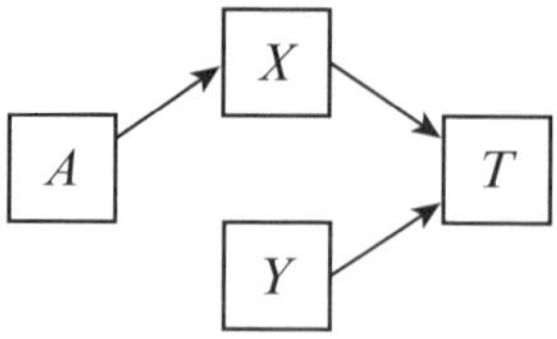

Figure 6.5
Alternative structure to test decision-making algorithm.

either randomly between A and X or on the basis of value-irrelevant factors (e.g., perceptual salience). If actions on A and X have identical impacts, then we seem to have no basis for picking one rather than the other. At the least, it is straightforward to develop experimental stimuli for which "always act on X" is not the predicted action. In contrast, the present algorithm predicts that people will always choose to intervene on X. Of course, for all these experiments, it is important that people learn the causal structure without reflecting deeply on it; if they have ample time to think about all the possibilities, then even the present algorithm predicts that people should make optimal choices. Nonetheless we have straightforward empirical tests for a novel decision-making algorithm prompted by modeling our causal knowledge as a DAG-based graphical model.

6.3 Graphical-Model-Based Decision Making

The previous two sections showed ways in which decision making can use graphical-model-based cognitive representations, both in the context of traditional models of decision making and to suggest novel algorithms (that remain to be empirically tested). Those demonstrations do fall short, however, of what was shown in chapters 4 and 5, where graphical models played an integral role in understanding the very cognitive processes; those representations were not simply (optional) inputs to the process. This section aims to show that graphical models can similarly play a central role in decision making. The DAG-based graphical models in the previous sections treated every node identically: they all represented variables that could take different values. The factors that are relevant to a decision-making situation are not, however, all of the same type. Rather, it seems natural to distinguish four different types of things that we would like to represent in our model: actions, values, factors in the world, and the decision-making method itself. The variables that we have seen all along in our graphical models correspond to the factors in the world; to incorporate the other three, we need to expand the representational language of our graphical models.

Decision networks, also called influence diagrams, are DAG-based graphical models containing four distinct node types corresponding to the four types listed earlier (Howard & Matheson, 1981; Shachter, 1986). I will follow standard notational conventions and represent the different node types using different shapes. Nodes corresponding to events or factors in the world (i.e., outside the decision agent herself) are drawn in ovals, and all edges into them correspond to causal connections. Nodes representing the actions taken by the decision maker are drawn in rectangles; edges into such nodes capture informational or cognitive connections. Value nodes are denoted by diamond shapes, and edges into them indicate the factors that determine the value that the decision maker receives at a moment in time. Finally, the decision-making process itself is drawn in a triangle and is typically required not to have edges into it. This is all quite complex in the abstract, so it is perhaps easiest to understand by working through an example. Consider the simple problem of deciding whether to turn on the lights in a room with windows, where we assume that the decision maker wants to be able to see but does not want to waste electricity. A plausible decision network for this situation is shown in figure 6.6.

Time of day encodes whether it is daytime or nighttime, which is obviously outside the control of the decision maker. *Max utility* indicates that the decision maker is using a decision process in which she attempts to maximize her utility; for probabilistic decisions, one could instead use a strategy such as "choose the action that has the maximal probability of yielding a utility of at least *U*." The *Flip switch* node represents the action

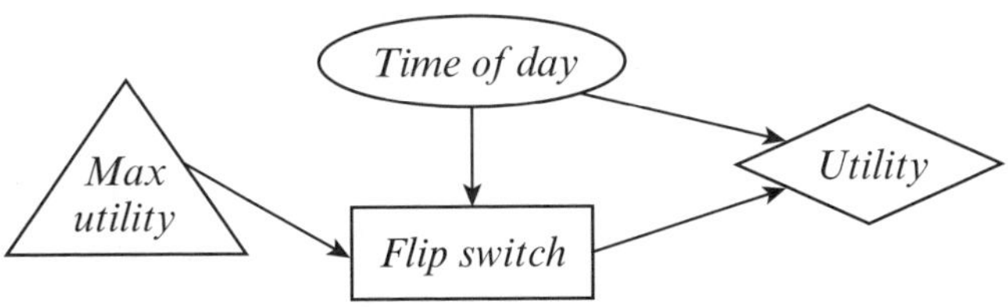

Figure 6.6
Example decision network.

that the decision maker actually takes, either "yes" or "no." That action is determined by the decision-making process (*Max utility*) given information from *Time of day*. Finally, *Utility* is a function of the time of day and the action, where her value presumably depends on (a) being able to see, but with (b) a cost for using electricity.

If we have a fully specified decision network, then we can use information about the world to derive a probability distribution for the possible actions (perhaps concentrated entirely on one choice, if we use a decision rule such as "maximize expected utility"). More generally, a decision network provides a representation of the decision situation that is faced by the decision maker, and so it encodes (in a graphical model) exactly the information required to make a decision in accordance with the specified decision rule (see also Solway & Botvinick, 2012). By providing additional information, a decision network goes beyond the types of graphical models that we have seen in previous chapters. For example, consider trying to represent the decision problem of "should I turn on the lights?" in an "ordinary" DAG-based graphical model. The causal structure is clear: *Light switch* → *Ability to see* ← *Time of day*. But that causal graph tells us nothing about what I value, my abilities or capacities for action, or how I make decisions. These additional node types are required to make sense of decisions using just a graphical model.

These observations might seem to be in tension with sections 6.1 and 6.2, since I argued there that decision making could be understood using "ordinary" DAG-based graphical models. In those sections, however, the graphical model was actually *not* sufficient to explain the full decision-making process; it only captured one informational component or cognitive representation, rather than all elements of the process. The other relevant pieces (e.g., value function, decision-making process, etc.) were contained in processes or algorithms that sat outside the DAG-based graphical model, though they obviously used that graphical model. In contrast, the decision network framework enables us to put all those pieces into a single graphical model, thereby providing a much stronger graphical-model-based unification of the relevant decision-making representations. For example, the iterative decision search algorithm discussed in section 6.2 operated on causal knowledge but also used values, costs, thresholds, and other elements that were not in the causal graphical model. Using decision networks, we can represent almost all the pieces of that algorithm in a single graphical model: (a) add a single value node that is the child of only the target variable; (b) for every variable on which I can act, include an action node that is its parent; and (c) add a single decision rule node that is the parent of every action node and has the iterative procedure as its value. The resulting decision network makes the same predictions as the algorithm from section 6.2, though at the cost of including more graphical nodes. These additions are worthwhile, however, precisely because they force us to be clear about the relevant elements, and also reveal assumptions (e.g., only single actions are allowed) that could naturally be relaxed. Similar characterizations can be provided for all of sections 6.1 and 6.2, not just the iterative decision algorithm.

All these observations about decision networks leave unaddressed the key descriptive question: do people's actual decisions suggest that they represent particular decision situations using decision networks? This question turns out to be trickier to answer than we might have expected, as most standard decision-making experiments do not test predictions that are relevant to this question. Instead those experiments typically focus on how people determine the value of a choice with multiple attributes, or how those values are used in choice, or both. Put into the language of decision networks, those experiments aim to determine the settings of the decision process and value nodes, rather than understanding and exploring the broader causal/informational structure in which they reside. At the same time, experiments that estimate those values are easily captured using decision networks precisely because they do not specify the settings of those nodes a priori. Standard decision-making experiments thus help to estimate some "free parameters" in the decision network graphical model, rather than testing the overall viability of the framework. To see whether people's choices can be understood as if they represent situations using decision networks, we need to find choice problems with more complex causal/informational structure.

Because the decision networks framework is still quite new in cognitive science, relatively few experiments have directly investigated it. Some such experiments do exist that explore distinctive predictions of decision networks, however, and they suggest that decision networks provide good (graphical) models of our cognitive representations of some decision situations. One set of experiments explores the ways in which decision networks can support inferences about the preferences of *other* people, given observations of their choices. That is, if people understand their own choice situations using decision networks, then they plausibly represent others' choice situations in the same way. And just as decision networks can be used to generate my own choices, they can also provide the foundation for "backward" inference about others, from their choices to their preferences. For example, Jern and Kemp (2011) looked at inferences about the complex, structured preferences of others from pairwise choices over sets of objects. They found that participants' inferences about others' preferences (based on the choices that the others made) corresponded closely to the inferences that result from trying to estimate parameters in a decision network. That is, the conclusions we draw about what someone else likes or dislikes can naturally be understood as inferences about a decision network that models the other person's choices.

A second, and more interesting, set of experiments examines how we use observations of someone's choices to learn more about what they know and can do (Jern, Lucas, & Kemp, 2011). For example, suppose someone is playing a game in which the computer displays five letters on a screen, and the player has to write down a sixth letter that is different from the others. Additionally, suppose that a cover over part of the screen can obscure one or more of the letters. If I observe only the six letters (five from the computer, one from the contestant), can I learn the shape of the cover? Intuitively, the answer is clearly yes: the contestant would never knowingly choose a letter that matches one of the computer's letters (assuming she understands the game, responds sensibly, and so forth), and so if there is such a match, then that letter must be covered on the screen. Standard models of decision making cannot easily handle this type of situation, since they do not have a transparent representation of these types of informational links. In contrast, the player's choice problem can readily be modeled as a decision network, where the structure of the cover implies missing informational links. In fact, we can represent all the different decision networks that correspond to all the different covers that could be placed over the screen. Learning the structure is then just a matter of learning which decision network is the actual one; that is, learning is determining which decision network best predicts the player's actual choices. Jern et al. (2011) performed experiments structurally similar to this one and found that people gave responses that closely tracked the decision network predictions. Although experiments about decision networks in cognition have only just begun, these results—coupled with the ability of decision networks to capture many standard results—give reason to suspect that many of our decisions are made using cognitive representations much like decision networks.

A general concern, however, lingers about *any* approach (including decision networks) that attempts to model choices as occurring within the causal structure of the world. From the decision maker's perspective, choice is almost always understood as exogenous and lying outside the relevant causal structure; if I think that my decisions are interventions (which has been repeatedly demonstrated), then I cannot think that they are caused by factors in the decision situation. Moreover, most models of decision making mirror this stance: standard decision theory, for example, represents the decision maker's choice as "free" and unconstrained by the other represented factors. From an outside observer's perspective, however, one can frequently understand a choice as being caused by other factors in the environment. For example, the outside temperature is clearly a (partial) cause of whether I decide to wear a sweater to work. In fact, whole research programs center on understanding the ways in which external factors (rather than rational deliberation) can cause our choices (e.g., the work described in Ariely, 2008). Whether anything causes choice thus depends on one's perspective (Sloman & Hagmayer, 2006), and uncertainty about the proper perspective might underlie self-deception phenomena (Fernbach, Hagmayer, & Sloman, 2014; Sloman, Fernbach, & Hagmayer, 2010). Moreover, this ambiguity and uncertainty raise concerns about the coherence between deliberation/choice and self-prediction (Levi, 1997, 2000, 2007; Rabinowicz, 2002), and even of standard decision theory itself (Kusser & Spohn, 1992), though decision theorists have resources with which to respond (Joyce, 2002). More generally, the worry is that graphical models, and decision networks in particular, cannot possibly provide a model of our cognitive representations about choice if we have no coherent understanding of choice in the first place.

The fundamental incompatibility between these two perspectives on the causal status of choice—outside versus inside the causal structure of the decision situation—arguably underlies the difficulties posed by Newcomb-type problems (Glymour & Meek, 1994; Hagmayer & Sloman, 2006). Newcomb's problem (Nozick, 1970) supposes that a decision maker is confronted with a seemingly simple choice between receiving the contents of (i) one covered box or (ii) that same covered box plus a transparent box that has $1,000 in it. The tricky part of the problem comes in the way that the contents of the covered box are determined: an incredibly accurate (in the past) predictor places $1,000,000 in that box if she predicts that the decision maker will make choice (i), but nothing at all if the prediction is choice (ii). If we think about choice as exogenous, then it seems clear that the decision maker should choose both boxes. The prediction has already been made at the time of choice, and so the money is either in the covered box or not. Since the choice is outside the causal structure of the world, the *actual* decision cannot change whether the money is there. One should thus take both boxes, thereby receiving $1,000 more than whatever is in the covered box. If we instead adopt the perspective of choice as part of the causal structure of the world, then we understand our choices as presumably caused by our earlier selves. Those earlier selves can be known by the predictor, and so one's actual decision is *not* independent of whether the money is there; rather, both are effects of a common cause—namely, one's earlier self. Thus, given that the predictor has been accurate in the past, the decision maker should make choice (i) to maximize the chance that $1,000,000 is in the covered box.

Our responses to Newcomb's problem depend on whether we understand choice as exogenous or endogenous—outside or inside the causal structure of the world, respectively. These perspectives are incompatible with each other, however: we cannot simultaneously understand our choices as *both* exogenous *and* endogenous but rather must choose a perspective at a moment in time. As a result, Newcomb's problem has been thought to pose a challenge to all precise models of decision, whether based on graphical models or not. I suggest, however, that graphical models are particularly well situated to respond to Newcomb's problem, precisely because the perspective that one takes in a moment is transparently represented in the corresponding graphical model. In a decision network, actions are always understood to be "regular" causal nodes that can be influenced or shaped by other factors (e.g., the temperature outside). If choice is understood as endogenous, then there is nothing more to be done; the representation already captures the idea that my actions are caused by the world around me. If, however, choice has an exogenous component, then we simply add a decision process node with an edge into the action node; the addition of such a node exactly encodes the idea that some part of choice lies outside the rest of the causal structure (since decision process nodes never have edges into them). These two perspectives on choices are truly irreconcilable, so no single framework can represent both simultaneously. The best that we can ask is that the framework clearly represent each possibility, as well as the different inferences that can be drawn in each. The graphical models framework does exactly that (see also Fernbach et al., 2014).

Over the course of the past three chapters, we have seen how the graphical models framework can represent the knowledge structures that underlie three major areas of cognition: causal learning and reasoning, concept acquisition and application, and decision making of different types. The next chapter turns to the challenge of putting these pieces together into a single cognitive architecture.

7 Unifying Cognition

7.1 Shared Representations and Unified Cognition

The previous three chapters explored three distinct types of cognition, focusing on causation, concepts, and decision making. Although these cognitive processes were considered separately, the analyses were bound together by the thread of graphical models: all three types of cognition were understood using that computational/mathematical framework. This chapter now argues for the position that was explicitly introduced in chapter 1 but left largely implicit in chapters 4 through 6: I contend that large swaths of human cognitive activity can fruitfully be understood as different operations on a shared representational store, where those cognitive representations are (approximately) graphical models. In some ways, this is a tricky argument to make, as there are not clearly articulated alternatives against which I can juxtapose this account. In particular, as we will see in the next chapter, most other prominent cognitive architectures unify cognition through shared processes or model schemata, rather than shared representations. The remainder of this section is thus devoted to clearly articulating my account of unified cognition, including a description of some alternatives that it is *not*.

Before turning to that task, though, I must address a lingering ambiguity.[1] The previous chapters all used the same framework of graphical models. However, the existence of a common mathematical representation for two systems does not imply the existence of something shared that is substantive or metaphysically "real." For example, the motion of a weight on a spring and the steady state of an AC electrical circuit can both be represented using the same sinusoidal function, but we do not believe that the two systems share any deep metaphysical similarity or identity.

Analogously, the "mere" fact that the same mathematical framework can model the cognitive representations used in multiple types of cognition does not imply that there is necessarily any *actual* similarity or overlap between the representations used in those different cognitions. Such unification is perhaps nontrivial from a mathematical point of view, but that does not necessarily imply anything about cognition. The concern is that the same mathematical framework might be applicable to different cognitions only because they happen to share some qualitative features, just as the (metaphysically quite different) causes in the weight/spring and electrical circuit systems share certain qualitative properties.

The overall argument in this chapter is decidedly *not* this simplistic (and invalid) inference from shared mathematical description to metaphysical identity. I am not confusing mathematics and metaphysics but am instead making a more substantive claim. The argument in this chapter for the existence of a shared representational store—that is, some measure of metaphysical identity—is that it provides the best explanation for the range of empirical data presented in section 7.2, principally about what we might call "cross-cognition transfer" (in contrast to the more commonly studied "cross-domain transfer"). I argued in chapter 2 that representational realism implies a complex array of empirical commitments that are not implied just by the computational specification of a particular cognitive theory. The work of this chapter is to explicate those commitments for the particular case of shared cognitive representations structured as graphical models and then to provide both actual and potential empirical data about them.

To understand the commitments of this cognitive architecture, we need some understanding of the "possibility space" of accounts that can predict and explain the shared (or not) nature of cognitive representations. However, there are no obvious extant accounts that we can use to stake out positions in that possibility space; the extent to which one's cognitive representations are shared across cognitive processes seems to have been relatively little considered, at least in the psychological literature. We can nonetheless consider some natural "points" (i.e., cognitive architectures) in this space. First, one might think that cognitive processes form "silos" such that there is no cross-process representation sharing.[2] On a natural implementation of this view, the representations that result from the process of causal learning would be simply unavailable to, for example, the process of feature inference. Causal learning can produce a cognitive representation of causal structure, but that representation would be inaccessible when using partial observations to make inferences about other properties of an individual. Importantly, the silos here do *not* correspond to multiple memory systems; the discussion of shared representations in this chapter will be largely orthogonal to issues about, for example, the distinction (if any) between semantic and episodic memory. Rather, the notion of a silo concerns a set of cognitive representations, regardless of which part of memory happens to encode them.

The overarching idea of silos actually corresponds to a whole family of views, depending on exactly how we individuate a cognitive process or its corresponding silo. At one (implausible) extreme, we could do an extremely fine-grained individuation, such that processes as closely related as causal learning and causal reasoning end up in different silos. This extreme view cannot be correct, as numerous psychological experiments have shown representation sharing between these types of very close processes, either explicitly in participant responses or implicitly because the experimental design makes no sense without such sharing. However, many slightly "coarser" individuations seem more plausible: for example, perhaps causal cognition is one silo, conceptual cognition forms a second one, and so forth. Of course, an extremely wide range of possible nontrivial individuations exists, and they need not track our intuitions about distinct cognitive operations.

A second cognitive architecture in the "representation sharing" space arises naturally from the maximally coarse individuation in which just one silo includes all cognitive processes. At this endpoint, no cognitive process is isolated (in cognitive representations) from any other. Importantly, this proposal is not that there is just one single, enormous representation; rather, there can be many distinct representations, though they must be in some shared (in a sense discussed later in this section) cognitive space. This "one silo" (or rather, "no silo") view suffers from an important ambiguity. If multiple relevant[3] cognitive processes can access the same cognitive representation(s), then we need to be clear about (a) which cognitive processes are active at any particular moment, and (b) how to resolve conflicts if two cognitive processes are trying to make incompatible changes to some shared representation. One cannot simply stop after saying that representations are shared, as they could be shared in many different ways among multiple processes. Moreover, note that this issue does not arise if there are multiple nontrivial silos, as the silos presumably include only cognitive processes that are unlikely to be simultaneously active. For example, we have little evidence that people learn and reason about the same causal structure simultaneously, though they may rapidly cycle between these processes.

I will not attempt to map out all possible accounts of how cognitive representations could be shared across multiple processes, but rather focus on two natural alternatives. First, one might suppose that (a) all cognitive processes are, in some sense, active at all times, while being optimistic that (b) all incompatibilities are quickly resolved and so no significant conflict resolution method is required. This view might seem hopelessly Panglossian, but it is actually a natural way to think about the idea that our representations are "maximally informative." More precisely, suppose that one thinks that we humans always aim to make fully informed inferences and decisions. As a result, we are constantly trying to operate with accurate and fully specified cognitive representations of the world (though we may fall short of this ideal in local instances). That is, our cognitive representations might (aspire to) be close to maximal, and approximately veridical, representations of the external world. Something like this view is implicit in threads of human vision research that aim to understand it as yielding veridical, three-dimensional representations of our environment (e.g., Marr, 1982). And a similar idea is actually quite natural for other parts of cognition: namely, that we are trying to understand the complete structure and constituents of our world by any means necessary. In this cognitive picture, the mind is presumably structured such that any cognitive process can influence any representation at any time, and the external world then provides the constraints that preclude (long-term) incompatibilities.

In contrast, one might think that very few cognitive processes—perhaps only one—are active at any particular moment. In that case, we do not need to worry about possible incompatibilities, since any representation that is modified by multiple processes would be changed sequentially, rather than simultaneously. For example, the processes of causal learning and feature inference might both access the same cognitive representation, but the cognizer would be engaged in only one of these processes at a time. This view is naturally suggested by introspection, and also by considering the relatively sequential nature of problem solving and goal satisfaction. Of course, ample evidence shows that some cognitive processes function entirely implicitly or unconsciously and so we should not overweight the importance of introspective judgments. It is however plausible (or at least possible) that many types of higher-order cognition run in a more serial fashion rather than in parallel.

If these processes modify cognitive representations sequentially, then the issue of incompatibilities simply does not arise, though there could be cycles of changes in which (i) process P_1 changes the representation to R, followed by (ii) P_2 changing it to something R^* that is incompatible with R, followed by (iii) P_1 changing it back to R. The possibility of such cycles highlights that this account implies that the content of our representations should exhibit significant order or process effects. Any particular learning or reasoning process presumably depends on only some of the information in the environment and thus will only use or modify the cognitive representation along those lines. For example, feature inference depends on only the probabilistic structure of a category, not its causal structure. Learning based on feature inference should thus not, in a single-process account, lead to changes in one's representation of causal structure. In particular, if I have not yet learned the causal structure, then if feature inference is the only learning process at work in me, then I will continue to not know the causal structure. This contrasts with the multiple-process learner who does feature inference learning and causal learning all at the same time. The single-process account predicts that our cognitive representations should carry detectable residues of our cognitive process histories, precisely because we do not try to learn and reason about everything.

We have identified three salient cognitive architectures in the "possible theory space" depending on the number of representational stores and the number of simultaneously active processes: (i) the *multiple-stores* view (for which it does not matter how many processes are simultaneously active); (ii) the *single-store, multiple-processes* view; and (iii) the *single-store, single-process* view. At a high level, the number of representational stores matters for the "portability" of representations between cognitive processes, while the number of simultaneous processes determines the maximality (versus task dependence) of the representations that are acquired and used. For each type of account, we can thus make some high-level predictions about the kinds of behavior that we should expect to see.

For the multiple-stores accounts, we should expect to find very little cross-cognition transfer. Representations acquired through one cognitive process should be relatively inaccessible to other types of cognitive processes, or accessible only after substantial transformation or deformation. This lack of cross-cognition transfer is just what it means to have multiple representational stores rather than a single one and thus is an important empirical constraint implied by these accounts. Moreover, since each representation comes from just one (or a few) cognitive process, we should expect to find "marks" of those processes in the representations. That is, a close connection should exist between the particular cognitive learning process and the resulting representational structure and content. In contrast, the single-store, multiple-process account predicts substantial cross-cognition transfer, since the different cognitive processes can access and modify the same information, leading to full encoding of the knowledge required for the transfer task. For example, even when causal learning does not require category information, this account predicts that people's categorization performance (after causal learning) should be approximately as good as if that were the focal task. That is, since multiple cognitive processes are running simultaneously, the information in the representation should be (close to) maximal. We should thus expect to not see substantial task or process dependence in the representational structure or content: people should (in these accounts) be extracting most of the information available to them, regardless of the particular task they have been provided.

The single-store, single-process accounts carve out an intermediate position between the other two. On the one hand, they predict that significant cross-cognition transfer should occur, since there is a single representational store that all (relevant) cognitive processes can access. Information acquired using one cognitive process should be available to many other cognitive processes; causal learning, for example, should yield representations usable for categorization. On the other hand, the representations should show signs of the cognitive processes by which they were learned or used, since only a single cognitive process modifies them at each point in time, and so only the information relevant to the focal task should be encoded or learned. This process or task dependence is predicted to manifest in distinctive patterns during the cross-cognition transfer. For example, if a representation is acquired through causal learning, then categorization behavior based on it should be different than if the representation were acquired through "standard" category learning.

7.2 What Do the Data Say?

Empirical data discriminating between these different kinds of architectures come in two types. Data about whether there is any substantive cross-cognition transfer at all can distinguish between the multiple-store and single-store accounts. To the extent that such transfer occurs, the level and pattern (if any) of process or task dependence can distinguish between the single-process and multiple-process versions of the single-store accounts. The published literature, however, contains relatively little empirical data of either type: cross-cognition transfer is an understudied part of cognitive science. Moreover, the few experiments that aim to explicitly study such transfer have tended to focus on whether transfer occurs at all, not what patterns arise in the posttransfer cognition that could provide insight into whether one or multiple processes access the representation(s). Thus, after considering the extant data in this section, I provide a number of novel experiments in section 7.3 that could be performed to gain more insight into cross-cognition transfer.[4]

In general, experiments on cross-cognition transfer ask people to learn through one cognitive process or with one cognitive goal, and then test people by asking them to use that knowledge in the same situation, but with a different type of cognitive process. Cross-cognition transfer is thus importantly different from the transfer of learning from one problem situation to another that has been widely studied, particularly in educational psychology (Cormier & Hagman, 1987; Haskell, 2000; Singley & Anderson, 1989). Transfer of learning typically involves challenges in which the task is relatively constant but the situation changes. For example, one might examine whether people who have learned to solve one type of geometry problem can apply that knowledge to a new geometry problem. In contrast, I am interested here in cross-cognition transfer, where the situation is held relatively constant, while the task varies. Much of the research that is described as investigating "transfer" is thus not applicable to the study of cross-cognition transfer.

As an example of the kind of experiments that are relevant, consider a series of experiments performed by William Nichols and me (Nichols & Danks, 2007). Experimental participants were presented with two different possible causes of a plant blooming and were told that, after learning, they would pick one of the two factors to apply to a new plant. Moreover, they would receive a monetary bonus if the plant actually did bloom after applying the chosen factor. That is, from the participants' point of view, their task was to learn for decision-making purposes. After participants made their decision, however, we surprised them by asking about the causal *strength* of each factor. Causal strength information is not actually required to solve the decision-making problem; one could make an optimal decision by, for example, simply tracking whether there are more cases of the effect with factor 1 or with factor 2. More generally, the decision-making problem requires only knowledge of the rank order of the causal strengths, not their absolute strengths. At the same time, numerous causal learning experiments have shown that people are able to learn quantitative causal strengths when asked to do so (see the many references in sec. 4.2).

What would the different cognitive architectures outlined in section 7.1 predict for this experiment? It is not clear whether we should think that "learning for decision making" and "causal strength learning" fall into different representational stores (silos) in a many-stores account. If they do, then the prediction is that people's causal strength ratings should be close to random. In these many-stores accounts, people generate a representation of the situation to make a decision, but this representation is relatively inaccessible to causal reasoning processes, so the information required to answer the probe question will be unavailable. As a result, we should expect people to respond quasi-randomly; at most, their responses might have a rank order that justifies their decision, since we asked the causal strength question after the decision was made. If they chose factor 1, for example, then they might respond that factor 1 is stronger than factor 2, but only because it enables them to rationalize or justify the decision that was just made, not because they have a representation of the causal structure. There is no prediction that the responses should be close to the actual causal strengths.

Now consider the two single-store views. If multiple processes can access the single representational store, then we should expect people's causal strength ratings to be quite accurate. We know that people are capable of learning such strengths, and so the causal strength learning process should be able to encode that information in the shared representation, though it is not strictly required to make an appropriate decision. In contrast, if only a single process is (substantively) active at any point, then we would predict better-than-random causal strength ratings, though they should not be as accurate as in a standard causal learning experiment. The process of learning to make an appropriate decision will sometimes modify the shared representation, and as noted earlier, that process needs to learn only the rank order of the factors' strengths. Causal strength learning should thus be partially "impaired," though this decrease in accuracy should be restricted to the precise numeric values; both processes aim to learn the rank order (either explicitly or implicitly), so there should be no decrease in performance in that regard.

These three predictions exactly track the general pattern for which I argued at the end of section 7.1. In particular: (a) a many-stores account predicts essentially no transfer and thus very poor performance on the transfer task; (b) a single-store, many-process account predicts substantial transfer task learning (by the other process) and thus performance on the transfer task that is comparable to when that task is focal; and (c) a single-store, single-process account predicts that transfer task performance should depend on the learning task, and so people should exhibit a characteristic pattern of performance decrease on the transfer task. The data from two different experiments in Nichols and Danks (2007) best match prediction (c), which suggests a single-store, single-process account. In particular, we found that the quantitative strength estimates were skewed in particular ways: for example, when the weaker causal factor was a nonfactor (i.e., had zero causal strength), participants regularly reported that it actually had slightly *negative* causal strength (i.e., it prevented blooming). Thus option (b) does not seem to be correct in this setting. At the same time, participants in the experiments were excellent at reporting the rank order of the factors' causal strengths; more generally, their strength estimates were biased but clearly not random. A many-stores account thus also seems implausible in these experiments. Rather, it seems that there is a common representational store that is being modified in limited ways.

The Nichols and Danks (2007) experiments provide a nice illustrative example, but they suffer from some significant flaws. Most importantly, they were originally conducted simply to see whether people could use causal learning to guide their decisions (in the spirit of some of the theories discussed in sec. 6.1), rather than to study cross-cognition transfer. We thus had no measures to determine, for example, whether people's success at getting the rank order of the causal strengths was due to learning or post hoc rationalization of their previous decisions. Perhaps more importantly, we did not attempt to measure people's representations before learning, so we do not know exactly how the task dependence arose. One possibility is that people represented the situation using a "rich" causal representation (including numeric causal strengths), but the causal learning process was insufficiently active or influential to move the strength estimates to their proper values. An alternative possibility is that the framing in terms of a decision-making goal led people to use an impoverished representation involving only some combination of rank order information and more qualitative causal strengths (since that is all they require to succeed), and then they learned as much as possible about that reduced representation. That is, it is possible that learning began with a directed graphical model and only a qualitative representation of causal strengths (e.g., "none," "weak," "strong," or "very strong"). If the to-be-learned representation had this structure, then performance could decrease even if causal learning was constantly active. In general, this kind of underdetermination poses a problem for many experiments on cross-cognition transfer: it is often unclear whether there was reduced learning of a rich representation or full learning of an impoverished representation. More generally, learning and representations are remarkably hard to tease apart, and these studies are no different. I consider some ways to distinguish these possibilities in the next section, but this underdetermination may ultimately prove largely insurmountable (at least using typical behavioral data).

One final concern about the Nichols and Danks (2007) experiments is that the cover story (about plant blooming) was written using causal language. As a result, participants might have been primed to track (at least somewhat) the causal strengths. That is, perhaps a multiple-stores view is actually correct, but participants nonetheless partially learned the causal strengths because the cover story language suggested that they should. It would be preferable if the cover story used as little causal language as possible while the situation is still one in which decision making matters. We start to see these features in the next experiment we consider.

Hagmayer et al. (2010) presented participants with a control task in which they repeatedly chose actions (specifically, energy rays that stimulate brain areas) to keep a target (a mouse's neurotransmitter levels) at an appropriate level. The value of the target at each moment was a complex function of the action chosen and the previous state of the target. This dynamical system was thus reasonably complex and difficult to control, particularly since the participants only saw the impact of the chosen action (the brain area activations) and the resulting level of the target. Participants learned to control the system through repeated actions and improved over time at keeping the target close to the desired level. So far, this experiment simply tested people's ability to learn to control a dynamical system. The cross-cognition transfer arose because, unbeknownst to the experimental participants, some of the brain regions actually caused one another. We can thus use the representations that participants spontaneously learn about this between-region causal structure to determine their cross-cognition transfer. Hagmayer et al. (2010) are explicit that they have this goal: "We investigate whether decision makers *spontaneously* acquire causal models" (p. 145; italics in original). In terms of the three central theoretical options discussed in this chapter, the predictions are clear about what should be learned about causal structure: "many stores" says "nothing"; "single store, many process" says "as much as if causal structure learning were the goal"; and "single store, single process" says "only as much structure as is required to solve the control problem."

In both of their experiments, Hagmayer et al. (2010) found that a large majority of the participants in each experiment learned about the causal structure between the brain regions. In particular, when given a forced choice between (i) the structure with no causal connections between brain regions and (ii) the structure with a causal connection between one particular pair of brain regions, most (80–85 percent) participants correctly selected option (ii). This measure (and others discussed in the following paragraphs) suggests that the many-stores view is incorrect, since cross-cognition transfer does seem to occur. It is less clear what conclusions to draw about the process question. The relatively good performance might suggest that people are doing "full" causal learning, but this conclusion is too quick. The experimental measure of causal knowledge was relatively coarse, as it was simply a forced choice between two given options. More importantly, both experiments provided explicit temporal information to participants. That is, the causal learning data for participants involved not just co-occurrence of brain region activation but also timing information such that region *B* was frequently activated *after* region *A*.

This type of temporal information makes causal structure inference much easier, and people appear to exploit it spontaneously (Fernbach &

Sloman, 2009; Lagnado, Waldmann, Hagmayer, & Sloman, 2007). The causal structure learning in this experiment was thus arguably sufficiently easy that even single-store, single-process accounts can explain it. The single-process views hold only that performance should (potentially, depending on the learning task) decrease, not that *no* learning at all should occur. The forced-choice measure arguably has a sufficiently low threshold for success that no decrease in performance could be observed. As further evidence for this explanation, Meder and Hagmayer (2009) used a similar experimental design but asked participants to produce the full causal structure, rather than make a forced choice. They found that participants "spontaneously" learned causal structure but were much worse at reporting the exact structure. For example, 40 percent of the participants in their experiment 2 produced causal graphs that were inconsistent with even just the temporal aspects of the learning data. The two papers together suggest that forced choices over two causal structures do not provide sufficiently fine-grained information to distinguish single- and many-process accounts.

Hagmayer et al. (2010) also assessed causal learning using more indirect measures, such as predictions about what would happen if various interventions were performed on the brain regions directly (thereby potentially breaking causal connections). These measures provide additional evidence that experimental participants learned about the causal structure, and so the many-stores view is unlikely to be correct. At the same time, people's performance exhibited substantial deviations from the normatively correct responses that they should have given if they had learned the full causal structure (including numeric causal strengths). However, these deviations do not automatically imply that a single-process view is correct, since they have at least two alternative explanations. First, as discussed in section 4.3, people's causal reasoning typically exhibits some systematic deviations from the normative responses. The errors found in these experiments could be a product of whatever reasoning process generates those errors. Second, participants did not reach perfect performance on the learning task (i.e., figuring out how to control the dynamic system), and so it is possible that people simply failed to fully learn the quantitative structure. Nonetheless these experiments suggest that something like the single-store, single-process view might be right. Also, although graphical models are not the main focus of this chapter, it is interesting to note that those studies consistently found support for that representational framework. People's performance was suboptimal, but their pattern of behavior was still best explained as operations on graphical model representations, rather than one of the other decision-making representations that Hagmayer et al. (2010) considered.

As noted at the start of this section, relatively few experiments have directly investigated cross-cognition transfer across different cognitive domains. Moreover, even some experiments that appear relevant at first glance turn out not to be particularly informative. For example, Waldmann and Hagmayer (2006) examined the impact of previously learned concepts on causal learning from data and argued that people learn causal graphs using their preexisting concepts as nodes. No real transfer occurred in their experiments, however, since the previously learned concepts functioned simply as labels in the data and nodes in the graph. In particular, the causal learning parts of their experiments did not use anything about the structured representations underlying the concepts, so the only "transfer" was one cognitive process passing a label to another.[5] Similarly, Lien and Cheng (2000) showed that people spontaneously construct novel categories that are maximally helpful in causal reasoning. That is, their results demonstrate that unsupervised concept learning can be guided by the role of the concepts in the subsequently learned causal structure.[6] As with Waldmann and Hagmayer (2006), though, these concepts simply provided nodes for the subsequent causal learning; there was no interesting transfer of the representation of the concept itself.

We can, however, find relevant data and experiments if we look for indirect evidence of cross-cognition transfer. Many of the studies cited in previous chapters already provide quite a lot of indirect evidence. For example, causal reasoning has been assessed by asking people to choose particular interventions (e.g., Gopnik et al., 2004). This measure depends implicitly on there being some level of cross-cognition transfer: if the products of causal learning could not be used for this type of decision making, then people should be unable to appropriately select interventions. Similarly, almost all the experiments on causal graph-based decision making use response measures that necessarily depend on decision-making processes having some level of access to causal knowledge. When we combine this wealth of indirect evidence with the data already mentioned, it becomes extremely hard to see how any strong form of the many-stores view could be correct. Any defense of such a view would require not only explaining away the mathematical commonalities described in the previous chapters but also accounting for how all these experimental measures end up working at all, let alone so successfully. To my knowledge, no such explanations have been proposed, and it is hard to see how they could be made sufficiently compelling to offset this diverse empirical data.

This conclusion nonetheless leaves open the question of number of processes. On this point, we have both direct and indirect evidence from within the cognitive domain of concepts. Since this research is within a particular domain, it cannot speak to the issue of number of stores, but it can still be informative about the number of processes. In terms of research directly on this problem, consider the experiments of Ross (1997, 1999, 2000; see also Jee & Wiley, 2007). Participants were taught how to classify individuals into a particular category; for example, they were taught to classify people as suffering from one or another disease. The participants then had to use their knowledge of the individual's category to perform a second task (e.g., choose a treatment option); the two judgments—classification and secondary task—were performed either sequentially or in separate contexts. The key twist to the experiments was that some of the category features were relevant to the second task but not to classification. On a many-process account, these features should be (mostly) ignored whenever people classify, regardless of whether they had made the additional judgments. The "classification learning" process should, on this account, always be active, so the concept representation should continue to accurately encode the information required for classification, regardless of any additional tasks. In contrast, a single-process account predicts that people's classification judgments should be influenced by the additional treatment judgments, since the "learning to treat" process will potentially modify the representation of the concept without the "learning to classify" process being able to maintain the previously learned content. The results of the experiments clearly support a single-process account: after participants learned to perform the second task, their classification judgments were now influenced by factors that were previously (and correctly) ignored (Jee & Wiley, 2007; Ross, 1997, 1999, 2000).

In contrast, research that speaks only indirectly to the number of processes can be found in investigations of learning format effects in concept acquisition. Recall that the discriminating feature between the single-process and many-process accounts is whether behavior on the transfer task depends in part on the learning task (assuming different learning tasks involve the same data). Single-process accounts predict that there will usually be such learning dependence, while many-process accounts predict that it should be less likely. There are two major learning tasks used in the experimental study of concept learning, and a substantial amount of research has investigated learning task effects on the cognitive representations that are actually acquired (Chin-Parker & Ross, 2002, 2004; Hoffman & Rehder, 2010; Markman & Ross, 2003; Yamauchi & Markman, 1998; Yamauchi, Love, & Markman, 2002). Both of these cognitive tasks were discussed in more detail in section 5.3.

Given a sequence of individuals, one way to learn a new concept is through classification learning in which I am told the category for each individual, perhaps after making an initial guess about its category. For example, I might be shown a picture of an animal and have to guess whether it is a dax or a grom (i.e., one of two made-up categories). I am provided feedback about whether I categorized the animal correctly and then move to the next image. This process continues until I can correctly classify the animals into their groups. A different learning task is feature inference, where I am shown an individual and told its category and then must infer one or more of its features. For example, I might be shown a picture of an animal known to be a dax and asked to determine how many legs it has. I receive feedback about my inference and then move to the next animal until I can correctly infer the relevant features. One nice feature of these two different learning tasks is that it is possible to present participants with exactly the same data, regardless of the learning task. For both tasks, people receive feedback and so end up having full knowledge of the individual and its category; as a result, the learning data can be perfectly matched.[7] If there were no learning task dependence, then we would expect people to learn essentially the same concepts regardless of learning condition (as predicted by Anderson, 1991b). Instead many different experiments have revealed substantial learning task effects in this cognitive domain (Chin-Parker & Ross, 2002, 2004; Hoffman & Rehder, 2010; Markman & Ross, 2003; Yamauchi et al., 2002; Yamauchi & Markman, 1998; Zhu & Danks, 2007).

Mere dependence is insufficient to support a single-process account; the dependence must match the account's predictions. In this case, the prediction is that people should be accurate about only those factors that are relevant or necessary for success in the learning task, and should fail to represent (or should represent inaccurately) aspects of the concepts that are relatively irrelevant to the learning task. A central intuition for single-process accounts is that the limits on process access to the shared cognitive representations imply that people should learn—more generally, modify their representations—in highly limited ways. In this experimental context, this intuition implies that people should learn (alternately, represent or encode) only those aspects of within-concept structure and between-concept differences that are meaningful for the goal at hand. When we look to the empirical data, we find exactly this pattern of learning task effects: classification learning leads people to learn substantially more about the features that distinguish between categories, while feature inference results in learning more about the between-feature correlations within each particular category. This large body of experimental work thus strongly suggests a single-process view, at least within this cognitive domain. Of course, that does not show that a single-process account is correct across many cognitive domains, but it provides significant indirect support for such an idea.

7.3 Novel Predictions, New Experiments, and Open Questions

Many of the experiments in the previous section provide only indirect evidence or discrimination between the different theoretical alternatives proposed in section 7.1. Other experiments, however, can potentially examine the issue more directly. This section outlines some of those experiments to give an idea about how to further test this cognitive architecture, as well as potentially resolve some ambiguities in the framework. To begin, notice that all the experiments discussed so far assume (perhaps implicitly in the data analysis) that there are no significant individual differences. That is, they all assume that people are generally the same in their cross-cognition transfer. That assumption helps to justify the inference from nonrandom, task-dependent patterns in cross-cognition transfer to a single-store, single-process account. If we drop that assumption, then a different explanation arises for the data we have seen: perhaps everyone has multiple representational stores, but some people simply like learning new representations. That is, perhaps there is no cross-cognition transfer whatsoever, but some individuals learn multiple representations of the experimental system (one per store or process) because of their particular personality traits. If we consider only average performance, then there is not necessarily any difference predicted between (i) everyone being single-store, single-process cognizers, and (ii) a mixed population in which some people learn everything while some learn only the focal learning task.

To separate these two possibilities, we need to collect more fine-grained data. One option is to examine the individual responses, since option (ii) predicts that the distribution of responses should be strongly bimodal, where the two modes correspond to fully accurate and close-to-random responses. A closer examination of the Nichols and Danks (2007) data reveals no evidence that we had a mixed population of learners; the response distributions show no sign of being bimodal, though some are admittedly rather diffuse. Of course, this evidence comes from only one set of experiments that were not explicitly designed to look for different learning strategies. It is entirely conceivable that a more targeted experiment would find important differences in whether people learn about aspects of the world that are not immediately goal relevant. A different option is to try to determine whether an experimental participant is likely to be someone who tries to learn everything about an experimental situation. This type of intellectual curiosity has been examined under the name "need for cognition" (Cacioppo & Petty, 1982; Cacioppo, Petty, & Kao, 1984). More practically, well-studied scales seem to provide a good estimate of whether someone is likely driven to understand all of a situation, even when success at the learning task does not require such complete knowledge. In future experiments, it will be important to try to distinguish between options (i) and (ii), using both more careful data analysis and also more sophisticated measures of the individual participants.

Most of the experiments discussed in section 7.2 explored the interactions between some cognitive domain and decision making. The skeptic might argue, however, that such experiments do not actually provide a strong test of the single representational store account, since it is (the skeptic argues) entirely unsurprising that decision making uses representations from other cognitive activities. According to this line of argument, decision making does not produce representations but only consumes them to generate actions. Decision making thus necessarily relies on cross-cognition transfer, precisely because it is (in this argument) qualitatively different from cognitive activities such as categorization or causal reasoning. Of course, decision-making processes are clearly involved in learning. For example, participants in the Hagmayer et al. (2010) experiments (discussed in sec. 7.2) learned to control a dynamical system by making decisions and observing the outcomes. The skeptic maintains, however, that learning and decision making are separable processes: given some representation *R*, I make a decision, and then the outcome information is used by some other process to modify *R*. On this view, it is completely unsurprising that decision making shares representations with other cognitive processes or domains, since it must get them from somewhere and cannot produce them itself. Experiments involving decision making do not, on the skeptic's view, give us any particular reason to think that there is a rich representational store that is shared across multiple cognitive processes that do not involve decision making.

One problem with this skeptical position is that it presupposes that we can cleanly carve out the set of "decision-making processes" that only consume representations, rather than modifying them directly. For example, the skeptic must show how to divide causal reasoning—making predictions, generating explanations, and so forth—into parts that modify representations and those that actually make a decision in a way that changes nothing about the representation. Similarly, the skeptic must maintain that reasoning about concepts is divisible in this way. The problem is that our cognitive reasoning processes just do not seem to be neatly separable in this way into distinct components; the same reasoning that leads to a choice can also modify the representations over which the reasoning occurs (Williams & Lombrozo, 2010). The skeptical position seems plausible only if we *define* decision making to be those cognitive processes that use representations without modifying them but that begs the question against the single-store theories. More importantly, such a definition would be counter to the standard method of defining cognitive processes by their input, output, and function and thus requires much more justification than just a general skeptical worry.

The skeptic's argument, however, does contain a kernel of truth: the experiments on cross-cognition transfer have been restricted to always using decision making, and so the single-store account has not yet received the strongest possible test. Thankfully, obvious experiments can directly test this account. For example, one might ask participants to learn the causal structure M_1 underlying a set of animals and then separately learn a causal structure M_2 for different animals. If there is a single representational store (and if some concepts are defined by shared causal structure), then these causal structures should provide natural candidates for categorizing novel instances. That is, people should naturally group novel animals based on whether they appear to have causal structure M_1 or M_2, even though they have never been told that those causal structures each pick out a category. On standard accounts of concept learning, people need either explicit instruction (e.g., labels) when engaged in supervised concept learning, or explicit contrasts for unsupervised concept learning. In this experiment, participants receive neither: there are no category labels or other markers indicating that the causal structures correspond to concepts, and the causal structure learning occurs in distinct episodes, so there are no (explicit) contrasts. If people nonetheless learn novel concepts based on those causal structures, then we have reason to think that there is a shared representational store.[8] Although some experiments have tried to link causal learning and our concepts (Lien & Cheng, 2000; Waldmann & Hagmayer, 2006), they have not looked for this type of *direct* transfer of representations between cognitive processes.

A similar experiment would reverse the order of operations: start with learning multiple categories, each determined by a different causal structure, and then ask participants to design novel interventions on members of those categories. A number of experiments have explored whether people's concepts exhibit structural features that are plausibly explained using graphical models, and causal models more specifically (see chap. 5). Those experiments have not, however, examined the intervention choices that people can or do make on the basis of that (conceptual) knowledge. As a result, it is unclear whether people are always learning *causal* structure when they learn concepts from data through categorization or feature inference learning.[9] We can thus perform an experiment in which participants learn concepts through one of the standard methods (e.g., categorization), where the concepts are actually defined in terms of shared causal structure. Once people have learned several such categories, they are then presented with new instances of those categories and asked to make (or reason about) interventions on the novel individuals. If representations are shared across multiple cognitive processes, then we should expect people to succeed at these inferences, at least to the extent that they actually learn causal-structure-based categories. That last qualifier is necessary, since "failure to transfer" is not necessarily disconfirming evidence if people never learned an appropriate cognitive representation in the first place. If, for example, someone learns an exemplar-based category instead of a causal-structure-based one, then it would be entirely unsurprising (and unproblematic for my view) if they could not design appropriate interventions. It will thus be important to determine the cognitive representations that people actually learn, albeit in a way that does not prime participants to necessarily think causally.

The previous two experiments would look simply for successful cross-cognition transfer, but as we saw in section 7.2, it can also be illuminating to look for patterns in the cross-cognition transfer that can reveal details about the learning and reasoning processes operating in particular situations. The Nichols and Danks (2007) experiments point toward the possibility of a general pattern: people learn only as much as they need to learn to solve the learning task at hand. This "minimalist" learning contrasts with a more "maximalist" type of learning in which people learn all that they can about a situation, regardless of whether the additional information seems immediately relevant. As noted earlier, minimalist strategies fit naturally with single-process accounts, while maximalist ones cohere better with a many-process view. One could perform many different experiments to distinguish between these possibilities.

In general, the types of learning task dependence predicted by single-process views fit cleanly with an overarching goal dependence of learned representation, regardless of whether there is any cross-cognition transfer. For example, Rehder, Colner, & Hoffman (2009) used eye-tracking data to argue that feature inference learning focuses on the *expected* question items, rather than on learning all the relevant (internal) statistics. Sarah Wellen has recently developed (in collaboration with me) several experiments that explicitly explore whether people extract minimal information to succeed at their learning goals or rather learn maximal information about their situation. For example, suppose that people are confronted with four buttons, where pressing a button causes a number from 1 to 100 to be displayed. The numbers for any particular button are randomly generated from a probability distribution with unknown average and variance. Participants also know that, after learning, they will select a button to be pressed one more time, and their payment will go up if the number is either very large or, in a different condition, very small. That is, half of the participants are trying to figure out which button produces the largest numbers on average, while the other half are trying to determine which yields the smallest numbers on average. In actuality, two of the button averages are close together and small, and the other two are close and large. The true averages might, for example, be 20, 30, 70, and 80. All participants see the exact same sequence of button values, regardless of whether they are trying to find the largest or smallest button. After the learning phase, we surprise participants by asking them not just to select a button but also to report the average values for all four buttons.

A maximalist learner should track all four button averages and thus give reasonably accurate estimates for all of them after learning. The responses should not vary as a function of the learning goal. In contrast, a minimalist learner can quickly detect (after only a few trials) that two of the buttons are almost certainly not winners, since they are either much too low or much too high (depending on whether the goal is to find the largest or smallest button, respectively). The minimalist learner can then focus her attention on only the pair of buttons that might be appropriate choices in the end. As a result, she should be reasonably accurate about the two buttons that match the learning goal, but be much less accurate about the two that are irrelevant for the goal. The prediction is obviously not that the minimalist learner will know *nothing* about the buttons that do not match the learning goal but that her learning should be significantly worse than individuals for whom the learning goal *does* match those particular buttons. That is, people are predicted to extract different information from the same sequence, based solely on whether their goal is to find the largest or smallest (on average) button. In preliminary versions of this experiment, we have found exactly the pattern of results predicted for the minimalist learner. People are quite good at learning which button best satisfies their goal, and even the precise values of the buttons that are plausible candidates for their goal. They learn much less about the buttons that are far from their goal, and thus the learning goal significantly affects the resulting representations. There appears to be a general goal dependence on learning that is consonant with the single-process views in which representations are modified only by learning processes that are directly or immediately relevant to one's goals.

Wellen has also designed an experiment to test a different type of potential goal dependence in causal learning. In general, one can make successful predictions from observations without actually having the correct causal structure. In contrast, if I know the full, correct causal structure, then I can infer key (conditional) probabilities based on either observations or interventions, perhaps with some systematic biases (as discussed in chap. 5; see also Rottman & Hastie, 2014). Thus, consider an experiment in which all participants are provided with the same data about variables A, B, and X, where the true causal structure is $A \rightarrow X \rightarrow B$. Half of the people are tasked with learning to infer values of X based on A and B, while the other half are charged with learning the underlying causal structure. After learning, all participants are asked *both* types of questions—causal structure and observational inference. The maximalist learning prediction is that there should be no difference between the two groups; all participants receive the same data, and so both groups can learn an equal amount about the situation. In particular, if the situation is one in which the causal structure is actually learnable,[10] then all participants should perform well on both tasks. In contrast, the minimalist learner should exhibit goal dependence in her learned representations. If her goal is to learn the full causal structure, then the minimalist will perform well on all questions (again, subject to potential systematic biases in causal reasoning). In contrast, if the learning goal is simply to make observational inferences about X, then the participant needs only to learn the conditional probability of X given values of A and B. That particular conditional probability is consistent with the incorrect causal structure $A \rightarrow X \leftarrow B$. The minimalist learner is thus predicted to make systematic errors on the causal structure questions (relative to participants who have the causal structure learning goal). The extent of people's minimalism in experiments such as this one is currently unknown.

Across many different experiments, there does seem to be a consistent theme of people behaving like minimalists who learn just what is required to succeed at the learning task, rather than like maximalists who attempt to extract maximal information about their situation. Moreover, this pattern of experimental data fits nicely with some results about causal misconceptions in everyday life. As just one (extreme) example, many medical professionals and some textbooks (at least in the 1980s) believed that a larger heart caused an increased risk of congestive heart failure (Feltovich, Spiro, & Coulson, 1989). The view was that the heart failed *because* it got too big and so lost the ability to pump blood effectively. Even at that time, though, the correct causal structure was known to be that congestive heart failure is caused by a failure of the heart muscles to be properly activated or "energized," which thereby leads to an enlarged heart. That is, the true causal relationship between *Heart failure* and *Heart size* is exactly backward from the causal relationship as understood by medical professionals (again, at least at that time). One might think that this misconception revealed some sort of failing on the part of the medical professionals, as many of them had incorrect beliefs while the truth was readily available. Importantly, however, the "backward" conception still enables successful inference by the medical professionals; their observational predictions do not suffer by virtue of believing the wrong causal model. Of course, their postintervention predictions *would* suffer from using the wrong causal model, but those predictions arise only if one can intervene directly on *Heart size* or *Heart failure*, which was not an option in the 1980s. The maximalist conception of learning cannot explain the medical professionals' seeming lack of concern about having incorrect causal beliefs (Feltovich et al., 1989), since the correct causal structure was learnable by them. Minimalist learning can, however, account for their behavior. If medical professionals have the learning goal (for this system) solely of observational prediction, then they have not made a mistake using the "backward" conception, since it fully satisfies that learning goal.[11]

The experiments discussed in this section have focused on predictions of the single-store, single-process view. However, another key theme of this book (albeit one that has mostly resided in the background) is that it is important for our cognitive representations to encode relevance information. For the most part, I have not explicitly discussed this theme, since one of the main reasons to consider graphical models is precisely that they compactly represent relevance relations. All the arguments for graphical models as the proper framework for (many of) our cognitive representations are thus also arguments that our representations can, and do, encode relevance. At the same time, we could conduct experiments that attempt to directly test whether people are appropriately sensitive to relevance relations. Many experiments have shown that people attend to different parts of the environment to extract information that is (or is believed to be) relevant to the current cognitive task (e.g., Desimone & Duncan, 1995; Downing, 2000; Huang & Pashler, 2007; Pashler & Harris, 2001). The key question for the cognitive architecture presented here is: do people's attentional or information-seeking strategies track relevance information in the way that the graphical model claims to represent? For example, if people learn that $A \rightarrow B \rightarrow C \rightarrow D$ and are then asked to predict the value of D, do they first check the value of C? Many more complex examples could easily be constructed and even integrated with some of the other experiments outlined in this section. There are significant methodological challenges for investigating information-seeking strategies (e.g., the complexity of eye-tracking data). Those costs will be worthwhile, however, to the extent that these experiments can test the hypothesis that our cognitive representations track relevance relations approximately as a graphical model does.

Overall this chapter has aimed to present a clear, well-defended cognitive architecture in which (a) there is a single representational store of (b) cognitive representations structured as graphical models, where (c) only single cognitive processes modify those representations at a time, such that (d) cross-cognition transfer exhibits predictable patterns of dependence on the tasks and goals during the learning of that representation. This psychological account is the key positive proposal of the book, and the point toward which all the previous chapters have built. In the final two chapters, I consider a set of open issues that remain about this cognitive architecture. First, I have argued that this account unifies cognition in a deep and novel way, but there have been many proposals for how to "unify the mind." The next chapter thus shows how my account differs in key ways from previous proposals, in both details and broad approach. Unification through shared representations is an interestingly different tactic than what is employed by most unifying cognitive architectures. Second, one might wonder whether this account really matters; perhaps it is simply a lot of mathematics to say something that we already knew. I hope this chapter has already dispelled that concern, as I have provided both interpretations of previous experiments and predictions for novel experimental designs. Nonetheless, I step back in chapter 9 and ask about the broader morals and conclusions that one can draw from this cognitive architecture.

8 Alternative Approaches

8.1 Different Approaches for Unifying the Mind

The previous chapter provided an integrated cognitive architecture that aimed to unify many aspects of cognition as different processes on a shared store of cognitive representations, structured as graphical models. The goal of a unified model of much of cognition is obviously not new but rather has been a perennial target; we can even understand Plato's account of the soul in the *Phaedo* as an attempt to build a unified understanding of the mind. The belief that my mind actually is a relatively unified, coherent object or process naturally arises from both self-introspection and other-observation. Demonstrations that aspects of cognition are not integrated are interesting to cognitive scientists precisely because unification and coherence are typically the (implicitly) assumed default state. All these observations suggest that we should expect cognitive architectures, and even many cognitive models, to explain cognitive unification. Models of "local" parts of cognition (e.g., causal inference) are valuable because they tell us what must be unified, but we should aspire to build accounts of human cognition that explain how those various local elements combine and interact.

Many different routes and strategies have been followed in pursuit of the goal of cognitive unification. In this book, I have argued for unification through shared representations: our cognition is unified because we have stable, persistent cognitive representations that are shared across multiple cognitive processes and domains. In contrast, the vast majority of other approaches to unifying cognition have pursued different strategies. This chapter explores several of those alternatives to show how they differ from the account that I have offered. Each of these accounts could be, and typically has been, the subject of a book in its own right. My presentations and discussions will thus necessarily be quite high-level, rather than getting into the technical and empirical details. My principal focus will be to illustrate important differences between my account and previous unifications.

At a high level, we can group alternative cognitive unifications into two types: schema-centered unifications and process-centered unifications. This way of grouping unifications is not necessarily standard and puts together accounts often thought to be quite different. Nonetheless this taxonomy appropriately highlights important conceptual and thematic similarities between different accounts. Schema-centered unifications arise when we have a collection of distinct cognitive theories and models that are nonetheless all instantiations of the same type of structure (in some sense). In other words, schema-centered accounts argue for cognitive "unification" in virtue of some common template that is shared by all the individual cognitive models, rather than through shared cognitive elements (representations, processes, or both) across those models.[1] Of course, some elements might actually be shared—either cognitively or neurally—between different cognitive processes or representations, but that overlap does not play any central role in the unification. Rather, these accounts unify by having a few model schemata, often just one, that are instantiated all throughout the mind. For example, there are many different connectionist models of parts of cognition (e.g., Hummel & Holyoak, 2003; Rogers & McClelland, 2004), each of which tries to develop a neurally plausible model of some part of cognition.[2] At the same time, essentially no *single* connectionist model ever attempts to explain a wide range of cognitive processes and objects (though see Eliasmith et al., 2012). Cognition is instead supposed to be unified by virtue of these models all being instances of a single underlying type; that is, the mind consists of many distinct instantiations of the same type of object. Schema-centered unifications are typically not explicitly described in this way (though see Griffiths, Chater, Kemp, Perfors, & Tenenbaum, 2010; McClelland et al., 2010), but much of the scientific motivation for using the same schema for multiple cognitive models presumably comes from such a source. There are too many different schema-centered unifications to survey all of them; I focus in section 8.2 on two that have been deeply influential over the past thirty years: connectionism (sec. 8.2.1) and Bayesianism (sec. 8.2.2).

Process-centered unifications pursue the quite different strategy of trying to show how coherent cognition arises from shared processes, where those processes are typically small building blocks that combine to yield complex cognition. The "processes" that are shared in these unifications are much more restricted than the cognitive processes that I have previously discussed (e.g., causal reasoning). Nonetheless, by combining these elements in appropriate ways, a process-centered unification produces the appropriate range of cognitive activities. For example, the Soar cognitive architecture is based on production rules—roughly, complex if-then rules—that can be retrieved from memory and flexibly combined in working memory to determine a set of cognitive and motor actions (Laird, 2012; Laird, Newell, & Rosenbloom, 1987; Newell, 1990). That is, it unifies different aspects of cognition by basing the architecture on a small(er) set of operations that are shared across multiple cognitive activities. Process-centered unifications arguably do not directly compete with my architecture, since the mind could (in theory) be unified in both representations *and* processes.[3] In practice, however, process-centered unifications typically use much simpler representations than graphical models, though whether that is the correct choice remains an open question. As with schema-centered unifications, many different process-centered unifications have been proposed, and in section 8.3 I consider three salient ones: ACT-R (sec. 8.3.1); Soar (sec. 8.3.2); and Sigma (sec. 8.3.3), a recently developed cognitive architecture that also uses graphical models, though differently than in this book.

Throughout these discussions, a theme will consistently emerge: the ideas that I have proposed in this book are, in important ways, fully compatible with multiple different cognitive architectures that have been proposed. My system rarely directly competes with other proposals; it is instead complementary to many of them, precisely because I focus on representations, while they focus on schemata or processes. At the same time, many open questions and challenges must be resolved before my proposed cognitive architecture can be integrated substantively with any of these other proposed cognitive unifications. My cognitive architecture and these alternative unifications place constraints on one another (in the sense of chap. 2) without one being reducible to the other. Part of each section thus focuses on barriers that would need to be overcome to carry out this type of integration.

8.2 Schema-Centered Unifications

8.2.1 Connectionism

In general, schema-centered unifications aim to understand the mind through the use of a common cognitive "schema" or pattern across different cognitive activities. Such an approach rarely attempts to build a single model or architecture that can, by itself, predict and explain multiple cognitions (though see Eliasmith et al., 2012). Rather, the motivating idea is to show that the same general class of model can explain various cognitive activities, coupled with the argument (or sometimes just the assertion) that instances of this class could potentially be found throughout the mind or brain.

Connectionism encompasses perhaps the best-known schema-centered unification and provides an excellent example of this type. The connectionist starts with the observation that human cognition and behavior can be exceptionally complicated, but individual neurons are quite limited and simple. An individual neuron, for example, does not have cognitive representations but rather seems to be much more limited computationally. Nonetheless complex human behavior and cognition are generated (at least in the physicalist view) just through the processing of, and interactions between, these neurons. Moreover, we have essentially no evidence that individual neurons play causally critical roles; there does not seem be a proverbial "grandmother neuron" that encodes the one and only representation of your grandmother. Rather, cognition (somehow) emerges through the interactions of many neurons in structured networks. The core connectionist intuition is that we can significantly advance our understanding of cognition by trying to model those networks. Cognitive science has a long history of formal models of networks composed of neuronlike elements (Minsky & Papert, 1969; Rumelhart, McClelland, & PDP Research Group, 1986); those explicitly called "neural networks" make up only a subset of the many different efforts. I am not concerned here with any single method but rather focus on connectionism more generally.

Connectionism is an incredibly broad area of research, and so I make no claims to comprehensiveness. Rather, my discussion will explain just enough about connectionism to justify my claim that it is a schema-centered unification, and to see the similarities and differences with the architecture that I have advocated.[4] Much more information about connectionist networks can be found in many standard texts (e.g., many of the references in McClelland et al., 2010; Rogers & McClelland, 2004). Typical connectionist networks are composed of simple units, often called "neurons," since they are supposed to be computationally somewhat similar, but there is no necessary commitment to any sort of biological realism (for reasons I explain later in this subsection). In a basic connectionist network, these units are grouped into "layers" (analogous to neural layers), where most or all units in one layer are causes of units in the next layer. One layer is designated as the "input" layer, and the activation levels of those units are set from outside the connectionist network; the analogy here is with phenomena like visual perception, where the activation of cells in my retina is driven by factors outside my brain. The activation in the input layer then propagates forward in the network by causing the activation levels of units in the next layer, which then cause the activation levels of units in the layer after that, and so on. Eventually there is activation of units in the so-called output layer that encodes the product of the network, which can range from classification of some input into a particular category, to a sequence of motor actions, to a linguistic utterance.

Given a particular activation of the input units, it is simple to use a specific connectionist network to generate a particular output, as it is just a matter of propagating the input activations forward in the network until the output activations stabilize. In many cases, however, we want to have the network learn from data; we do not want to have to specify all the connections and their strengths in a purely a priori manner. A huge range of different learning methods have been proposed for connectionist networks, but it will suffice here to consider just the one that is arguably most common, back-propagation (Rumelhart et al., 1986). For this learning method, we first construct a connectionist network using between-layer connections with random strengths. This network will obviously do a terrible job of producing the proper output given some input; its output will be essentially random for each input. Now suppose that we also have some way of "teaching" the network; that is, when the network produces this random result, we can provide the correct answer (at least sometimes). Back-propagation uses the network's error—the difference between its actual output and the output it was supposed to produce—to make small, directed changes in the connection strengths so that the network's output for that input moves closer to the correct output. If the network is "taught" many times in this way, then its structure and connections will converge to reliably produce the correct output for inputs; in many cases, connectionist networks can actually learn to produce (approximately) any arbitrary function from the inputs to the outputs (Hornik, Stinchcombe, & White, 1989).

We can add many complications to connectionist networks, such as allowing later layers to cause earlier ones—so-called recurrent networks (Elman, 1991)—to encode information about timing or sequence. Other changes lead to more computationally sophisticated connectionist networks that can learn faster, represent more complex functions, and encode functions in a more compact manner. We can also alter the connectionist networks to make them more biologically plausible in different ways, such as using units that more closely model actual neurons, or incorporating additional pathways by which activation can spread. These various complications, however, do not change the basic structure of connectionist networks: units are activated as input; that activation propagates throughout the network; the resulting activation encodes the network's output; and errors in the network's output can be used to help the network "learn" to perform better in the future.

One of the most interesting features of connectionist networks is the structure of their representations. One might have thought that particular units would, through learning, come to correspond to particular aspects of the world; a connectionist network for classification might, for example, have a unit that is active just when the input image is a dog. In practice, however, connectionist networks essentially never develop this way. Instead they almost always end up using some manner of distributed representation. For example, the category DOG will be represented in a typical connectionist network by a pattern of activations across multiple units in an intermediate layer (or possibly multiple layers). More concretely, suppose we have a simple connectionist network with three layers—input, output, and a "hidden" layer in between—where the hidden layer has five units. The activation levels of those five hidden units determine a five-dimensional "activation space," where any particular point in that space corresponds to particular activation levels for each of the five units. We can then understand the representation of DOG as a region inside that space: any set of activations (for the five units) that falls inside that region corresponds to the network "thinking" DOG. No symbol or object corresponds to the network's representation of DOG; rather, the distributed representation means that representation of any particular concept is an emergent matter that occurs only because of the whole network (or at least a significant part of it).

Distributed or emergent representation is often taken to be one of the hallmarks of a connectionist network and seems to present a very different model of cognitive representation from the one that I have used. One standard nonconnectionist picture is that cognitive representations are the discrete physical entities or symbols that are the objects of cognitive processing. Something like this view has arguably been in the background of this whole book (though I suggest later in this subsection and in section 9.3 that it might be dispensable). The phenomenon of distributed representation, however, suggests that cognition involves nothing of the sort. Connectionist networks contain no persistent mental objects that could play the role of representations; cognition instead involves the distributed transformation of distributed information without any explicit or symbolic representation of entities and properties in the mind and the world. Of course, there is a sense in which the hidden unit activation levels at some particular moment do "represent" a particular dog in that moment, but this form of "representation" is radically different from that assumed by cognitive architectures based on discrete, persistent symbols.

At the same time, it certainly seems as though we do have persistent cognitive representations, and so something also seems to be wrong with the connectionist picture. The standard connectionist reply is to suggest that this apparent structure actually resides *in the world*, rather than in our minds. We do not, in the standard connectionist picture, actually have concepts, words, and so forth in our minds, but only distributed and emergent activation patterns. However, those activation patterns approximate the function of such objects because the patterns arise from learning about the external world, and the world (that our brains aim to track) is filled with things like natural kinds, words, and so forth (McClelland et al., 2010). For connectionists, the apparent structure of our cognition arises because of structure in the world, rather than (necessary, foundational, representational) structure in our cognition, cognitive architecture, or cognitive representations.

Connectionist models have been developed to explain many different cognitive phenomena, including learning and reasoning with concepts (Rogers & McClelland, 2004), relations and relational concepts (Doumas,

Hummel, & Sandhofer, 2008; Hummel & Holyoak, 2003), language acquisition (Mayor & Plunkett, 2010), language difficulties (Plaut & Shallice, 1993), memory systems (McClelland, McNaughton, & O'Reilly, 1995), and motor control (Wolpert & Kawato, 1998). Many connectionist models explicitly aim to capture developmental phenomena (e.g., Mayor & Plunkett, 2010), where the idea is that the development and learning of the connectionist network can provide interesting insights into the way that a child might develop. In addition, connectionist networks have been used to investigate the cognitive effects of brain lesions (Hinton & Shallice, 1991; McClelland et al., 1995; Plaut & Shallice, 1993). More specifically, the research idea here is to train a connectionist network, induce "lesions" in it by destroying some of the units, and then examine whether the resulting network exhibits behavior similar to humans who have sustained similar (in some sense) brain lesions. An exhaustive survey of all connectionist models would require its own book but thankfully is not required here. The important observation is that researchers generally do not build single connectionist networks that capture many different types of cognition. Connectionist models unify the mind not through positing a single underlying system but rather through a coherent modeling perspective in which all aspects of cognition are (hopefully) understood through a common lens. In contrast with the process-centered unifications discussed in the next section, there need not be a single "engine" driving all cognition; many different processes, networks, modules, or whatever could underlie cognition. It is nonetheless a unification, however, precisely because the goal is to understand all those elements in terms of connectionist networks.

Connectionist networks are sometimes thought (particularly by those who do not use them) to be intended as biologically realistic models of the human brain. In practice, however, they rarely are; there are many differences between actual human brains and most connectionist networks, and only a few connectionist models aim to provide detailed, systematic models of biological processing (e.g., Eliasmith et al., 2012). The lack of biological grounding is not a problem for the connectionist unification, however, as that unification does not require the building of a single, massive, connectionist "brain." The explanations offered by connectionist models differ from those that result from direct maps of the underlying neural system. First, connectionist networks can provide "how possibly" explanations for human cognition, as they can reveal how various behaviors could or could not be generated by a network of computationally simple units. In particular, connectionist networks can provide constraints on the plausible neural underpinnings for some cognitive activity. For example, if networks of a particular structure are unable to predict or explain some actually observed (in humans) empirical phenomena or behavior, then we can conclude that our brains do not have that structure (McClelland et al., 1995). Second, connectionist networks can arguably play a deflationary role: they appear to demonstrate that there is no particular need for the types of complex symbolic models sometimes offered in cognitive science (McClelland et al., 2010). These deflationary claims are quite contentious, however, since it is unclear whether connectionist models are really nonsymbolic in the relevant ways (e.g., Fodor & Pylyshyn, 1988; though there are many responses to their arguments).

The deflationary implications of connectionist models seem to speak directly against the cognitive architecture that I have presented in this book. If the brain functions anything like a connectionist network, then it seems that there just cannot be persistent cognitive representations involving objects such as graphs, nodes, or edges. Hence there cannot be anything like graphical models underlying our cognition. This argument moves too quickly on at least two related fronts, however. First, recall that I argued that representation realism is best understood as a set of commitments about future behavior in different tasks that engage the same putative representation. I deliberately did not include any commitment that we have the ability to point toward particular objects in our brains, since we know too little about how the brain both represents and processes information about the world (see also sec. 9.3). As a result, my representation realism requires only that people behave in systematic (and systematically interpretable) ways that are best explained as operations on graphical models. That is, I commit myself to a realism about representations that is entirely consistent with them being neurally distributed or emergent, as long as the distributed representations are appropriately *stable* across tasks and environments. The second, related point is that the deflationary view privileges a particular type of model when trying to understand the mind. In contrast, my view is that a model's value comes from what it can help us to understand, predict, and explain. In some contexts, connectionist networks might be best; in others, symbolic models may prove most fruitful; and in yet a third type of setting, we might gain the most value by considering multiple types of models. The value of the cognitive architecture that I have proposed should be assessed not through a priori condemnation of its use of graphical models (i.e., symbolic representations) but by whether it can help us to better understand cognition.

If we adopt that stance, then we can see that graphical models can provide significant value in understanding some of the ways in which cognition is unified; this book has attempted to do exactly that. Moreover, this approach can help us to understand the source of some challenges faced by connectionist networks themselves. One notable lacuna in the empirical phenomena explained by connectionist models is causal learning from observations. There are connectionist models of causal learning for situations in which the individual can intervene on the system (Rogers & McClelland, 2004), and of aspects of causal reasoning (Van Overwalle & Van Rooy, 2001). No connectionist models, however, exhibit the human behavior of observing some system and then accurately predicting the results of interventions that have never been observed (Waldmann & Hagmayer, 2005). When we think about this problem using graphical models, it is easy to see why this is hard for connectionist models. If I learn $C \rightarrow E$ and need to predict the outcome of a hard intervention on E, then I should break the $C \rightarrow E$ edge and use the graphical model in which there is no edge. (See chaps. 3 and 4 for more details and explanation.) That is, human behavior requires exactly that we *not* simply track or mirror the world; we instead need to be able to reason about possibilities that are inconsistent with every observation that we have ever had. This behavior does not fit the standard connectionist deflationary picture in which the structure of our cognition is due to the world's structure, not anything in our minds. Of course, this does not imply that a connectionist model is impossible, only that this causal learning and reasoning behavior presents a significant open challenge and research question for connectionist modeling (for an initial attempt to address this question, see, e.g., Beukema, 2011). More importantly, it highlights the value of using multiple approaches to understand the nature of cognition, rather than taking deflationary suggestions to an unjustified extreme.

8.2.2 Bayesianism

A very different type of schema-centered unification can be found in Bayesian models of human cognition that argue that much of human cognition can be understood as Bayesian updating, at least at a computational or rational analysis level (Chater & Oaksford, 2008; Chater, Tenenbaum, & Yuille, 2006; Griffiths et al., 2010; Griffiths, Kemp, & Tenenbaum, 2008; Oaksford & Chater, 2007). Recall that $P(A \mid B)$ denotes the conditional probability of A given B; that is, it is the probability that A obtains once we know B. Importantly, $P(A \mid B)$ can be quite different from $P(B \mid A)$, both in value and in difficulty of computation. I do not know the value of *P*(*Is pregnant* | *Is female*)—that is, the probability that someone is pregnant, given that she is female—for the worldwide population, since I do not know (and it would be quite costly to determine) what proportion of women worldwide are currently pregnant; all I know is that the number is much less than 1, as there are many women who are not pregnant. In contrast, I know that *P*(*Is female* | *Is pregnant*) is 1, simply as a matter of (human) biological fact; every pregnant individual is a female. These two conditional probabilities are different, but we can readily transform one into the other using a simple fact about probabilities:

$$P(A \mid B) = \frac{P(B \mid A)P(A)}{P(B)}$$

Bayesian updating is the process of transforming conditional probabilities in this way, but with a particular interpretation for A and B originally provided by Thomas Bayes and posthumously extended by his literary executor, Richard Price, in 1763. Suppose we have some theory of interest T, whether large-scale and grandiose (e.g., quantum mechanics) or small-scale and local (e.g., the center switch controls the lights in this room). If we get some evidence E that is relevant to T, then we may want to know how likely T is in light of that evidence. That is, we arguably want to know $P(T \mid E)$. This conditional probability is frequently quite hard to determine directly, but it might be much easier to compute $P(E \mid T)$, as this quantity is just the likelihood of seeing E if the theory T were actually true. We can now see how to use the equation displayed earlier: let A be the theory of interest and B be our evidence. We can then compute the quantity of interest—$P(T \mid E)$—in terms of other quantities that are often much easier to determine: $P(E \mid T)$, and the prior probabilities (before seeing E) of T and E, $P(T)$ and $P(E)$.

A *Bayesian model* is any model in which cognition, usually learning and inference, proceeds through application of Bayesian updating of the sort just outlined. To see exactly how this could work, consider a simple example of causal learning. Suppose one is trying to determine the causal structure in some situation based on a sequence of observations, and suppose further that one has background knowledge that only three structures are possible: a common cause model M_{CC} ($A \leftarrow B \rightarrow C$), a common effect model M_{CE} ($A \rightarrow B \leftarrow C$), or no causal connection at all M_{NC} ($A \quad B \quad C$). Before making any observations, the Bayesian learner has some *prior probability* that each of these models could be true; that is, we have $P(M_{CC})$, $P(M_{CE})$, and $P(M_{NC})$, where these must sum to exactly one (since one, and only one, of these three models is correct). As we receive evidence E, we need to update these prior probabilities to the *posterior probabilities*: $P(M_{CC} \mid E)$, $P(M_{CE} \mid E)$, and $P(M_{NC} \mid E)$. Looking back at the earlier equation, we see that we can do this by multiplying the prior probability by the so-called *likelihood function* for each model: $P(E \mid M_{CC})$, $P(E \mid M_{CE})$, and $P(E \mid M_{NC})$. If our causal models are standard DAG-based graphical models, then these likelihoods are easy to calculate; recall that a major reason to use those graphical models is precisely that they provide a compact encoding of a probability distribution, so it is easy to determine the probability of any particular data point.[5] Finally, we also need to divide by $P(E)$, but this term is the same for all the models, so it really just acts as a normalization factor that ensures that the numbers coming out of the equation are still probabilities. If we subsequently receive more evidence, then we can simply use these posterior probabilities as our new prior probabilities. That is, Bayesian updating can be performed iteratively on each data point as it arrives, or in a batch after collecting multiple data points. This posterior probability distribution over the causal models can then be used whenever necessary to select, either explicitly or implicitly, a particular causal model using some decision procedure (e.g., probability matching or utility maximization, though see Eberhardt & Danks, 2011).

Bayesian models have been developed for many different types of cognition, including the focal topics of this book: causal learning and reasoning (Bonawitz, Griffiths, & Schulz, 2006; Griffiths & Tenenbaum, 2005; Lucas & Griffiths, 2010; Sobel, Tenenbaum, & Gopnik, 2004; Steyvers, Tenenbaum, Wagenmakers, & Blum, 2003), category learning and inference (Goodman, Tenenbaum, Feldman, & Griffiths, 2008; Heit, 1998; Kemp, Perfors, & Tenenbaum, 2007; Piantadosi, Tenenbaum, & Goodman, 2012), and decision making of many different types (Jern & Kemp, 2011; Jern, Lucas, &

Kemp, 2011; Kording & Wolpert, 2006; Lee, 2006). Bayesian models have also been offered for cognitive activities ranging from lower-level phenomena such as object perception (Kersten & Yuille, 2003) and memory effects (Schooler, Shiffrin, & Raaijmakers, 2001; Shiffrin & Steyvers, 1997) up to higher-level phenomena such as pragmatic inference in language (Frank & Goodman, 2012) and complex social cognition (Hamlin, Ullman, Tenenbaum, Goodman, & Baker, 2013; Ullman et al., 2009).

To understand what binds these models together, it is important to note that Bayesian models of cognitive phenomena have generally been offered at the so-called computational level (Marr, 1982). Recall from section 2.2 that computational-level accounts specify the problem and environment that the cognitive agent confronts, as well as the behavior that would (optimally or rationally) solve that problem in this environment. As such, these models remain largely agnostic about the underlying cognitive mechanisms that produce the behavior; they offer explanations of *why* some behavior occurs (namely, because it is the rational thing to do) rather than *how* some behavior is generated (Danks, 2008). Researchers have started working on the problem of how (approximately) Bayesian behavior could actually be generated (Denison, Bonawitz, Gopnik, & Griffiths, 2013; Griffiths, Vul, & Sanborn, 2012; Kruschke, 2006; Shi & Griffiths, 2009; Vul, Goodman, Griffiths, & Tenenbaum, 2009a; Vul, Hanus, & Kanwisher, 2009b), but there is still little agreement about the underlying mechanisms or representations that generate this behavior. Rather, the tie that binds together multiple Bayesian models into a single unification of cognition derives from the shared schematic structure of the different models.

As a result of this focus on the computational level, proponents of most Bayesian models are not committed to any particular claims about how the (approximately) Bayesian behavior is generated, but agree only that people do behave in this way, and that the Bayesian predictions are (approximately) rational or optimal. Three distinct arguments commonly support the rationality of Bayesian models. First, Bayesian methods exhibit long-run properties that any rational agent should exhibit (Perfors, Tenenbaum, Griffiths, & Xu, 2011): in many circumstances, they provably, reliably converge to the (learnable) truth (Gaifman & Snir, 1982), and no learning or inference method can systematically arrive at the truth faster (Schulte, 1999). Second, if the probabilities all correspond to strengths of belief, then given certain assumptions about how belief manifests in action, changing beliefs through

Bayesian updating is the only way to avoid incoherent actions over time (Teller, 1973, 1976). That is, if rationality requires that our actions in the future be coherent (in a precise, restricted sense) with our actions now, then under certain circumstances, Bayesian updating is the only rational way to learn. Third, we live in a noisy, probabilistic world, and so we might think that our cognition should rationally be based in probabilities (rather than, say, formal logic). The equation at the heart of Bayesian updating is a fact of probability theory, so we rationally ought (according to this argument) to follow it (Oaksford & Chater, 2007). If we accept these three different, independent arguments that acting in a Bayesian manner is rational, then we seemingly have an explanation for *why* people (might) act like Bayesians: they behave this way—engage in this cognition or behavior—precisely because it is the right or rational thing to do.

All Bayesian models, regardless of cognitive domain, scale, or content, are built from the same basic mathematical machinery. Part of the argument in favor of this particular machine is precisely that the same computational framework seems to be able to provide powerful explanations of why people act or think in particular ways across all those different domains and scales. In contrast with the process-centered unifications discussed in the next section, the focus on the computational level means that the shared mathematical machinery does not necessarily extend to any shared underlying mechanisms or representations. One might thus justifiably fear that the unification provided by Bayesian models is as spurious as the "unification" (mentioned in sec. 7.1) of a weight's motion when on a spring, and the steady-state behavior of an AC electrical circuit. The (purported) rationality of Bayesian updating critically provides a response to this worry, however, as we can attempt to unify the mind based on the why-explanations that Bayesian models aim to provide. That is, the shared mathematical structure across many different cognitions and behaviors can be understood to reveal a different type of unity to the mind: namely, that the mind systematically responds to its environment (approximately) rationally. The different Bayesian models all have the same underlying schema that (putatively) picks out the rational cognition or behavior, and so we have a unification of cognition as rationally (i.e., in a Bayesian manner) solving the problems that the cognitive agent confronts.

This unification and accompanying justification conflate, however, three terms—*Bayesian*, *probabilistic* or *generative*, and *rational*—that frequently co-occur in cognitive science discussions of Bayesian models but are justified by different features of a model: the processes, representations, and performance, respectively. First, the term *Bayesian model* refers to any model in which cognition is based on the application of Bayesian updating. Second, a *probabilistic or generative model*[6] is one in which the cognitive representations in the model are structured representations of probabilities that can be used to generate novel cases. The graphical models that I have used throughout this book are some of the most prominent types of probabilistic, generative models, though certainly not the only ones. Third, a *rational model* is one that characterizes the rational behavior or cognition for an agent, where I am deliberately agnostic about exactly what "rational" means (though see chap. 2). That is, the model, whatever its structure, has some plausible claim to being rational for the cognitive agent in its environment.

When these terms are described in this way, it is easy to see that they are conceptually independent of one another. A Bayesian model uses a particular process for learning and inference, but that implies no (obvious) commitments about representation or evaluation. A probabilistic, generative model uses cognitive representations of a particular sort but could use seemingly any learning or inference process and so need not meet any particular evaluative criterion. For example, the cognitive models that I offered in chapters 4 through 7 used generative models, but many of the learning and inference algorithms discussed there were decidedly non-Bayesian. Finally, there are many different standards of rationality, so there is no necessary reason that a rational model must use either Bayesian updating or probabilistic, generative models. In particular, all three of the arguments for the rationality of Bayesian updating turn out to show, when we use plausible assumptions, only that Bayesian updating is *one* way to be rational, not that it is the *only* way to be rational; Bayesianism is only uniquely rational if we make implausible assumptions (Eberhardt & Danks, 2011).

Although these three terms are conceptually distinct, it is unsurprising that they are frequently blurred together in the cognitive science literature on Bayesian models. Suppose that you want to build a Bayesian model (in the sense that I use that term) of some aspect of cognition. If we look back at the equation for transforming conditional probabilities, we can see that Bayesian updating will be useful just when $P(E \mid T)$ is much easier to compute than $P(T \mid E)$. In practice, this usually happens when T is a probabilistic, generative model: by definition, those are exactly the models that easily generate "data" about the world and thus lead to straightforward calculation of $P(E \mid T)$. Given a DAG-based graphical model G, for example, it is easy to calculate the probability of getting any particular evidence or data set. Bayesian models thus almost always use probabilistic, generative models or representations, though such representations can also be used in non-Bayesian models. Now suppose that one has a Bayesian model in hand and wants to know *why* people behave in this way. As noted earlier, there are at least three independent arguments that Bayesian models are rational, and so proponents of Bayesian cognitive models should emphasize the rationality of Bayesian models, at least if they think that some behavior being rational provides an explanation for why that behavior occurs (though see Danks, 2008). Just as with probabilistic, generative models, however, Bayesian models do not have an exclusive claim to rationality.

I went on this digression about these three terms—*Bayesian*, *probabilistic/generative*, and *rational*—precisely because disentangling them enables us to see the principal difference between the Bayesian unification of cognition and the one that I have proposed in this book. Bayesian unifications argue that much of human cognition and behavior is the (approximately) rational response to the problems and challenges that we face. In contrast, I focus on the cognitive representations that actually (in the sense of realism introduced in chap. 2) underlie our behavior. Of course, the account that I have offered is based on graphical model representations and so is sympathetic to Bayesian models (since graphical models are generative models). In that sense, proponents of a Bayesian unification would presumably be amenable to the mathematical work done in this book (in fact, some of them generated or contributed to it) while disavowing the particular representation realism that I have espoused.[7] At the same time, Bayesians are committed to the use of a particular mathematical model (at least at the computational level) that I do not necessarily adopt; some of the algorithms or processes discussed earlier in the book used Bayesian updating—notably the categorization algorithm in chapter 5—but that was driven by the method's fit-to-data, rather than any particular commitment to building a Bayesian model. Finally, I have not attempted to give a rational explanation of human behavior, though the graphical model basis for our cognitive representations is, I suggest, quite sensible given the challenges that we face. The problem is that actually providing a why-explanation requires much more than simply demonstrating optimality (Danks, 2008), and Bayesian models almost never have a unique claim to rationality in any case (Eberhardt & Danks, 2011). My proposed cognitive architecture and Bayesian unifications share many mathematical features but fundamentally have different commitments and goals.

8.3 Process-Centered Unifications

8.3.1 ACT-R

I now turn to a quite different type of cognitive unification: process-centered unifications attempt to build models from a small set of relatively simple, widely shared processes, where single models should be able to predict and explain different types of cognition. More colloquially, these unifying cognitive architectures aim to discover the "machinery" of the mind. One of the best-developed cognitive architectures of the past thirty years has been ACT-R (Anderson, 2005, 2007; Anderson et al., 2004). Models in this architecture have been applied to a wide range of laboratory and real-world tasks (with a notable exception discussed at the end of this subsection); many examples can be found at the website of the ACT-R Research Group at Carnegie Mellon University, http://act-r.psy.cmu.edu. I focus here on how ACT-R provides a measure of unification to cognition.

At a high level, the ACT-R architecture comprises eight distinct modules, with the understanding that more will need to be added over time (Anderson, 2007). The input and output of the system are handled by modules for visual and aural processing, and for manual (hand) action and vocalization, respectively. Four modules are more traditionally cognitive, specifically for declarative memory, goals, procedures/processing, and the "imaginal" module, which largely handles working memory. Each of these eight modules is individually fast and mostly unconscious in terms of its internal operation. In many respects, these modules fit many of the criteria for a "cognitive module" articulated in Fodor (1983). Moreover, much of the recent research on ACT-R has aimed to identify specific brain regions for each of the modules, and experiments have yielded some impressive results correlating ACT-R (predicted) operations with actual brain activity measured using fMRI (Anderson, 2007; Anderson et al., 2008; Anderson, Qin, Jung, & Carter, 2007).

Each of the eight modules functions in relative isolation from the others, but they do need to communicate. The procedural module is the nexus of communication for the modules: the other seven modules all communicate with the procedural module, and it is the only one with connections to multiple modules. It thus functions as the hub of the cognitive architecture. The basic functional unit for the procedural module (though not for many of the other modules) is a so-called production rule: essentially a complex *if-then* statement that is (a) triggered when the antecedent *if* condition is satisfied, and (b) produces the consequent *then* statement. For example, one might have the production rule "*if* the goal is subtraction *and* the numbers are 17 and 4, *then* the output is 13." In practice, production rules in ACT-R are much more complicated than this example, though their basic structure is the same: antecedents include goals and system state information (including beliefs about the external world), and consequents provide the operation to perform when the antecedent is satisfied.

Production rules can come from many different sources, including deliberate reasoning, explicit instruction, learning over time (e.g., associative processes), or analogies with prior situations or experiences. Perhaps most interestingly, multiple production rules can be "compiled" together to form a new production rule based on their previous co-occurrence. At a high level, production compilation takes multiple operations and combines them into a single one; the new compiled production might be more complex than the input ones but need not be. As a simple example, suppose I repeatedly use the production rules "*if* goal *G*, *then* retrieve information *I*" and "*if* goal *G and* information *I*, *then* perform action *A*." Production compilation can yield the new production rule "*if* goal *G*, *then* perform action *A*." Obviously, much more complicated production compilation can occur. Moreover, production compilation is critical because, in contrast to some other cognitive architectures, only a single production rule can be active at any point in time in ACT-R.[8] The procedural system must choose, at each moment in time, from among the many different production rules that are potentially relevant to the current goal. In practice, the procedural system selects on the basis of the rules' expected utilities; that is, the system selects the production rule that it judges (typically based on past experience) will be most likely to lead to timely satisfaction of the current goal.

The procedural module contains and carries out the production rules but is a very different type of module from the other seven, since it has essentially no content itself. Rather, it must get the content for the rules (e.g., the exact numbers for a subtraction operation, or that the current goal is to subtract two numbers) from the other modules. In general, ACT-R assumes that each of the other seven modules communicates with the procedural module through module-specific "buffers" (analogous to buffers inside one's computer) that each contain only one piece of information at a time. These between-module buffers act as information bottlenecks that help to explain the sequential nature of much of human cognition. Although each individual module can process information in a fast and parallel manner, they can only communicate that information back to the central procedural module through a slow and serial buffer. The types of cognition on which I have focused depend most on communication between the declarative memory module and the procedural module, as the declarative module has much of the "knowledge content" that must be accessed for the proper functioning of the production rules. (The imaginal and goal modules will also sometimes be relevant, since they respectively encode the current problem representation and handle means-end reasoning, including planning and generation of subgoals.)

The declarative module contains what we typically call representations, whether of facts, theories, connections, or episodes. In ACT-R, these are called "chunks": the elements that are stored and retrieved together. A simple example might be something like "Abraham Lincoln was the sixteenth president of the United States," but chunks can have significant internal structure. In the use of concepts, for example, the chunks could be rules for categorization, or salient past exemplars of each category, or even a mixture of both in a single cognitive model (Anderson & Betz, 2001). The buffer between the declarative and procedural modules can contain only a single chunk at a time, so the chunks determine the "unit of information transfer" into the procedural module. Internal to the declarative module, chunk activation is determined by the basal activation level of that chunk (e.g., chunks that have been active in the recent past will tend to be more active in general), as well as two dynamic, context-specific processes. First, the procedural module can "query" the declarative module by asking for particular types of information. In response to such a query, the chunks that are most similar to the query (by some metric) will gain activation. Second, the previous activations of chunks can "spread" to less active chunks, where the spread is driven by between-chunk similarity; for example, activating the Abraham Lincoln chunk can lead to activation of other chunks about him (e.g., "Abraham Lincoln gave the Gettysburg Address"), or about other U.S. presidents, or perhaps even the number 16. The key observation about this process is that it implies that different chunks can implicitly be connected by similarity, whether in particular properties or in overall structure (depending on the particular similarity metric that is used).

We are now in a position to see how ACT-R aims to unify cognition. Although there is great diversity between the modules, and even between elements within a module, the cognitive architecture as a whole provides a single "machine" that can perform many different cognitive tasks. The same ACT-R system can be deployed to drive a (simulated) car (Salvucci, 2006), solve algebra problems (Anderson, 2005), or categorize new objects (Anderson & Betz, 2001). The different tasks depend to varying degrees on different modules; driving requires heavier use of the visual module than object categorization does, for example. Nonetheless the same integrated system—the same processes and representations (perhaps even the same brain areas; see Anderson et al., 2008), not just the same mathematics—underlies a wide range of cognition and behavior. Moreover, the central role of the procedural module and its exclusive use of production rules implies a further degree of unification, as ACT-R regards all cognition as fundamentally process driven. The core challenge in the development of an ACT-R model is often to determine the production rules that, when activated in an appropriate sequence, implement the underlying cognitive process. Although there is diversity between different modules, all cognition is ultimately (in ACT-R) unified by the underlying production rules. There are many different particular production rules, but all cognition (in ACT-R models) has the use of production rules at its core.

This unification focus stands in contrast with the representation unification that I have pursued in this book, but not necessarily in opposition. At least in theory, the unification that I have proposed here is consistent with the ACT-R cognitive architecture. In practice, however, there are substantial challenges. First, there do not seem to be any ACT-R models that use graphical models as their core representations. Even in the area of causal learning and reasoning where DAG-like cognitive representations seem almost obligatory, ACT-R models have not used graphical models. Instead causal knowledge has been represented either as declarative facts (Drewitz & Brandenburg, 2012) or as production rules that enable the cognitive agent to generate simulated system states (Schoppek, 2001). Moreover, this absence does not seem to be an accident of history but rather seems grounded in the nature of declarative memory and chunks in ACT-R. The standard assumption in ACT-R models is that declarative memory simply stores previously observed chunks (as well as their basal activation rates), and the spreading activation between declarative memory items is based simply on the between-chunk similarity. In this picture, we can think of chunks as essentially discrete units that move through the buffer.

The problem is that this picture does not fit cleanly with representations as graphical models. People seem to be capable of reasoning with large graphical models, such as when they engage in complex causal reasoning. Since chunks are supposed to be discrete units, this suggests that we should identify chunks with these large graphical models. At the same time, however, the between-module buffers can each hold only one chunk at a time, so it seems that a large graphical model is much too big to be a single chunk, particularly since a context or task change can lead people to use only a small part of that graphical model. The underlying issue is that ACT-R chunks standardly are understood to have rich within-chunk content, but only weak (perhaps only implicit) between-chunk connections. In contrast, graphical models are typically built on nodes that have very little internal content but have rich connections with many other nodes. Hence it is unsurprising that we cannot identify graphical models with chunks in the declarative module.

An integration of my cognitive architecture and ACT-R would presumably require a different strategy, perhaps one that gives up the ACT-R assumption that chunks are stored similarly to how they are passed through the buffer. More specifically, suppose that (part of) the declarative module contains representations structured as graphical models. If a chunk comes into the declarative module's buffer, then that action could trigger processing in the declarative module: either some graphical models in the declarative module could be updated in response to the new information in the chunk, or else one or more subgraphs could be activated in response to a query. Given sufficient activation, some subgraph could then be placed into the declarative module's buffer so that it could be used by the procedural module. The overall picture is one in which the chunks that appear in the declarative-procedural buffer are generated dynamically from the *un*-chunked content stored in declarative memory. That is, chunks would still be passed back and forth but would no longer be persistent objects that are simply activated in toto. Of course, some aspects of the procedural module would undoubtedly need to be changed to take advantage of chunks with graphical model content, rather than the current structured variable/property lists. In addition, we would also have to specify methods or strategies for partial chunk activation, as it needs to be possible for only a subgraph to be activated. Both of these adjustments face their own sets of challenges. While it thus seems possible that graphical model cognitive representations could be integrated into ACT-R, it would require substantial research efforts on both sides. As we will see in the next two sections, this reflects a general observation: combining process-centered and representation-centered unifications often seems possible in theory but faces significant practical obstacles.

8.3.2 Soar

The Soar cognitive architecture explicitly aims to provide a general model for intelligent agents, whether human or machine (Laird, 2012; Newell, 1990). Models built in the Soar architecture have been developed not only for standard cognitive science or laboratory tasks (Laird, 2012; Newell, 1990; Rosenbloom, Laird, & Newell, 1993) but also for natural language processing (Lewis, 1993; Rubinoff & Lehman, 1994) and many different real-world situations and applications including video game intelligence and multiple military-industrial problems (Gunetti & Thompson, 2008; Gunetti, Dodd, & Thompson, 2013; Laird, Derbinsky, & Tinkerhess, 2011; Wray, Laird, Nuxoll, Stokes, & Kerfoot, 2005). In fact, this focus on real-world domains has been a major driving force behind the development of Soar since its beginnings as a way to model and understand general problem solving (Newell, 1990). Soar shares with ACT-R the overall idea that cognition is unified through shared (micro)processes, but there are important differences in the details. In particular, where ACT-R has many different processes because each module has its own set of operations, Soar aims to unify cognition through a very small number of underlying cognitive processes, and perhaps only one.

A Soar model represents the world in terms of states: the current or start state, and a set (possibly just one) of desired goal or end states. The agent's behavior—both cognitive and motor—emerges from the agent's attempt to move from the current state to one or more of the goal states. Changes from one state to the next occur because of cognitive operations that transform the current state. This overall cycle of "state, operation, and result" is the original source of Soar's name, though it is now understood as a proper name, rather than an acronym. More precisely, a *state* is a representation of all relevant objects and variables in some situation; it is a complete description of the relevant aspects of a situation. An *operator* acts on a state and transforms it into a new one; Soar constrains operators to be production rules, as in ACT-R. The Soar architecture incorporates perceptual and motor systems, so all operators have the form "*if* the current state, perceptual input, and/or other operators meet some conditions, *then* do some combination of state change, operator change, or motor action." As this schema suggests, these operators can be incredibly complex and detailed, depending on the situation.

Cognition in Soar is "just" choosing a sequence of operators starting from the current state and perceptual input and (hopefully) ending at a goal state, so a key challenge is how to consider and choose particular operators. In Soar, three memory systems provide potential operators. Procedural memory encodes the agent's skills and abilities, and so its contents are already structured as operators. Semantic memory encodes facts about the world, which are better understood as "data chunks" (Rosenbloom, 2006) that can shape the state. Episodic memory encodes particular events in the agent's history, which Soar represents as essentially a list of prior (remembered) states (Nuxoll & Laird, 2012). When we are in a particular state, all the memory elements that are considered relevant, either through automatic retrieval or deliberate consideration, are placed in working memory as possible choices. The Soar agent decides between the possible operators using various preferences (perhaps from past learning; see discussion later in this subsection) or by treating the operator choice as *itself* a problem to be solved. In this latter case, Soar has a new, more immediate goal state—namely, picking a good operator—and attempts to reach that goal state successfully. This subgoal might, for example, be reached by finding an instance in episodic memory when the state was similar and one of the operators was used either successfully or unsuccessfully.

The set of operators that an agent has in memory is obviously not fixed; Soar agents can learn. For many years, the only learning mechanism in Soar was chunking (Laird, Rosenbloom, & Newell, 1986): essentially, one creates new operators by putting together a sequence of operators that was previously successful or even just repeatedly used. This process is similar to, but not identical with, production compilation in ACT-R. As a simple example, suppose O_1 is "if A, then B" and O_2 is "if B, then C." The chunking mechanism can generate the new operator O_3—"if A, then C"—that can be used as a single operator in the future and yield both new and more reliable behavior. In practice, chunking can be significantly more complex, since the operators rarely line up perfectly and one must be careful about the inputs and outputs of the newly chunked operator. Chunking alone is insufficient for all learning, though, so Soar now incorporates additional learning mechanisms. Reinforcement learning enables the Soar agent to attach values to the operators based on their past successes and failures, thereby enabling improved operator choices (Nason & Laird, 2005). Additional mechanisms allow for learning that changes semantic memory (Rosenbloom, 2006) and episodic memory (Nuxoll & Laird, 2012), and these different learning mechanisms can interact in interesting ways (Gorski & Laird, 2011).

In contrast with ACT-R, relatively little research has explored possible neural implementations of Soar-like models or attempted to correlate Soar operations with activity in particular brain regions. A relatively early version of Soar was implemented in a set of neural network models (Cho, Rosenbloom, & Dolan, 1991), which suggests that Soar is potentially neurally plausible (though neural networks are not necessarily biologically realistic). A different approach is to focus on working memory, which plays a central role in the Soar architecture and whose neural bases have also been extensively studied. Young and Lewis (1999) argue that the properties of the working memory module in Soar are consistent with what we know about the neural and cognitive features of actual working memory, though this is again not a particularly strong connection to neural implementations. This gap is, however, not necessarily a black mark against Soar; as I argue in section 9.3, there are many good reasons to articulate and investigate a model that is not (yet) grounded in any particular neural implementations.

The Soar architecture can lead to complex cognition because between-rule dependencies can develop that lead to extended chains of operator choices. Nonetheless the basic picture of cognition is still the repeated application of a single type of (complex) operator. According to Soar, the mind is unified and coherent because there is a shared set of processes that are dynamically invoked in different contexts. The different cognitive models cited in this subsection all have the same basic structure; they simply differ in the particular content of the operators residing in procedural memory and preferences for selecting among them (and occasionally the items in semantic or episodic memory). Because Soar is a process-centered unification, it could theoretically be consistent with the shared representational store account articulated in chapter 7, as the shared graphical model cognitive representations would presumably reside in semantic memory. The problem is that the current understanding of semantic memory in Soar does not allow for this type of rich, structured representations. As such, while the two architectures are compatible in theory, substantial barriers would have to be overcome for them to be compatible in practice.

8.3.3 Sigma

The final cognitive unification that I consider here begins to explore how to integrate graphical models with Soar, though in a quite different way from the one just suggested. Sigma is a recent cognitive architecture that starts with the same basic structure as Soar (Rosenbloom, 2009a, 2009b, 2011). Recall that, in Soar, operators that "match" the current (working memory) state are applied to update the cognitive system to a new state. These sets of operators—both active and stored in long-term memory—can naturally be understood as functions, albeit ones that are potentially incredibly complex. Soar thus models cognition as the repeated application of different functions to some initial state, where the functions are the items contained in long-term memory. The Sigma cognitive architecture is (roughly) the Soar cognitive architecture, but where all the operators are encoded as factor graphs (Kschischang, Frey, & Loeliger, 2001) rather than complex and diverse *if-then* production rules. To fully understand the difference between Sigma and Soar, we need to digress briefly into factor graphs.

In this book, I have focused on graphical models as representations of structure or situations in the world: they capture causal structures, or social networks, or relevance relations between features in a concept, or something similar. Factor graphs are graphical models that focus instead on representing *functions* (Kschischang et al., 2001). More precisely, a factor graph as a whole is a representation of a complex function f over some set of variables, where we assume that the complex function f can be decomposed into the product of simpler functions. As a concrete example, suppose we have $f(x, y, z) = (x^2 + 3x - 4y)(5y - z + 17)$. This function is clearly quite complicated, but it also has some definite internal structure. In particular, it is the product of two other functions, one that depends only on x, y and another that depends only on y, z. We can gain a number of computational advantages by explicitly representing this internal structure, such as increased speed in initial computation. Equally important, *re*computing f when one of the inputs changes can potentially be much faster: if z changes its value, for example, we need only to recompute the second subfunction to find the new value of f.

Technically, factor graphs are graphical models with two types of nodes in the graph, corresponding to variables and subfunctions. They explicitly represent the f-function decomposition with undirected edges between variable and function nodes, where there is an $X — f_i$ edge if and only if X is an argument of the subfunction f_i. There are no other edges in a factor graph; in particular, there are no variable-variable or function-function edges. Given a particular setting of some or all of the variable nodes, it is straightforward to compute f (or its possible values, if some variable values are unknown): simply set the variable nodes to the appropriate values (when known), compute the subfunctions (or their possible values) based on their adjacent variables, and then take the product of the function nodes. If one (or more) of the variables change values, then the new value of f can rapidly be computed through message passing: the changed variable node tells its (function node) neighbors about its new value, the function nodes update their values and pass update messages to their (variable node) neighbors, who update their values when appropriate, pass further messages, and so forth, until the factor graph as a whole settles into its new, stable state (Kschischang et al., 2001).

The Sigma cognitive architecture represents the complex, separable operators in Soar using a factor graph, and so the operation of the cognitive architecture is "just" updates within the factor graph (Rosenbloom, 2009a, 2009b). More specifically, long-term memory in Soar is (roughly) a set of production rules that can be accessed by working memory. In contrast, working memory in Sigma is (roughly) an exceedingly complex factor graph with edges into the nodes in working memory. These working memory nodes include perception nodes that are determined by influences outside the factor graph, and action nodes that change the external world. When values of working memory nodes change, messages are passed through the factor graph, leading (in some cases) to changes in other working memory nodes. In this way, Sigma efficiently computes extremely complex functions like Soar's conjunctions of operators, but in a modular, stable manner that is potentially quite fast (Rosenbloom, 2012). Sigma has further been extended to include various types of learning (Rosenbloom, Demski, Han, & Ustun, 2013), though it is currently only able to modify the subfunctions, not change their inputs. Put in graphical terms, the learning is restricted to parameter learning; there is no way to learn the factor graph structure itself. It is straightforward to see how factor graphs can encode procedural knowledge, since those operators are clearly functions. Sigma additionally includes episodic and semantic memory, though doing so requires using directed edges in the factor graph so that messages are passed only in certain directions (Rosenbloom, 2010). There are many important technical details about Sigma (e.g., how operators of various types "compile" into a factor graph), but those details can mostly be set aside. For our purposes here, the important point about Sigma is that it starts with the basic Soar architecture but replaces the operators—that is, the cognitive agent's "content"—with a graphical model.

Given this description, one might naturally wonder what differences really exist between my cognitive architecture and Sigma. We are both based on graphical models; we both aspire to explain many different types of cognition; we both have a fundamentally computational view of the mind; and so forth. More generally, there are close connections between factor graphs and some of the graphical models that I have discussed in this book. Many DAG- and UG-based graphical models are used to represent joint probability distributions, where the graph encodes direct probabilistic (or statistical or informational) relevance. A joint probability distribution can be understood as a function: given values for some of the variables, it outputs the probability of that particular state. Moreover, the joint probability distribution factors in exactly the way that a factor graph requires. The joint probability for a DAG, for example, can be written as the product of the probability of each variable, conditional on its graphical parents. In fact, the message-passing algorithm of Pearl (1988) for DAG-based graphical models turns out to be identical with the message-passing algorithm for factor graphs of that same distribution (Frey & Kschischang, 1996). Since graphical models of joint probability distributions can immediately be converted into factor graphs of that same distribution, we can at least entertain the possibility of, for example, using the results of chapter 5 within Sigma.

Those theorems enable us to convert (many) concepts into graphical models of probability distributions, which could then be translated into factor graphs and (one might hope) plugged straight into the semantic memory of a Sigma cognitive agent. Unfortunately it is not quite so easy.

While Sigma and my cognitive architecture share many thematic similarities, they also have some important differences.[9] First, for important but technical reasons the nodes in the Sigma factor graphs often correspond not to variables but to *sets* of variables. For example, instead of nodes for V_1, V_2, V_3, we might have nodes V_{12} and V_{13} whose values depend on two of the single variables (Rosenbloom, 2009b). We thus cannot simply substitute the graphical models from my cognitive architecture directly into the Sigma factor graphs, as they are defined on different types of nodes. Moreover, Sigma factor graphs typically have many more nodes than the "natural" graphical models in my architecture. On the one hand, these are purely formal differences, since there are algorithms to transform the "single-variable" nodes into "variable-set" nodes and vice versa. On the other hand, the use of variable-set nodes does have the effect of making the (sub) function nodes "primary" and the variable nodes "secondary" in importance. That is, the factor graph is constructed by first determining the subfunctions and then adding variable nodes as necessary.

This difference in emphasis points toward a crucial conceptual difference between factor graphs and the types of graphical models that I have used. Factor graphs are designed to factor a function, rather than encode relevance relations between variables or objects. That is, factor graphs put the function first; the graphical models that I have used put the variables (or objects, or individuals, and so on) first. Sometimes these two distinct perspectives will coincide. As discussed earlier, if I want to compute marginal or conditional probabilities for a joint distribution over some variables, then I can use either a factor graph or a more traditional DAG-based graphical model. The two models are essentially the same, though the notation is different. In other cases, however, the two ways of thinking about graphical models—function first or variables first—can come apart. For example, suppose that we have the causal structure $X \rightarrow Y \rightarrow Z$, and we want to determine the impact of a hard intervention on Y. This inference is easy in the causal graph framework as shown in chapters 3 and 4: one simply breaks the $X \rightarrow Y$ edge and then does observational inference on the resulting graph. In contrast, we cannot use a standard factor graph to perform this inference given an intervention, since the observational inference function is, in a sense, built into the graphical model. More precisely, three different causal graphs—the true one, $X \rightarrow Y \rightarrow Z$, but also $X \leftarrow Y \rightarrow Z$ and $X \leftarrow Y \leftarrow Z$—all have the same factor graph representation because they all can encode the same probability distributions (and so the same observational inference functions). That creates a problem for making inferences given an intervention on Y, however, since these three causal graphs make qualitatively different predictions about the impact of such an intervention, and so no transformation algorithm of the single (observational inference) factor graph can work for all three cases.

The more general issue is that I have used graphical models that provide stable representations on which many different processes can operate, rather than building those functions or processes into the graphical model itself. Thus factor graphs will be insufficient whenever one wants to apply multiple distinct processes to the same representation.[10] At the same time, there are at least two reasons that one might prefer factor graphs to the graphical models used elsewhere in this book. First, we are sometimes in a situation in which the function really is the important piece. For example, consider the ideal gas law: $PV = kT$ (where P = pressure, V = volume, T = temperature, and k is a gas-specific constant). One could have a graph with P, V, and T nodes with edges between all of them, but it is unclear how to interpret these edges. They should not be directed, since changes can "flow" between the variables in any direction (e.g., for fixed volume, increasing the pressure leads to an increase in temperature, but an increase in temperature also leads to an increase in pressure). At the same time, undirected edges obscure the single underlying function that binds them together. What we really want is exactly a factor graph, since its central node will be the ideal gas law function, which is the focus.

A second reason to perhaps prefer factor graphs is that I have used graphical models that are arguably "inert," in that their use requires the additional specification of an algorithm or process. A causal graphical model, for example, does not actually do any inferences at all; inference procedures must be provided. In contrast, factor graphs are fully specified in both content and operation, since there is only one inference algorithm for all factor graphs: the message-passing algorithm of Kschischang et al. (2001). In some cases, the representation/process separation might be useful; in this book, for example, it has been critical, since one of the claims throughout has been that the *same* representation can be used or modified by multiple cognitive processes. In other cases, however, there might be no clear distinction between the representation and the process, in which case factor graphs would be a more natural representation.

More generally, there are multiple cognitive elements—attention, working memory, some parts of perception—for which people have claimed that the representation/process distinction appears to be tenuous, if not absent. This is part of the reason why I have been careful to claim only that my cognitive architecture potentially unifies *some* parts of cognition, though they are important ones. A natural possibility is that factor graphs might be the appropriate way to unify other aspects of cognition, perhaps through a cognitive architecture like Sigma. Rosenbloom (2009b) noted that "graphical models provide untapped potential for cognitive architectures." He focused on the potential for factor graphs to compactly represent complex (Soar-style) operators. I have focused on the potential for other types of graphical models to compactly represent our transferrable or reusable knowledge of relevance relations. An intriguing open question is whether these two distinct cognitive architectures could be integrated into a single one that uses graphical models to capture *both* cognitive processes *and* cognitive representations.

9 Broader Implications

9.1 Rethinking the Notion of Modularity

At this point in the book, I want to step back from the details of particular cognitive models and architectures to consider some of the broader, more philosophical implications of the cognitive architecture that I have advanced and defended in previous chapters. That is, how (if at all) does it matter if our cognition really is partly unified by virtue of a shared store of cognitive representations that are structured (approximately) as graphical models? Many connections could be drawn, but I focus here on three topics for which there are both significant implications and also interesting open research questions. Section 9.2 examines the interplay between multiple types of relevance, and section 9.3 considers the relationship between cognitive/psychological and neural/biological models or architectures. First, however, I turn to one of the longest-standing debates about the nature of mind: namely, the extent and type of modularity in the mind/brain.

Essentially everyone agrees that there must be *some* differentiation within the mind and brain, but there is almost no agreement about what that differentiation might be, either in general structure or in specific content. At the least, there is clearly some degree of separation between the so-called peripheral and central systems, where the peripheral systems include elements such as primary perceptual systems, and the central system includes explicit causal learning, means-ends reasoning, and so forth. We arguably cannot draw a bright-line distinction between central and peripheral systems, but it is nonetheless a gradient that is useful when thinking about the organization of the mind. In particular, many of the more peripheral systems seem to function without substantive dependence on the more central systems. For example, many aspects of visual processing appear to proceed independently of our explicit beliefs. As just one instance, whether spatiotemporal contact is perceived as one object causing another to move does not depend on our causal knowledge about the underlying system (Schlottmann & Shanks, 1992), though other aspects of visual perception (e.g., temporal order) do seem to be sometimes influenced by causal beliefs (Bechlivanidis & Lagnado, 2013). There additionally seems to be at least some degree of independence between multiple peripheral systems (e.g., visual and auditory processing), though the separation is often less than we might think. One striking example of the apparent interaction between peripheral systems is the McGurk effect (McGurk & MacDonald, 1976), where people who hear the sound of one phoneme while watching someone utter a different phoneme report hearing yet a third phoneme. For example, if the sound [ba] is played while watching someone say [ga], people typically report hearing [da]. That is, visual perception influences (in some way) our auditory perception.

Despite these influences, ample evidence suggests that the mind/brain has some degree of differentiation. This observation leads naturally to the thought that perhaps the mind/brain is modular in some way, such as we saw in ACT-R (sec. 8.3.1). This idea is particularly compelling if one thinks that there is some degree of analogy between the mind/brain and other information processors such as computers. Just as my computer is organized into distinct units with distinct functions and information (hard drive, RAM, keyboard, etc.), so one might think that the mind/brain is formed from distinct, separable elements that each focus on only part of cognition. Of course, this proposal is relatively contentless in this vague, nebulous phrasing. Instead we need to provide much more specificity about just what a module is, how the mind/brain might be divided up into distinct modules, and the ways in which different modules can interact.

The most famous conception of modularity in the past thirty years is undoubtedly Jerry Fodor's notion (Fodor, 1983, 2001). Fodorian modules must have multiple properties to varying degrees, including rapid, relatively unconscious processing and functional dissociability (i.e., the ability to be selectively impaired or damaged). Probably the most important property for a Fodorian module is information encapsulation: the module can only use information that was either provided as input or already stored in the module. The irrelevance of causal mechanism knowledge to causal perception is a classic example of information encapsulation. The causal perception module—or more likely the visual perception module—operates using only visual input plus whatever content is stored in the module, rather than being able to access and exploit causal knowledge or representations stored elsewhere in the mind/brain. If the strong notion of Fodorian modularity applies anywhere, then it is almost surely only in the peripheral systems (though for a challenge of even that claim, see, e.g., McCauley & Henrich, 2006). Fodor himself argued that the "central processing system" is surely not modular in his sense (Fodor, 1983).

Nonetheless some degree of modularity does seem to arise in our more central or "higher" cognition. For example, language production and use appear to be distinct in important ways from the mental rotation of images of objects. This observation has led to the development of a different notion of modularity that is more commonly applied to "higher" aspects of cognition. This type of modularity emerges largely in the writings of those who take a more evolutionary approach to understanding the mind/brain, and often appears under the heading of the so-called massive modularity hypothesis (Barrett & Kurzban, 2006; Carruthers, 2006; Pinker, 1997; Tooby & Cosmides, 1992). The core idea here is that modules are characterized functionally as the bits of mind or brain that perform some particular function. For example, we might think that there is a distinct piece of mind/brain that handles explicitly logical reasoning such as *modus ponens* and *modus tollens*. This cognitive element would (if it exists) constitute a module precisely because it has a specific, well-defined function. Of course, this conception is relatively uninteresting without further constraints, as simply dividing up the mind/brain functionally does not lead to any particular predictions or explanations.

We thus typically find the further restriction that modules (and the processing that they perform) are relatively domain specific. In particular, the standard argument is that the mind, including the more central parts of it, must be composed of processing modules that enable us to solve domain- and context-specific challenges. For example, rather than having a domain-general logical or social reasoning mechanism, we might have a "cheater detection" module that reasons solely about possible cheating in social exchange situations (Cosmides & Tooby, 1992). This module—more precisely, the cognitive process it contains—is simply not triggered by other situations, and the relevant cognition is highly tuned and specialized to this particular situation. Evolutionary considerations are often invoked at this point, where the argument is that we humans could only evolve cognitive modules that solve problems that impact our fitness, and those fitness-relevant challenges fall into particular domains (e.g., social exchange). Hence (the argument continues) all cognitive modules of this functionally identified sort must be domain specific, and so we must have many distinct ones, resulting in a "massively modular" mind/brain (Barrett & Kurzban, 2006; Pinker, 1997; Tooby & Cosmides, 1992). Alternately, one can argue for massive modularity and domain specificity of modules on computational grounds. More precisely, one can argue that domain-general modules are simply computationally intractable for the difficult problems humans face, and so we must solve our challenges using more domain-specific methods (Carruthers, 2006).

Unsurprisingly, there have been long-running and contentious arguments about Fodorian modules, domain-specific modules, the massive modularity hypothesis, and the various cognitive, neural, evolutionary, and computational claims that have been advanced. I have no particular interest in wading into those murky waters. Instead I want to explore a common assumption underlying all these different notions of modularity: namely, modules should be individuated principally based on process, rather than representation. Almost all the properties that Fodor (1983) identified with modules are properties of processes. One might have thought that information encapsulation would be determined by the representations (if representation = information), but even that property is really about delimiting the content to which the modular process has access. Proponents of massive modularity have a similar background assumption: "The thesis of massive modularity is generally understood to apply only to *processing systems*, however, not to the representations that might be produced by such systems" (Carruthers, 2006, p. 3; italics in original). That is, modules are processing systems, so the cognitive process determines the module individuation. Similarly, domain-specific modules are defined in terms of domain-specific computational mechanisms or operations (Tooby & Cosmides, 1992): "The concept of modularity should be grounded in the notion of *functional* [i.e., process] *specialization*" (Barrett & Kurzban, 2006, p. 629; italics in original). Moreover, this focus on process extends beyond philosophical debates about what counts as a module. Cognitive architectures that explicitly self-describe as modular (e.g., ACT-R) also define their modules in terms of shared or single processing.

This almost-universal focus on the ways that cognitive *processes* can be modular is entirely understandable. A common intuition about the mind/brain is that it can be understood roughly as a giant box-and-arrow diagram or flowchart. In this picture, the boxes are individuated by their functions; each box does something distinct in the overall operation of the mind. Moreover, the notion of module is typically mapped onto these boxes, and so we get the natural assumption that modules should be individuated by cognitive processes. The cognitive architecture proposed in this book, however, forces us to recognize that the notion of modularity must also apply to representations, not just processes. More precisely, we must distinguish between "process modularity" and "representation modularity," where the latter is the idea that some information or representations are stored separately from others, rather than being integrated into a single representational store. In some ways, the notion of representation modularity is not a new one. In particular, theories of multiple memory systems—typically semantic, procedural, and declarative—are arguably representation modular in exactly this sense: content or representations stored in one memory are not integrated with those stored in another memory (Poldrack & Packard, 2003). Of course, interactions can occur between distinct memory systems or representation modules if content from each is accessed by some third module, but they are nonetheless distinct as long as there is no common store for the different contents.

Process and representation modularity are, in principle, relatively independent of each other. A standard reading of the massive modularity view is that it is both process and representation modular: we have many different processing modules, each of which has its own, domain-specific content. Of course, there may be a large representational store (a single semantic memory, perhaps) in addition to those domain-specific modules, but the overall architecture is one of modularity along both dimensions. Alternately, one could have a mind with a single massive (nonmodular) representational store but many process modules that access and manipulate it. For example, one might agree with the massive modularity hypothesis but think that all those processes access different parts of the same underlying representational knowledge; Samuels (1998) suggests something like this model in his library model of cognition. A third possibility is that one could have a single process module (at least for conscious cognition) but different modular representational stores. One example of such a position would be multiple memory systems conjoined with a single global workspace within which multiple processes operate. Finally, old ideas about the nature of the (conscious, higher) mind tended to involve no process or representation modularity: there was simply one integrated knowledge base and one "location" in which cognition occurred. We no longer think that this idea is empirically correct, but it completes the possibility space for different types of modularity.

The more general point is that we need to broaden our understanding and characterization of the notion of modularity. The almost-exclusive focus on processes as the individuating element for cognitive modules has led to either overlooking or conflating distinct possible cognitive architectures. We need to have a more nuanced view that recognizes that modularity in the mind/brain can vary along both process-focused and representation-focused dimensions. Previous accounts of modularity have been multidimensional; Fodor (1983), for example, argued that the degree of modularity depended on the degree to which the cognitive element displayed nine different properties (thus modularity was a nine-dimensional notion). However, those accounts have all failed to include an entirely different set of dimensions associated with representation modularity. We need a better understanding of both those dimensions and, even more importantly, the interactions between process and representation modularity.

These interactions are particularly important in understanding the "modularity" of my cognitive architecture. If we think solely about the three different cognitive areas on which I have focused, my view appears to have substantial process modularity. The different cognitive operations are, for me, certainly distinct in both their operation and the effects that they have on the common representational store. At the same time, I have argued that there is no representation modularity (at least in these areas of cognition), and so this position is quite different from the massive modularity hypothesis. The different processes do not have domain-specific knowledge; rather, they access different elements in a shared representational store. What appear to be domain-specific learning or representations are, in the cognitive architecture proposed here, simply the sorts of task-specific effects discussed in chapter 7. Of course, many open questions remain about exactly how to distinguish representation modularity from process modularity. Samuels's (1998) argument against the massive modularity hypothesis trades exactly on the difficulty of disentangling the two. Previous debates about the nature and extent of modularity in the mind/brain, however, have not even asked these kinds of questions. The cognitive architecture based on shared cognitive representations forces us to confront them.

9.2 The Challenge of Multiple Relevance Types

Much of this book has focused on arguing that graphical models provide a powerful framework for representing many of the cognitive representations that are accessible by multiple cognitive processes. One key advantage of this particular computational framework is that graphical models compactly represent relevance relations: *A* and *B* are connected by a graphical edge just when one is directly relevant to the other, whether causally, informationally, socially, or through some other type of relevance relation. As a result, many of the accounts of learning discussed in this book actually provide partial answers to the question of how people come to (mostly) attend only to relevant factors.[1] That is, one of the puzzles that prompted this book was how people—whether engaged in inference, learning, decision making, or some other cognitive activity—are capable of generally considering only elements of the world that might make a difference. The answer offered so far in this book is: they often can do so because graphical models directly capture those relevance relations, and so any cognitive processes that encode and exploit the "edge" information will automatically, and in some sense implicitly, focus on only the relevant items. A simple "message-passing" model of causal reasoning, for example, uses the graphical model structure to constrain the "direction" of spread, and so irrelevant (by the graph) nodes will simply never be updated. Both substantive and operational definitions of "relevance" mesh perfectly with the graphical models framework, and so we gain a partial solution to an old cognitive science challenge.

The story is not, however, quite as simple as I portrayed it in the preceding paragraph. For almost all standard types of graphical models—causal models, social networks, models of spatiotemporal diffusion using undirected graphs, and so forth—the edges in a particular graph all represent just one type of relevance relation; there is a single semantic interpretation of the edges in each graphical model. The relevance type for the edges can differ *between* graphical models, but it is essentially always the same *within* a graphical model. For example, every edge in a causal model captures a direct causal relation, while every edge in a social network represents a direct social exchange or connection. This restriction—one relevance type for the edges in a graphical model—was noted in chapter 3, but I did not emphasize it, since it did not matter for most of what followed. We have focused on cognitive representations that clearly only try to capture one relevance type at a time, so the appropriate graphical model (and semantic interpretation of the edge) has always been clear from context. My focus and challenge have instead been to show that graphical models with natural edge semantics could capture the learning, reasoning, inference, and decision-making behavior that people exhibit in a wide range of circumstances.

Our knowledge structures are not, however, neatly segregated into distinct cognitive representations defined by relevance type. Our cognitive representations instead often appear to include multiple relevance types in a single representation. For example, I know that the concept CAT bears a particular taxonomic relationship to the concept of ANIMAL, and so a relation of exclusion holds between CAT and MOUSE. At the same time, I know that instances of CAT sometimes stand in a predator–prey relationship with instances of MOUSE. More precisely, part of my knowledge of food webs includes a CAT → MOUSE edge, indicating that cats sometimes eat mice. In general, our knowledge appears to be even more integrated than I have previously considered; single cognitive representations seem to contain multiple edge types with different relevance semantics. As a result, it seems that there is something deeply flawed about my use of the graphical models framework, since it appears to rule out a priori some kinds of knowledge structures that we appear to have.

One response to this concern is to argue that it is based on a false description of the ways in which our knowledge structures are integrated. In particular, one could argue that our knowledge structures are connected only through "maps" that connect entities in one graphical model with those in another, rather than through direct integration of multiple graphical models. If we return to the previous example, this response would contend that we have (i) a taxonomic knowledge structure involving CAT and MOUSE (and other concepts); (ii) a food web knowledge structure encoding the predator–prey relationship CAT → MOUSE; and (iii) a map that tells us that the CAT and MOUSE nodes in the two graphs refer to the same things. If we have these three pieces, then there are no knowledge structures with multiple relevance types and thus no concerns about the graphical models framework being too limited. This response is one way to try to say the graphical model account, but it imposes significant, potentially empirically incorrect constraints on the representations. For example, expert bird-watchers use both taxonomic and ecological information in grouping birds (Bailenson, Shum, Atran, Medin, & Coley, 2002), suggesting that these two knowledge types are not independent in the way required by this response. Of course, this response might still be saved with further elaboration, but much more would need to be said about how the separate knowledge structures are integrated in reasoning.

Even if that were done, however, this response is unavailable to me for a deeper, more theoretical reason. In section 5.4, I argued that graphical models can capture "webs" of concepts through the introduction of new nodes corresponding to superordinate concepts. For example, we can unify DOG, CAT, MOUSE, and so forth into a single graphical model by introducing a node for MAMMAL. At a high level, suppose we want to integrate graphical models G_1, G_2, etc., that correspond to different concepts. (Recall that much of the point of chapter 5 was arguing that concepts correspond to graphical models in this way.) For convenience, we can further suppose that the concepts are mutually exclusive: any individual falls under only one of those concepts.[2] We then construct a graphical model over all nodes (i.e., anything found in one of the *G*s) plus a node indicating which concept is "active" for an individual. There are important details about exactly which edges to include and how to ensure that the quantitative component of the graphical model is coherent, but I provided those details in section 5.5.2. The key point is that this integration method assumes only that concepts correspond to graphical models; it does *not* assume that the graphical models are all of the same type. Thus the "combined" graph can involve both causal edges from a concept based on shared causal structure, and informational edges from an exemplar- or prototype-based concept. And even if we restricted the integration method by requiring all the *G*s to have the same edge types (and thus the same relevance types), we would still have problems owing to the edges from the new, "higher-level" node. Those particular edges are essentially taxonomic in nature, so they are certainly different from the edges for causal-model-based concepts, and perhaps also edges for exemplar- and prototype-based concepts. The integration method that I proposed to explain between-concept relations and inference (e.g., inductive reasoning) is thus almost guaranteed to produce graphical models that encode multiple relevance types in a single graph.

Given this inevitability (at least for me), I could instead argue (or hope) that the possibility of multiple relevance types in a single knowledge structure will not pose a long-term problem for the graphical models framework. That is, perhaps the restriction to a single relevance type per graphical model is just a historical accident, and so the assumption can be eliminated without problems. Unfortunately this hope is merely wishful thinking: significant problems of inference can arise when trying to reason with multiple edge types in a single graph. These issues can be illustrated with an example from Spirtes and Scheines (2004). They consider the causal relations between *Total Cholesterol* (*TC*) and *Heart Disease* (*HD*). The standard wisdom (at least several years ago) was that cholesterol causes heart disease, and the natural causal model would thus be $TC \rightarrow HD$. The problem is that *TC* is not actually the "right" causal variable,[3] as *TC* is the mathematical sum of three different variables—*LDL* ("bad" cholesterol), *HDL* ("good" cholesterol), and *Triglycerides*—where each factor has a different causal impact on *HD*. For convenience, we ignore *Triglycerides* and focus just on *LDL* and *HDL*. The full causal structure is shown in figure 9.1, where the dotted arrows indicate that *TC* is a mathematical function of *LDL* and *HDL*; specifically, $TC = LDL + HDL$.

Figure 9.1 is an example of a graphical model with multiple edge types: two of the edges correspond to causal connections, and two represent inputs to a mathematical function. For some kinds of inferences, this graphical model is perfectly acceptable. For example, given an observation of *TC*, we

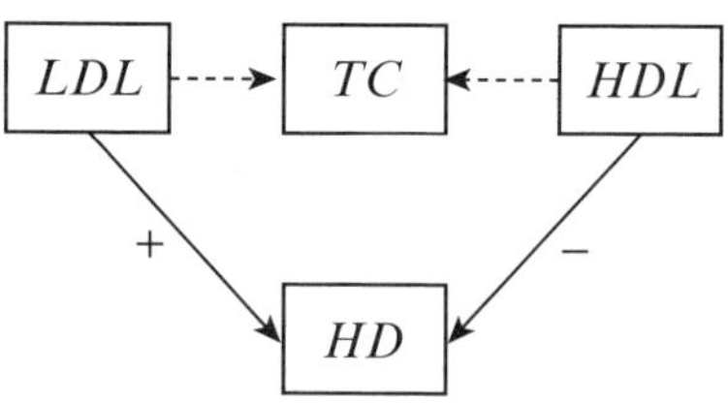

Figure 9.1
Partial causal structure for heart disease.

can determine the likelihoods of *HD* and various *LDL* or *HDL* levels. For other kinds of inferences, however, we run into some significant problems. In standard causal models, we assume that every variable could potentially be the target of an intervention, though we obviously need not have the technology or ability to perform those interventions ourselves (Woodward, 2003). Suppose that we intervene on *TC*; what does the graphical model in figure 9.1 predict for *HD*? The problem, as Spirtes and Scheines (2004) show in detail, is that the graphical model makes no determinate prediction at all. "Intervention on *TC*" is fundamentally ambiguous with respect to *HD* prediction, since the postintervention probabilities for *HD* depend on how the *TC*-intervention is realized. We get very different predictions if we set *TC* = 100 by intervening to produce <*LDL* = 90, *HDL* = 10> or by intervening to produce <*LDL* = 10, *HDL* = 90>. The variable *TC* is a mathematical aggregate of two different variables that are causally heterogeneous with respect to *HD*, and so interventions on *TC* are fundamentally ambiguous in terms of their impact on *HD*. We simply cannot use this graphical model to make predictions about *HD* given an intervention on *TC*.

This failure in predictive ability for figure 9.1 arises precisely because we have two different edge types in the graphical model. If the mathematical edges were instead causal (i.e., if the dashed edges were solid), then the graphical model would make determinate predictions given an intervention on *TC*. Our difficulties arise because we do not know how to derive, or even properly think about, interventions on mathematically defined variables. More generally, we do not know how to handle many types of inferences that involve multiple edge types and thus multiple relevance types. What is, for example, the probability that an animal eats mice given that we intervene to make it a mammal? Any assessment of that probability will require that we use multiple edge types, and the resulting prediction is simply undefined given our current understanding of graphical models.[4] One response would be to try to develop purely probabilistic readings for different relevance relations and thereby place all of them on a common footing. That is, if every relevance relation is a constraint on allowable (conditional) probabilities, then there would actually only be one foundational relevance relation, after all. Unfortunately this strategy will not work: although many, perhaps all, relevance relations imply such constraints, they are not defined by such constraints. As a result, we lose important information (e.g., about whether the relevance persists given an intervention) if we construe the relevance relations as only probabilities, and so can no longer do all the inference and reasoning that we require.

To extend the graphical models framework beyond the cognitive and knowledge domains I have discussed in this book, we require reasoning, inference, and learning methods that apply to graphical models with multiple edge types. This observation does not imply that there is any particular problem with the results in this book, particularly since I have never claimed (and, in fact, explicitly disavowed) universality for the graphical models framework. The cognitive architecture presented here does not depend on *all* cognitive representations being graphical models, so we could be relatively localist, if necessary. Having said that, I suggest that a more interesting option would be to develop graphical models that can capture multiple relevance types in a single graph.

Moreover, we already have a "proof of concept" of a graphical model type with multiple edge types. Decision networks (Howard & Matheson, 1981; Shachter, 1986) model decision-making situations (see sec. 6.3) and have four different node types, corresponding to (i) world factors, (ii) the decision maker's action, (iii) the decision-making process itself, and (iv) the value function for states of the world. More importantly, different edges in a decision network have different meanings, where the edge semantics are determined by the node type at the arrowhead end of the edge. Edges into world factors capture causal connections; edges into action nodes denote informational or cognitive connections; and edges into value nodes indicate the factors that jointly determine a state's value. (There are no edges into decision-making process nodes.) In other words, decision networks represent at least three different relevance types in a single graphical model. Moreover, there are standard, well-defined methods for all the standard learning and inference tasks in decision networks; none of the problems outlined earlier arise for them. Inferential or learning failures do not automatically arise for graphical models merely because they have multiple edge types, as some graphical models such as decision networks function just fine.

Decision networks avoid these issues in part by imposing some constraints on the graphical structure and semantics: decision process nodes never have edges into them; world-world edges are always understood causally rather than informationally; and so forth. That is, decision networks do not attempt to encode arbitrary groups of connections with multiple relevance types, but only particular combinations. Many of the cases discussed in this section are similarly nonarbitrary; for example, the new variables introduced to construct conceptual webs always have outgoing edges corresponding to taxonomic or informational relevance relations, regardless of the nodes to which they connect. As such, many of the worries expressed here might not arise, though that is an open question. Moreover, the proper response in some cases might simply be to say "not enough information is provided." For example, the problem of ambiguous manipulations seems to be a problem not with graphical models but with the proper specification of an intervention. If we are sufficiently clear about the nature of an intervention, then the problematic ambiguity does not arise (see also Eberhardt, 2014). The possibility of multiple relevance types still lurks as a potential problem, but we have many reasons to think that it is one that can be overcome.

9.3 Neurons, Processes, Rationality, and Representations

One notable absence throughout this book has been any serious engagement with, or even discussion of, neuroscientific data. If one thinks (as I and many others do) that the mind is fundamentally just the brain, then it might seem odd to have an entire book about the mind without ever discussing how it is, or could be, implemented neurally. Of course, this is not to say that cognitive science should simply be replaced by neuroscience, or that human cognition and behavior depend exclusively on the brain. Multiple perspectives on the mind/brain are surely valuable, and the body and environment clearly matter for our cognition. Even recognizing those complications, however, our knowledge of the brain has advanced considerably in recent decades, and so one might naturally expect that any serious cognitive science must engage (somehow) with neuroscience. Moreover, advocates of other cognitive architectures (e.g., Anderson, 2007) have pursued the goal of finding possible neural implementations. If the reader is convinced (as I am) that an important part of the explanation for our cognition is a shared representational store of graphical models, then a natural complementary question is how those representations are neurally implemented and accessed. Although I agree that the question is a natural and important one, neuroscience has gone relatively unmentioned in this book for two principal reasons. Discussion of each can help to illuminate and clarify aspects of my project.

The first reason is simply that relatively little extant neuroscientific research is directly relevant to the cognitive architecture proposed here. The different cognitive domains have unsurprisingly been studied using neuroscientific techniques. For example, both neuroimaging and surgical studies provide evidence that causal inference and causal perception occur in different parts of the brain (Blakemore et al., 2001; Roser, Fugelsang, Dunbar, Corballis, & Gazzaniga, 2005; Satpute et al., 2005). However, data of this sort do not enable us to learn about the representations underlying these cognitive capacities, as the data are too coarse-grained and focus on underlying processes rather than cognitive representations. Similarly, neuroscientific research on category learning and use has principally employed neuroimaging and neuropsychological methods (Ashby & Waldron, 2000; Ashby, Alfonso-Reese, Turken, & Waldron, 1998; Grossman et al., 2002; Humphreys & Forde, 2001; Patalano, Smith, Jonides, & Koeppe, 2001).[5] These methods can be valuable in trying to understand the coarse-grained structure of cognitive processes but are relatively uninformative about structural details of the underlying representations. For example, growing neural evidence suggests that category learning occurs through multiple cognitive processes (Ashby et al., 1998; Ashby & Waldron, 2000; Patalano et al., 2001), but that tells us relatively little about whether the learned representations of categories are structured (approximately) like a graphical model.

In contrast, there has been substantially more, and more fine-grained, investigation of the neural bases of decision making, in terms of both the diversity of neural phenomena and plausible neural models (Corrado & Doya, 2007; Daw, Niv, & Dayan, 2005; Frank & Claus, 2006; Gold & Shadlen, 2007; Holroyd & Coles, 2002; Knutson, Taylor, Kaufman, Peterson, & Glover, 2005; Rolls, McCabe, & Redoute, 2008; Schultz, 2006; Wickens, Horvitz, Costa, & Killcross, 2007). For example, one prominent strand of research has focused on learning to make decisions from repeated experiences, such as learning which bush tends to yield sweet berries rather than sour ones. That work has revealed critical roles, both biologically and computationally, for the dopamine system (Frank & Claus, 2006; Holroyd & Coles, 2002; Montague, Dayan, & Sejnowski, 1996; Wickens et al., 2007). At the same time, the resulting models focus on relatively "local" connections and thus do not tell us much about the nature of complex, structured representations. This research is surely valuable in trying to understand phenomena such as associative processes in causal learning, but it does not tell us about possible neural implementations of representations structured as graphical models (though it does suggest that we need associative models of causal structure learning like those in Wellen & Danks, 2012).

A related branch of research has looked explicitly at neural representations of probability and value (Glimcher & Rustichini, 2004; Knutson et al., 2005; Rolls et al., 2008; Schultz, 2006). In particular, this body of work has principally examined whether neural regions or even individual neurons seem to be doing something like expected utility calculations, and there do seem to be such neurons (perhaps in orbitofrontal cortex). Of course, such calculations are a far cry from complex, structured cognitive representations. Finally, there is widespread agreement that "sophisticated" decision making likely occurs in the prefrontal cortex, but little is known about representation in that brain region. Instead research on the prefrontal cortex has tended to focus on deficiencies found in lesion patients (Bechara, Damasio, Damasio, & Anderson, 1994; Bechara, Tranel, & Damasio, 2000; Shallice & Burgess, 1991), which provides relatively little insight into the fine-grained neural implementations underlying the cognitive representations.

The moral of this quick survey of neuroscientific research is that we do not yet have the data or models that we require to develop a neurally plausible implementation of a cognitive architecture with shared cognitive representations, such as the one that I have developed throughout this book. In fact, our ignorance is even worse than this, since we do not even have a clear understanding of how to encode a graphical model in something like neurons. Some recent research has argued that neural firings can sometimes be understood as the brain doing (in some sense) Bayesian inference (Deneve, Latham, & Pouget, 2001; Doya, Ishii, Pouget, & Rao, 2007; Knill & Pouget, 2004; Kording & Wolpert, 2006; Lee & Mumford, 2003; Paulin, 2005; Pouget, Beck, Ma, & Latham, 2013; Rao, 2005). More precisely, this work argues that parts of the brain seem to be computing conditional probabilities, and specifically the probabilities of various possibilities given sensory input or evidence. Some of this work has even argued that the particular inferences mirror the computations that one would do in a graphical model (Lee & Mumford, 2003; Rao, 2005), and so we might think that we have the beginnings of a suitable analysis.

The problem, however, is that these models only perform one particular type of Bayesian inference or updating, so they cannot capture or explain the full range of human inferences and reasoning. For example, suppose that we want to do inference on the graphical model $C \rightarrow M \rightarrow E$. In this case, we have neurally plausible systems that can compute the probability of C given an observation of E and even some evidence that inferences of this type occur in the visual cortex (Rao, 2005). The neural systems, however, are constrained to compute only one or a few conditional probabilities. In contrast, at the behavioral level, people are capable of making relatively arbitrary inferences using that graphical model: they could instead determine the probability of E given M, or the probability of M given observations of both C and E. The neural implementations fall short precisely because they are for particular *inferences*, rather than for the graphical model itself. Moreover, the gap is even wider when we consider people's ability to dynamically adjust their cognitive representations—their DAG-based graphical models—when reasoning from interventions or actions (Glymour & Danks, 2007).

We simply do not know at this point what kinds of neural structures might even *possibly* implement graphical model representations, much less where those structures might be found or what neural data could provide evidence for their existence. All of this obviously does not imply that no such models are possible,[6] but our current ignorance means that substantial theoretical and empirical work must be done to establish these connections. That is, there is a huge research project here that is only just beginning (as in, e.g., Shi & Griffiths, 2009). More generally, this lack of knowledge partly explains my choice in chapter 2 to focus on a quasi-operationalized notion of "representation," particularly in the context of representation realism. One common alternative view about representation realism is that it is a commitment to the existence of something "real" that is located "down in the neurons." The problem is that we have essentially no understanding of how graphical models could exist "in the neurons," so we have little idea about what this type of representation realism about graphical models would imply or involve (except some vague promises about the future). In contrast, the understanding of representation realism for which I argued provides clear constraints and predictions about future behavior precisely by not tying the realism to any particular neural structures. In such cases, it is more appropriate to remain with cognitive or behavioral characterizations.

At the same time, different theories inevitably place constraints on one another, so it is eminently sensible to try to establish some of the constraints that any such model must satisfy. For example, one might have wondered whether people are actually capable of arbitrary inference with cognitive representations structured as graphical models. If they are not, then our neural implementations can be restricted suitably. This observation leads to the second reason that I have not been concerned about my lack of attention to neuroscience. The cognitive architecture outlined in chapter 7, and the graphical models view more generally, places many constraints on any purported account of (many of) our cognitive representations. These constraints can play a crucial role in the development of future theories, such as neural implementations (at "lower" levels) or models of social interaction (at "higher" levels). For example, our investigations of neurally plausible models can proceed with an understanding of some of the phenomena that they must capture to accurately model (something like) the complexity of human behavior. This book helps to provide us with a clearer picture of the constraints that a successful neural model must satisfy, and so can help to guide our questions. As we gain a clearer picture of how the mind functions (including what it computes), we can ask more focused and precise questions about how the brain implements those functions. These constraints obviously do not determine the other theories but can significantly help to speed and advance our scientific understanding. More generally, part of the value of the present cognitive architecture is exactly that it can help us—in fact, already has helped us—ask better and more targeted questions about the underlying neural structures and phenomena.

10 Conclusions, Open Questions, and Next Steps

10.1 Where Do We Go from Here?

This book has covered a lot of ground to characterize and evaluate the integrated cognitive architecture, but much remains to be done. On the empirical front, many different experiments should be run (and some are in progress) to better specify aspects of the architecture. In earlier chapters, I described multiple experiments that should be informative about the exact cognitive representations and processes within each type of cognition. Perhaps more importantly, many experiments remain to be done to better understand exactly what types of learning and goal effects arise from multiple processes acting on the same, shared representation. For example, suppose that I have a goal that requires that I use only some of the information that is presented in learning. The single-store, single-process view predicts that people will learn relatively little about the unnecessary information, which is what we seem to find empirically. How does this happen? One possibility is that I use a cognitive representation that could (in some sense) represent the full learning input but I only attend to a subset of the information. A different possibility is that I actually use a more restricted cognitive representation, perhaps re-encoding the input information along the way. That is, people could be doing limited learning about a rich representation or rich learning about a limited representation (or something else altogether). We can experimentally separate the roles of attention and encoding in learning effects, though it is quite difficult in practice. The result of such experiments would be a more detailed and nuanced view of the internal structure of a single-store, single-process account.

I have also focused on limited subsets of cognitive domains and types of graphical models, and it is an open empirical question whether other areas of cognition might also be based on (other types of) graphical models. For example, people have significant knowledge about the structure of their social relationships (Watts, Dodds, & Newman, 2002); are our cognitive representations of social systems structured as graphical models? This seems quite plausible, not least because social network graphical models are widely used and easily understood in computer science as visual representations of social group structure. At the same time, this empirical question—whether people's representations are actually structured in this way, not just whether people can easily interpret such graphs—seems not to have been extensively explored. Similarly, I used decision networks in chapter 6, but we still have only a limited empirical basis for the claim that our cognitive representations of (many) decision situations are structured along those lines. More generally, I stated explicitly in chapter 1 that I claim no universality for my architecture: I certainly do not claim that all our cognitive representations are structured (approximately) like some type of graphical model. At the same time, however, I suspect that more cognitive representations than just those I have explored in this book are structured as graphical models. How widely the graphical models framework applies to cognitive representations is an important open question.

A similar diversity of open questions persists about the underlying theory and formalism. For example, I observed in section 9.2 that we do not yet know how to use graphical models with certain mixtures of relevance types. We need both formal, computational extensions for models with such mixtures and also methods for incorporating those extensions into the cognitive architecture proposed here. Other open theoretical questions abound in this area. Most notably, spatiotemporal relations are clearly important for much of our cognition, but graphical models are currently limited in their ability to represent spatiotemporally continuous relations and processes. Time is usually represented as discrete timesteps, but many interesting phenomena occur smoothly over time. Similarly, various formal tricks can capture spatial information, but space is not naturally represented in a graphical model. The core issue for both space and time is that the graph component carries only topological information about adjacency—that is, direct relevance—between factors. Current graphical models are thus fundamentally ill-suited to express spatial or temporal *distance*, which is critical for representing spatiotemporal relations. At the same time, there does not seem to be any principled barrier to developing graphical models that use richer graphs, as shown by various preliminary attempts (Nodelman, Shelton, & Koller, 2002, 2003; Wang, Blei, & Heckerman, 2008). The hard part is performing the formal, mathematical, and computational work to get all the representational pieces to line up in the correct way. Such an advance would, however, be incredibly valuable, as it would open the door to potentially using graphical models to capture the cognitive representations produced and used by many other parts of cognition, such as causal perception.

There are also multiple theoretical questions that are more distinctively cognitive in nature. On several occasions, I raised the challenge of developing neurally plausible implementations of graphical models that can support the different cognitive processes that people appear to use. This problem is currently a theoretical one: is there *any* way to do it, and if so, what are the properties, capacities, and shortcomings of the implementation? Of course, numerous empirical questions will naturally arise once we understand how graphical models could be represented in more realistic neural architectures, but the first challenge is computational. I also argued in chapter 8 that my cognitive architecture is complementary to existing process-centered unifications, such as ACT-R and Sigma, but researchers must overcome significant theoretical barriers before any such integration can occur. We thus face a large set of open questions about how, for example, graphical models can be understood in terms of ACT-R chunks, or factor graphs can be integrated with other types of graphical models.

Finally, in addition to these more focused open questions and next steps, several notable lacunae exist in the current cognitive architecture. Most obviously, I have largely set aside the role of language in human cognition, despite its ubiquitous presence in almost all our conscious thoughts and actions. Of course, language has played an indirect role in this cognitive architecture, both because there are presumably close connections (though not necessarily identity) between our concepts and the words that we use, and because many of the experiments discussed earlier depend on people's linguistic competence. I have not, however, seriously engaged with any linguistic or psycholinguistic research in this book. There are reasons to think that at least some of the cognitive representations underlying language phenomena might fit well with the graphical models framework. For example, reading time and fluency depend in part on our expectations about word location and order (Smith & Levy, 2013). That is, reading arguably involves the (implicit) computation of probabilities, and graphical models excel at the rapid computation of conditional probabilities. Alternately, Sloman (2005) has argued that many phenomena in pragmatics depend on our causal knowledge and could thus be translated into operations on graphical models. These observations are obviously speculative, but they do suggest that it would not be foolhardy to investigate the possible roles of graphical model cognitive representations in language production, comprehension, and processing.

Similarly, I have had relatively little discussion of social cognition, with the exception of a brief mention of social reasoning—specifically, inference about others' preferences from their choices—in chapter 6. Humans are deeply social creatures, and we spend substantial cognitive resources thinking and reasoning about others. In modern society, it is arguably an open question whether physical or social factors place more constraints on our everyday lives and decisions. Certainly, we frequently notice the social factors more readily. We might thus naturally hope that a cognitive architecture that aims to unify multiple types of cognition would extend to learning and inference about other individuals and our relationships with them. The cognitive architecture presented here would be even more persuasive if much of social cognition could be understood as operations on a shared store of cognitive representations structured as graphical models. This turns out to be an extremely challenging task, as we often do not have precise theories of social cognition and so are not even sure exactly what needs to be modeled and explained. Of course, that gap in our understanding raises the possibility of using the graphical models framework not just to explain existing theories but to significantly advance the field. For example, recent research has shown that our inferences about others' goals and intentions can fruitfully be understood as inferences in a graphical model (Baker, Saxe, & Tenenbaum, 2009; Hamlin, Ullman, Tenenbaum, Goodman, & Baker, 2013; Jern, Lucas, & Kemp, 2011). This work has actually revealed new empirical phenomena, in part by approaching a social cognition problem from the graphical models perspective. At the same time, social cognition involves an enormous variety of cognitive representations and processes, and so incorporating it into the present graphical-models-based cognitive architecture will require substantial theoretical and empirical research.

One might think that these open questions and challenges somehow reveal a defect in the view that I have developed throughout this book, as it has failed to answer all questions. I view them instead as evidence of the fruitfulness of adopting the graphical models perspective in trying to understand the nature of human cognition and cognitive representations. We do not arrive at the end of this book with nothing left to investigate but rather have a brand new set of problems and puzzles to address. No model, architecture, or theory is ever complete, just as no map is ever perfect, and so there will always be further questions. Graphical models are not the only objects in our mind, and this framework is not the only tool that we should (or will) use to better understand our thought and behavior. However, good accounts of our cognition can help us to understand the processes and representations that underlie it, as well as how our cognition enables us to navigate successfully through an exceedingly complex world. This book has proposed that important parts of our cognition can be understood as different operations on a shared store of cognitive representations that are structured as graphical models. This integrated cognitive architecture can explain the seamless, free-ranging nature of much of our cognition, as well as our ability to (mostly) focus on the information that is relevant to solving a particular problem. It enables us to better understand the seeming unity of our cognitive lives, as well as the errors that we sometimes make. In sum, we can better understand and explain our minds if we understand the roles played by our minds' graphs.

Appendix: Graphical Models and Concepts*

This appendix contains proofs for all the theorems stated and used in section 5.5. To my knowledge, these theorems have not appeared elsewhere, and so the proofs are provided for completeness, but without any comments or discussions.

Theorem 5.1: For all $S_E(\mathbf{X})$, there exists a P_E such that $S_E(\mathbf{X}) \propto P_E(\mathbf{X} \cup U)$, where U has e many values (and measure zero of the P_E's violate Faithfulness).

Proof of theorem 5.1: Without loss of generality, assume the exemplar weights of S_E are normalized: $\Sigma W_k = 1$. Define a probability distribution in terms of the Markov decomposition of the figure 5.1 graph: $P(U = j) = W_j$; and $P(X_i \mid U = j) = s_i(\,|X_i - E_i^j|\,) \,/\, Z_i$, where $Z_i = \int_0^\infty s_i(\epsilon)d\epsilon$. Because *Sim* is a proper similarity function, Z_i is always well-defined and finite. If every exemplar has the same value for some F_i, then $P(X_i \mid U = j) = P(X_i \mid U = k) = P(X_i)$ for all j, k. Reorder the features so that the first c features are those for which this is true, where possibly $c = 0$. Let G be the edge-deletion transform of the figure 5.1 graph that removes the $U \rightarrow F_i$ edge for $i \leq c$; $P(\mathbf{X})$ clearly satisfies the Markov assumption for G. $P(\mathbf{X})$ is positive (since every s_i is positive), and condition (b) for P_E is satisfied, since the relevant conditional probabilities are defined directly in terms of the (normalized) s_i's. For condition (c), if $Q_{ik} = E_i^k - E_i^1$, then

$$P(X_i + Q_{ik} \mid U = k) = \frac{s_i(|X_i - E_i^k + (E_i^k - E_i^1)|)}{Z_i} = \frac{s_i(|X_i - E_i^1|)}{Z_i} = P(X_i \mid U = 1)$$

All that remains is to prove that $P(\mathbf{X})$ satisfies Faithfulness for G, which requires proving that all appropriate associations hold. We do this with two lemmas, one for the adjacent variables U and F_i ($i > c$), and the other for connected-but-not-adjacent variables F_i and F_j ($i, j > c$).

Lemma 5.1.1: For all $i > c$, F_i and U are associated conditional on any $\mathbf{S} \subseteq \mathbf{V} \setminus \{F_i, U\}$.

Proof of lemma 5.1.1: Proof by contradiction: suppose there is some S such that F_i and U are independent conditional on S. Therefore, for all X_i, u, s, $P(X_i \,\&\, U = u \mid S = s) = P(X_i \mid S = s)P(U = u \mid S = s)$. Also, by Markov decomposition, for all X_i, u, s, $P(X_i \,\&\, U = u \mid S = s) = P(X_i \mid U = u)P(U = u \mid S = s)$. P is a positive probability distribution, so for all X_i, u, s, $P(X_i \mid U = u) = P(X_i \mid S = s)$. Therefore, for some fixed s, we have $P(X_i \mid U = u_1) = P(X_i \mid U = u_2)$ for all X_i, u_1, u_2. Since $P(X_i \mid U = u)$ is maximal at E_i^u, this equality implies that $E_i^{u1} = E_i^{u2}$ for all u_1, u_2. But $i > c$ implies $E_i^j \neq E_i^k$ for some j, k. Contradiction. ■

Lemma 5.1.2: For all $i \neq j > c$ and measure one of the $P(\mathbf{X})$, F_i and F_j are associated conditional on any $\mathbf{S} \subseteq \mathbf{V} \setminus \{F_i, F_j, U\}$.

Proof of lemma 1.1.2: Proof by contradiction: suppose there is some S such that F_i and F_j are independent conditional on S. Therefore, for all X_i, X_j, s, $P(X_i \,\&\, X_j \mid S = s) = P(X_i \mid S = s)P(X_j \mid S = s)$. Also, for all X_i, X_j, s, $P(S = s)P(X_i \,\&\, X_j \,\&\, S = s) = P(X_i \,\&\, S = s)P(X_j \,\&\, S = s)$. The Markov decomposition of P implies these probabilities can all be expressed as weighted sums over values of U. Many of the terms do not depend on X_i or X_j: $f(s, u_1, u_2) = P(U = u_1)P(U = u_2)P(S = s \mid U = u_1)P(S = s \mid U = u_2)$. Algebra yields: for all X_i, X_j, s,

$$\sum_{u_1} \sum_{u_2 > u_1} f(\mathbf{s}, u_1, u_2)(P(X_i \mid U = u_1) - P(X_i \mid U = u_2))$$
$$(P(X_j \mid U = u_1) - P(X_j \mid U = u_2)) = 0$$

We must now show that this double summation is not trivially true.

Claim: There exists $u_1 \neq u_2$ such that $P(X_i \mid U = u_1) \neq P(X_i \mid U = u_2)$ and $P(X_j \mid U = u_1) \neq P(X_j \mid U = u_2)$ for more than measure zero of the X_i, X_j.

Proof of the claim: Let $I_1, \ldots, I_k$ be a partition of the values of U such that each partition element contains all u that share a maximal point for $P(X_i \mid U = u)$. Note that $k > 1$, since $i > c$. If F_i is binary, then for each u, $P(X_i \mid U = u)$ equals either α_i or $(1 - \alpha_i)$ for some fixed α_i, since s_i is the same function for all exemplars. Therefore the distributions corresponding to U-values in two different partition elements can only be equal if $\alpha_i = 0.5$, which implies that $P(X_i \mid U = u)$ does not depend on u, which contradicts $i > c$. If F_i is continuous, then the distributions corresponding to U-values in two different partition elements can only be equal for measure one of the space if $s(\varepsilon)$ is constant for measure one of the space, which implies that the integral of

$s(\varepsilon)$ cannot be finite, which is a contradiction. Distributions whose u falls in different partition elements thus must differ for more than measure zero of the X_i. We can similarly define $J_1, \ldots, J_l$, which will have all the same properties as the I-partition. Thus the proof of the claim reduces to proving that there is some u_1, u_2 such that both (i) $u_1 \in I_a$ and $u_2 \in I_b$, where $a \neq b$; and (ii) $u_1 \in J_r$ and $u_2 \in J_t$, where $r \neq t$.

Consider some arbitrary $u_1 \in I_a$ and $\in J_r$ for some a, r, and all u_2 such that $u_2 \in I_b$ where $a \neq b$. Note that there must be at least one such u_2, since $k > 1$. If there exists $u_2 \in J_t$ with $r \neq t$, then the claim is proved. Thus suppose that $r = t$ for all such u_2. If I_a contains only one element (u_1), then every u is in the same J-partition element, and so $l = 1$, which is impossible. Therefore consider all u_1^* such that $u_1^* \in I_a$ and $u_1^* \neq u_1$. If all $u_1^* \in J_r$, then we again have $l = 1$, which is impossible. Therefore there exists $u_1^* \in I_a$ such that $u_1^* \in J_t$ where $r \neq t$. Therefore, since all $u_2 \in J_r$, we have a suitable pair in u_1^* and any $u_2 \in I_b$ for $a \neq b$. ■

The solutions for a nontrivial polynomial are Lebesgue measure zero over the space of parameters of the polynomial (Meek, 1995; Okamoto, 1973). Since the double summation is nontrivial, F_i and F_j are independent given **S** for only measure zero of the possible parameter settings. Thus measure one of these probability distributions are Faithful to G. ■

Since $P(\mathbf{X})$ satisfies all the relevant conditions, it is a member of P_E. By construction, $S_E \propto P(\mathbf{X})$, and so the theorem is proved. ■

Theorem 5.2: For all $P_E(\mathbf{X} \cup U)$, there exists an S_E such that $S_E(\mathbf{X}) \propto P_E(\mathbf{X} \cup U)$, where S_E has u exemplars.

Proof of theorem 5.2: It suffices to provide $\mathbf{E}^i$, W_i, and $s_i(\epsilon)$ for each $i \leq u$. Let $\mathbf{E}^j = \mathbf{R}^j$, the point of maximal probability given $U = j$, and set $W_j = P_E(U = j)$. Define $s_i(\,|X_i - E_i^j|\,) = P_E(X_i \mid U = j)$. Because the U-conditional probability distributions are identical up to translation, $s_i(\epsilon)$ is identical regardless of choice of j. Set $Sim(\mathbf{X}, \mathbf{Y})$ to be the product of s_i's. Condition (b) clearly holds, as the s_i's inherit all the characteristics of the U-conditional distributions. Finally,

$$\int_0^{\infty} s_i(\epsilon)d\epsilon = \int_{-\infty}^{\infty} P_E(X_i \mid U = j)dX_i = 1 < \infty$$

Thus condition (c) is satisfied, and so $S(\mathbf{X})$ is a member of S_E. And by the Markov decomposition of P_E, $S(\mathbf{X}) = P_E(\mathbf{X} \cup U)$. ■

Theorem 5.3: For all $S_{P1}(\mathbf{X})$, there exists a P_{P1} such that $S_{P1}(\mathbf{X}) \propto P_{P1}(\mathbf{X})$.

Proof of theorem 5.3: For the empty graph, the joint probability is simply the product of the variable-specific probabilities, and so it suffices to set $P(X_i) = s_i(\,|X_i - R_i|\,) / Z_i$, where $Z_i = \int_0^{\infty} s_i(\epsilon)d\epsilon$. The resulting distribution is Markov to the empty graph, and Faithfulness imposes no constraints given the empty graph. Moreover, the $P(X_i)$ "inherit" all the necessary properties from the s_i's, and so all the conditions are satisfied for $P(\mathbf{X})$ to be part of P_{P1}. Finally, by construction, $S_{P1}(\mathbf{X}) \propto P_{P1}(\mathbf{X})$. ■

Theorem 5.4: For all $P_{P1}(\mathbf{X})$, there exists an S_{P1} such that $S_{P1}(\mathbf{X}) \propto P_{P1}(\mathbf{X})$.

Proof of theorem 5.4: The construction in this proof is exactly the reverse of the one used for theorem 5.3, as we simply set $\mathbf{R}$ to be the point of maximum probability for $P(\mathbf{X})$ and then set $s_i(\,|X_i - R_i|\,) = P(X_i)$. All the relevant properties for s_i are immediately satisfied, and by construction, $S_{P1}(\mathbf{X}) = P_{P1}(\mathbf{X})$. ■

Theorem 5.5: For all $S_{P2}(\mathbf{X})$, there exists a P_{P2} such that $S_{P2}(\mathbf{X}) \propto P_{P2}(\mathbf{X})$, where there is an edge in the P_{P2} UG for each second-order feature in S_{P2} (and measure zero of the P_{P2}'s violate Faithfulness).

Proof of theorem 5.5: Let M be a UG over the m first-order features with F_i — F_j if and only if there exists a second-order feature defined on F_i and F_j (i.e., a nontrivial $h_k(\varepsilon_i, \varepsilon_j)$). To fully specify M, it suffices to specify each clique potential. Let N_i be the number of cliques containing F_i, N_{ij} be the number of cliques containing both F_i and F_j, and d be the size of clique D.

If $\varepsilon_i = |X_i - R_i|$ and $t_{ij}(\varepsilon_i, \varepsilon_j) = s_k(\,|h_k(\varepsilon_i, \varepsilon_j) - h_k(0, 0)|\,)$, then for each maximal clique $\mathbf{D}$, set $f_{\mathbf{D},ij}(\varepsilon_i, \varepsilon_j) = s_i(\epsilon_i)^{\frac{1}{N_i(d-1)}} s_j(\epsilon_j)^{\frac{1}{N_j(d-1)}} t_{ij}(\epsilon_i,\epsilon_j)^{\frac{1}{N_{ij}}}$, using the positive roots for even N_i and N_{ij}; and $g_D(\mathbf{X}) = \prod_{i,j\in \mathbf{D}} f_{\mathbf{D},ij}(\epsilon_i,\epsilon_j) = \prod_{i\in \mathbf{D}} s_i(\epsilon_i)^{1/N_i} \prod_{i,j\in \mathbf{D}} t_{ij}(\epsilon_i,\epsilon_j)^{1/N_{ij}}$. Note that t_{ij} is included only when F_i and F_j are both in clique $\mathbf{D}$, and so t_{ij} is necessarily nontrivial. Clearly, all g_D are functions only of variables in $\mathbf{D}$, and by construction, $P(\mathbf{X}) = \prod g_D(\mathbf{X}) / Z \propto S_{P2}(\mathbf{X})$ whenever the normalization constant Z is finite. Because S_{P2} is a proper similarity function, it immediately follows that $Z = \int \prod g_D(\mathbf{X})d\mathbf{X} = \int S_{P2}(\mathbf{X})d\mathbf{X} < \infty$. By construction, $P(\mathbf{X})$ satisfies the Markov assumption for M and the appropriate clique potential decomposition constraint. $P(\mathbf{X})$ also has all the appropriate symmetry properties by virtue of the definition in terms of s_i functions. The only thing that remains is to show that (measure one of the) $P(\mathbf{X})$ satisfy the Faithfulness assumption for M; we do this through two lemmas, one for adjacent variables and one for nonadjacent variables. For both lemmas, we use the same proof strategy as lemma 5.1.1 of finding nontrivial polynomials, which implies that the set of parameters for that equality are Lebesgue measure zero.

Lemma 5.5.1: For all adjacent F_i, F_j, and for measure one of the above-defined $P(\mathrm{X})$, F_i and F_j are associated conditional on any set $\mathbf{S} \subseteq \mathbf{V} \setminus \{F_i, F_j\}$.

Proof of lemma 5.5.1: Assume there is some suitable S such that F_i is independent of F_j conditional on S. Since $P(\mathbf{X})$ is positive, this implies that, for all X_i, X_j, s, $P(X_i \,\&\, \mathrm{S} = \mathrm{s})P(X_j \,\&\, \mathrm{S} = \mathrm{s}) = P(X_i \,\&\, X_j \,\&\, \mathrm{S} = \mathrm{s})P(\mathrm{S} = \mathrm{s})$. Let **A** be the set of all possible combinations of values for $\mathbf{V} \setminus \mathrm{S} \cup \{F_i, F_j\}$ (i.e., everything not mentioned in the independence statement), and let **a** and **b** be particular combinations. For each $\mathbf{a} \in \mathbf{A}$, denote the value of the neighbors of either F_i or F_j (excluding F_i and F_j, since they are each other's neighbors) by $\mathbf{N_a}$, and the values for the other variables as $\mathbf{D_a}$. The values in $\mathbf{N_a}$ and $\mathbf{D_a}$ for variables in **S** will be constant for all **a**, as those were fixed by specification of **s**. Each of the probabilities mentioned to this point in the proof can be expressed as the sum of probabilities for the fixed values and **a**. (This proof is expressed in terms of summations, but everything transfers straightforwardly to integrals, since we know that the probability density is well behaved in the relevant senses.)

The equality at the beginning of the proof can be rewritten as follows: for all X_i, X_j, **s**,

$$\sum_{\mathbf{a},\mathbf{b}\in\mathbf{A}} P(\mathbf{D_a}|\mathbf{N_a})P(\mathbf{D_b}|\mathbf{N_b})\sum_{F_i,F_j}(P(X_i \,\&\, F_j \,\&\, \mathbf{N_a})P(F_i \,\&\, X_j \,\&\, \mathbf{N_b}) - P(X_i \,\&\, X_j \,\&\, \mathbf{N_a})P(F_i \,\&\, F_j \,\&\, \mathbf{N_b})) = 0$$

where **a** and **b** range over all possible values of **A**. Since $P(\mathbf{D} \mid \mathbf{N})$ is always nonzero, this complex polynomial will be nontrivial (i.e., not identically zero) just when the following claim holds:

Claim: There is a set of X_i, X_j, F_i, F_j, **a**, **b** with nonzero measure such that $[P(X_i \,\&\, F_j \,\&\, \mathbf{N_a})P(F_i \,\&\, X_j \,\&\, \mathbf{N_b}) - P(X_i \,\&\, X_j \,\&\, \mathbf{N_a})P(F_i \,\&\, F_j \,\&\, \mathbf{N_b})]$ is not identically zero.

Proof of claim: Substitute in the clique potentials and take the sum over possible settings of **D**. Since clique potentials depend only on the variables in the clique, we can factor out the sum over **D**, where the factored-out potentials are irrelevant for whether the term in brackets is identically zero. For simplicity, we harmlessly abuse notation by using the variable names to actually denote the corresponding ϵ. Let D_i (D_j) denote the cliques with F_i but not F_j (or vice versa), and D_{ij} denotes the cliques with both. Since the two products in the subtraction term both involve X_i, X_j, F_i, F_j, $\mathbf{N}_a$, and $\mathbf{N}_b$, we can factor out all the s and t functions involving only variables other than F_i and F_j. We also factor out any terms involving just i, as those are shared in both terms. (We could alternately factor out terms involving just j, which would produce an analogous equation below.) The resulting equation for the purposes of determining nontriviality is:

$$t_{ij}(X_i, F_j)t_{ij}(F_i, X_j)\prod_{k\neq i,j} t_{jk}(F_j, \mathbf{N}_a(k))t_{jk}(X_j, \mathbf{N}_b(k)) -$$

$$t_{ij}(X_i, X_j)t_{ij}(F_i, F_j)\prod_{k\neq i,j} t_{jk}(X_j, \mathbf{N}_a(k))t_{jk}(F_j, \mathbf{N}_b(k)) = 0$$

Suppose the variables are binary. If $\mathbf{N}_a = \mathbf{N}_b$, $F_i = (1 - X_i)$, and $F_j = (1 - X_j)$, then the two terms in the equation reduce to $t_{ij}(0, 0)t_{ij}(1, 1)$ and $t_{ij}(1, 0)t_{ij}(0, 1)$. Nontriviality of the second-order feature implies that these terms are not equal, and so the original equation is not trivially zero.

Suppose instead that the variables are continuous, and assume that the equation holds for measure one of X_i, X_j, F_i, F_j, **a**, and **b**. If F_i and F_j have no neighbors, then this equation reduces to $t_{ij}(X_i, F_j)t_{ij}(F_i, X_j) = t_{ij}(X_i, X_j)t_{ij}(F_i, F_j)$ for measure one of X_i, X_j, F_i, F_j. But for any arbitrary F_i, F_j in this space, there exist $f()$ and $g()$ such that $t_{ij}(X_i, X_j)$ is expressible as $f(X_i)g(X_j)$ for measure one of X_i, X_j, which contradicts the nontriviality of the second-order feature. Suppose instead that either F_i or F_j has at least one neighbor, and assume without loss of generality that F_j has a neighbor. For any arbitrary setting **q** (in the measure one set in which the equation is satisfied) of everything except X_j and $\mathbf{N}_a(k)$, we can rewrite the above equation as follows: for measure one of X_j, $\mathbf{N}_a(k)$, we have $t_{jk}(X_j, \mathbf{N}_a(k)) = \alpha_q \dfrac{t_{ij}(F_i, X_j)}{t_{ij}(X_i, X_j)} t_{jk}(F_j, \mathbf{N}_a(k))$ for some $\boldsymbol{q}$-dependent constant α_q. But this implies that $t_{jk}(X_j, \mathbf{N}_a(k))$ can be expressed as the product of $f(X_j)$ and $g(\mathbf{N}_a(k))$, contra the assumption of nontriviality for second-order features. Thus the equation cannot hold for measure one of X_i, X_j, F_i, F_j, **a**, and **b**, and so the claim is established. ■

Since the claim holds, we know that the original complex polynomial is not identically zero for measure one X_i, X_j, **s**, and so X_i and X_j are independent conditional on $\boldsymbol{S}$ for only measure zero of the probability distributions. Thus lemma 5.5.1 holds. ■

Lemma 5.5.2: For all nonadjacent F_i, F_j and for measure one of the above-defined $P(\mathbf{X})$, if there is a path between F_i and F_j, then they are associated conditional on any set $\mathbf{S} \subseteq \mathbf{V} \setminus \{F_i, F_j\}$ such that $\mathbf{S}$ does not separate F_i and F_j.

Proof of lemma 5.5.2: The initial section of the proof for lemma 5.5.1 did not use the adjacency of F_i and F_j, and so we only must prove that there is a set of X_i, X_j, F_i, F_j, **a**, **b** with nonzero measure such that $[P(X_i \,\&\, F_j \,\&\, \mathbf{N_a})P(F_i \,\&\, X_j \,\&\, \mathbf{N_b}) - P(X_i \,\&\, X_j \,\&\, \mathbf{N_a})P(F_i \,\&\, F_j \,\&\, \mathbf{N_b})]$ is not identically zero. Since **S** does not separate F_i and F_j, **S** cannot contain either every variable adjacent to F_i, or every variable adjacent to F_j. Without loss of generality, assume that there is at least one neighbor of F_j, call it F_k, that is not contained in S.

We again express this difference in terms of (sums of products of) clique potentials and factor out terms that appear in both sides of the difference. If $Ne(j)$ is the set of features adjacent to F_j, then it suffices to prove: There is a set of X_i, X_j, F_i, F_j, **a**, **b** with nonzero measure such that the following equation is nontrivial:

$$\prod_{l \in Ne(j)} t_{jl}(F_j, \mathbf{N_a}(l))t_{jl}(X_j, \mathbf{N_b}(l)) - \prod_{l \in Ne(j)} t_{jl}(X_j, \mathbf{N_a}(l))t_{jl}(F_j, \mathbf{N_b}(l)) = 0$$

If the variables are binary, then let $F_j = (1 - X_j)$, $\mathbf{N_a} = \mathbf{N_b}$ except for F_k, and $\mathbf{N_a}(k) = (1 - \mathbf{N_b}(k))$. The difference in products then becomes the difference between $t_{jk}(0, 0)t_{jk}(1, 1)$ and $t_{jk}(0, 1)t_{jk}(1, 0)$. The nontriviality of second-order features implies that this difference cannot be zero.

Suppose instead that the variables are continuous and the difference is identically zero for measure one of the variables. Then for any arbitrary setting $\boldsymbol{q}$ of variables other than X_j and $\mathbf{N_a}(k)$, we have: for measure one of X_j, $\mathbf{N_a}(k)$, $t_{jk}(X_j, \mathbf{N_a}(k)) = \beta_q \dfrac{\prod_{l \in Ne(j)} t_{jl}(X_j, \mathbf{N_b}(l))}{\prod_{l \in Ne(j) \setminus k} t_{jl}(X_j, \mathbf{N_a}(l))} t_{jk}(F_j, \mathbf{N_a}(k))$

where β_q is a $\boldsymbol{q}$-dependent constant. Thus t_{jk} can be expressed as the product of $f(X_j)$ and $g(\mathbf{N_a}(k))$, contradicting the nondecomposability of t_{jk}, and so there must be a set of nonzero measure such that the product difference is not identically zero. F_i and F_j therefore must be associated conditional on $\boldsymbol{S}$. ■

Given those two lemmas, we can conclude that $P(\mathbf{X})$ is a member of P_{P2}. ■

Theorem 5.6: For all $P_{P2}(\mathbf{X})$, there exists an S_{P2} such that $S_{P2}(\mathbf{X}) \propto P_{P2}(\mathbf{X})$, where S_{P2} has a second-order feature for each edge in the P_{P2} UG.

Proof of theorem 5.6: Clique potentials are only defined up to a multiplicative constant, and so assume without loss of generality that $g_D(\mathbf{R}) = 1$ for all $\mathbf{D}$. For convenience, let $\mathbf{X}[Y_i]$ denote the point $\mathbf{X}$, but with the value Y_i for F_i; that is, we substitute a value on one dimension. There is a general underdetermination problem for second-order features: we care about $s_k(\,|h_k(\varepsilon_i, \varepsilon_j) - h_k(0, 0)|\,)$, but there will always be infinitely many s_k and h_k function-pairs that yield the same similarity judgments. Hence we focus on the composite $t_{ij}(\varepsilon_i, \varepsilon_j) = s_k(\,|h_k(\varepsilon_i, \varepsilon_j) - h_k(0, 0)|\,)$. If d denotes the size of clique $\mathbf{D}$, then we define the s_i and t_{ij} functions to be:

- $s_i(\epsilon) = \prod_{\mathbf{D}:i\in\mathbf{D}} g_D(\mathbf{R}[X_i])^{1/d}$

- $t_{ij}(\epsilon_i,\epsilon_j) = \prod_{\mathbf{D}:i \text{ or } j\in\mathbf{D}} \dfrac{g_D(\mathbf{R}[X_i,X_j])}{g_D(\mathbf{R}[X_i])^{\frac{(d-1)}{d}}\, g_D(\mathbf{R}[X_j])^{\frac{(d-1)}{D}}}$

Clearly, all the s_i and t_{ij} functions are uniquely defined, and all the necessary symmetry properties are inherited from those of $P_{P2}(\mathbf{X})$. If $\prod_{\mathbf{D}:i \text{ or } j\in\mathbf{D}} g_D(\mathbf{R}[X_i,X_j])$ could be decomposed into $f(X_i)g(X_j)$, then X_i and X_j would be unconditionally independent, which would contradict Faithfulness. Thus the second-order features cannot be decomposed in this way, and so they are nontrivial. All that remains is to show that $S(\mathbf{X}) \propto P_{P2}(\mathbf{X})$. Since we have m first-order features and q second-order features, we have:

$$S(\mathbf{X}) = \prod_{i=1}^{m}\prod_{\mathbf{D}:i\in\mathbf{D}} g_D(\mathbf{R}[X_i])^{\frac{1}{d}} \prod_{k=1}^{q}\prod_{\mathbf{D}:i \text{ or } j\in\mathbf{D}} \frac{g_D(\mathbf{R}[X_i,X_j])}{g_D(\mathbf{R}[X_i])^{\frac{(d-1)}{d}}\, g_D(\mathbf{R}[X_j])^{\frac{(d-1)}{d}}}$$

After removing terms that equal one, the first double product is $\prod_{\mathbf{D}}\prod_{i:X_i\neq R_i} g_D(\mathbf{R}[X_i])^{\frac{1}{d}}$; and the second double product is $\prod_{\substack{i\neq j:X_i\neq R_i \\ \text{or } X_j\neq R_j}}\prod_{\mathbf{D}:i \text{ or } j\in\mathbf{D}} \dfrac{g_D(\mathbf{R}[X_i,X_j])}{g_D(\mathbf{R}[X_i])^{\frac{(d-1)}{d}}\, g_D(\mathbf{R}[X_j])^{\frac{(d-1)}{d}}}$. The terms in the second double product can be separated into two groups based on whether (a) both or (b) only one of X_i, X_j differ from their $\mathbf{R}$-values. Since $g_D(\mathbf{R}[X_i, X_j]) = 1$ if both $F_i, F_j \notin \mathbf{D}$, the numerator for group (a) is $\prod_{\mathbf{D}}\prod_{\substack{i\neq j:X_i\neq R_i \\ \& X_j\neq R_j}} g_D(\mathbf{R}[X_i,X_j])$. Let b_D

denote the number of features in clique **D** whose values differ from their **R**-values. For any i such that $X_i \neq R_i$, there are $b_D - 1$ other features in **D** that also differ in their **R**-values. The denominator for group (a) can thus be rewritten as $\prod_{\mathbf{D}} \prod_{i:X_i \neq R_i} \left(g_D(\mathbf{R}[X_i])^{\frac{d-1}{d}} \right)^{b_D - 1}$. In group (b), for each i such that $X_i \neq R_i$, there are $d - b_D$ features in clique **D** that *do* have their **R**-values, and $g_D(\mathbf{R}[X_i, X_j]) = g_D(\mathbf{R}[X_i])$ for those features. Thus group (b) can be rewritten as $\prod_{\mathbf{D}} \prod_{i:X_i \neq R_i} \left(g_D(\mathbf{R}[X_i])^{\frac{1}{d}} \right)^{d - b_D}$.

The first double product, group (b), and the denominator of group (a) are all identical except for exponents. Combining them with the group (a) numerator yields: $S(\mathbf{X}) = \prod_{\mathbf{D}} \prod_{i:X_i \neq R_i} \frac{1}{g_D(\mathbf{R}[X_i])^{b_D - 2}} \prod_{\substack{i \neq j: X_i \neq R_i \\ \& X_j \neq R_j}} g_D(\mathbf{R}[X_i, X_j])$. The pairwise decomposability of the clique function implies $g_D(\mathbf{R}[X_i]) = \prod_{k \neq i} f_{\mathbf{D},ik}(\epsilon_i, 0)$ and $g_D(\mathbf{R}[X_i, X_j]) = f_{\mathbf{D},ij}(\epsilon_i, \epsilon_j) \prod_{k \neq i,j} f_{\mathbf{D},ik}(\epsilon_i, 0) f_{\mathbf{D},jk}(\epsilon_j, 0)$. If we substitute these into the previous expression for $S(\mathbf{X})$ and cancel terms appropriately, we find that $S(\mathbf{X}) = \prod_{\mathbf{D}} \prod_{\substack{X_i \neq R_i \\ \& X_j \neq R_j}} f_{\mathbf{D},ij}(\epsilon_i, \epsilon_j) \prod_{\substack{X_i \neq R_i \\ \& X_k \neq R_k}} f_{\mathbf{D},ik}(\epsilon_i, 0) = \prod_{\mathbf{D}} g_D(\mathbf{X}) \propto P_{P2}(\mathbf{X})$. ■

Notes

1 "Free-Range" Cognition

1. The ability to account for such data would be unilluminating if the graphical models framework were universal, in the sense of being able to express any possible theory. As I show in chapter 3, however, this is not the case: there are many possible cognitive theories that cannot be captured using graphical models.

2 Computational Realism, Levels, and Constraints

1. In this book, I do not engage with the long history of arguments that conclude that the mind cannot be fully understood as a computational device (Harnad, 1994; Searle, 1980). First, I simply lack space to address all potentially relevant issues. Second, these arguments all focus on cognition as a whole, but I make no claims of completeness for the account offered in subsequent chapters. I am obviously not trying to capture all aspects of cognition, so these arguments have relatively little bite. Third, I adopt a relatively pragmatic attitude toward scientific theories: they are valuable just in case they help us to understand, predict, explain, and control our world. I contend that computational approaches to the mind have proven helpful along all these dimensions and so are useful to consider. Subsequent chapters will hopefully establish this for the particular case of the graphical-models-based account.

2. The terminology that I introduce in this section is not completely settled in the broader cognitive science community. However, the definitions that I propose are relatively standard, with the possible exception of "theory."

3. As a personal example, I would advocate using a neural framework to understand low-level visual perception, rather than the more symbolic framework advocated here.

4. In practice, Marr's levels are almost always applied to cognitive models, rather than frameworks or architectures. To maintain generality, however, I will talk about

theories, though these issues are obviously most directly relevant to cognitive models of the same phenomena.

5. For example, many of the early debates about neural network models of cognition were exactly about what reality to attribute to the various parts of the model; were the networks, for example, supposed to map onto actual neural structures? These debates were exacerbated by the fact that publications with neural network models were rarely sufficiently specific about their realist commitments (or lack thereof).

6. Note that, in this characterization, we can also have stable, persistent representations of processes (e.g., if some cognitive algorithm is "stored" in some way in the brain).

7. To be clear: I do not claim that prediction is the only epistemically important function of a theory, but simply that it is a major one. It is thus a useful way to think about the epistemological commitments of a particular set of realist commitments for a theory.

8. As a concrete example, there was an exchange of papers in the 1990s between Shanks and Melz et al. (Melz et al., 1993; Shanks, 1991, 1993) in which a significant part of the debate was exactly about the intended scope of one model of causal learning: specifically, was the ΔP model supposed to capture all causal judgments (Shanks's reading) or only those made at asymptote (Melz et al.'s position)?

9. A full explication of this intertheoretic relation would require an explicit measure of approximation, as well as some account of how inputs and outputs in one theory map to inputs and outputs in another theory. These details will be highly dependent on the particular domain and theory, so there is no particular reason to expect any unified notion of input—output approximation that applies in all, or even many, situations.

10. My focus is on reductions between theories at different levels of description, called reduction$_1$ by Nickles (1973). A different notion of reduction—Nickles's reduction$_2$—focuses on theories at the same level, as when relativistic mechanics is said to reduce to Newtonian mechanics in the limit of $(v / c)^2 \rightarrow 0$.

11. As reduction is always a relation between a higher-level and lower-level theory, I use *H* and *L* throughout to refer to these two relata.

12. The story is obviously more complicated than this, but the details have been worked out (Moulines & Polanski, 1996).

13. Or rather, the phenomena covered by *H* are a rough subset of the phenomena covered by *L*.

14. The issue is complicated by the fact that *T* will typically reduce to *S* only given certain initial or background conditions. If the actual initial or background condi-

tions are not those required for *T*, then it is unclear whether to say that *T* is false or simply inapplicable. In either case, the truth-values of *S* and *T* can arguably be pulled slightly apart.

15. Concretely, *D* might be the Rescorla-Wagner model (Danks, 2003; Rescorla & Wagner, 1972) and *A* the conditional ΔP theory (Cheng & Novick, 1992). Or *D* could be the noisy-OR-based dynamics (Danks, Griffiths, & Tenenbaum, 2003) for A = the causal power theory (Cheng, 1997). See chapter 4 for more on these particular theories.

16. This extreme case is unlikely; the more realistic situation is: if *A* is true, then only a few "cognitively plausible" *D*s could be true.

17. In fact, it is the principal strategy in this book: graphical models provide a framework for representations in many different domains and processes, and so the unifying theory is more likely than one would expect from each separate success.

3 A Primer on Graphical Models

1. Semantic heterogeneity may pose a problem for some inference methods. This issue will arise again in sec. 9.2.

2. At least for linear systems. In a nonlinear system, zero correlation is necessary but not sufficient for independence.

3. Unfortunately, the exact connection between a statistical test and in/dependence judgments is frequently misunderstood or misrepresented in scientific practice (Harlow, Muliak, & Steiger, 1997).

4. The assumptions are sometimes stated in their contrapositive form; for example, the Markov assumption is sometimes "if two nodes are dependent regardless of conditioning set, then they are graphically adjacent." Also, Faithfulness is sometimes not explicitly stated, but it is almost always used in the corresponding learning, estimation, and inference methods.

5. Discrete variables with many possible ordered values (e.g., height, weight) are often more easily modeled as continuous variables.

6. If one has a mix of discrete and continuous variables, there are various ways to merge the two types of quantitative components.

7. Various alternative formulations exist, but they are all equivalent for the cases we consider here. See Lauritzen (1996) for technical details.

8. Also, one central debate has been about whether one can learn causal structures from data in a reliable or systematic manner. This issue is clearly irrelevant to the question of whether cognitive representations are (approximately) graphical models.

9. There is a theory of cyclic graphical models (Richardson, 1996, 1997), but it describes feedback systems that have reached an equilibrium state, rather than the short-run dynamics leading to such a state.

10. More precisely, the data space is not constrained by the quantitative component if we have sufficient flexibility in its specification (e.g., allowing for nonlinear relationships in a DAG). If the quantitative component is restricted, then there can be additional, parameter-based constraints on the data space that can be perfectly represented.

11. We can make similar observations about any unshielded collider, though we might additionally need to condition on a set of variables.

4 Causal Cognition

1. Though we can have temporally extended feedback loops (e.g., supply—demand cycles), as discussed in sec. 3.2.

2. Of course, I actually learned about this causal relation because people told me about it. The important point here is that causal inference provides a way that I could have learned this causal relation if no one had told me.

3. This is not quite right, since these theories often never converge. More precisely, the conditional ΔP values are the stable points of Rescorla-Wagner-based dynamical theories.

4. In general, these models provide estimates of the expectation of E. If E is 0/1 binary, then the expectation is the same as the probability of $E = 1$. I focus on that case, since the quantitative component of the graphical model is not fully specified given a function only for E's expectation. Everything said about equation (4.2) holds, however, if the probability of E is replaced with an expectation over E.

5. A technical aside: in all the psychological theories, the causal strength of the background is given by $P(E \mid \neg C_1, \neg C_2, \ldots, \neg C_n)$, regardless of the equation used to infer the causal strengths of the C_i's. That is, the background's causal strength is not necessarily computed by using B as the "cause" in the psychological theory's inference equation.

6. If some of the cause variables are not binary, then one can complicate equation (4.3) in various natural ways to allow for partial causing or blocking.

7. In fact, if we explicitly incorporate upper and lower bounds on E's value, then we can derive a natural functional form that behaves like (i) a weighted sum when E ranges over the real numbers; (ii) the noisy-OR/AND function when E is 0/1; and (iii) an interesting, but complicated, function when E ranges over a bounded interval of reals. That is, there is potentially a single (complex) functional form that sub-

sumes both of these sets of cognitive models in a principled way. No one, however, has systematically explored this more general functional form; in particular, no experiments have tried to determine what behavior people exhibit in situation (iii).

8. As an aside, the difficulty of knowing exactly where to discuss this issue actually lends support for the "single representational store" thesis of this book. Inference about features in a causal-structure-based category seems to simultaneously involve causal reasoning and reasoning about concepts, although those two cognitive domains are often studied separately.

9. Of course, it would need to be a representation of asymmetric, intransitive relations, which rules out simple associative strengths. However, one could have a model of "directed associations" that was noncausal but nonetheless sufficed for inference from observations.

10. Similar observations can be made about research on the importance of "normative considerations" in causal attribution (Alicke, 1992; Hitchcock & Knobe, 2009; Knobe & Fraser, 2008). There are significant disagreements about the exact phenomena, and even more disagreement about what "norms" are. In light of this, it is unclear what the graphical-models-based framework would be expected to capture. Having said that, David Rose and I have proposed such a theory, based on the idea that people are selecting "reliable" causes, that fits nicely with (some of) those data (Rose & Danks, 2012).

11. I use the word "mechanism" to mean something both broader and weaker than the mechanisms discussed in some recent philosophy of science (Craver, 2007; Machamer, Darden, & Craver, 2000).

12. On the other hand, it is surprising that people weight mechanism knowledge so heavily given that they often have much less of it than they think (Rozenblit & Keil, 2002).

13. More precisely, these forces are vectors that combine using standard vector addition.

14. In general, interventions can be understood as changes (from outside the causal system) in one or more of the terms in the Markov factorization. In the case of hard interventions, this can involve changing a conditional probability term into an unconditional probability term, as in the example of an intervention on M in the main text. But in general, many other kinds of changes are possible, corresponding to "softer" interventions. Eberhardt and Scheines (2007) provide a systematic characterization of interventions, broadly construed.

15. There are also versions of this situation in which the driver's being drunk did matter, though he was stopped at a light. For example, perhaps he did not stop in the proper location because he was drunk. Those are not the cases that I have in mind.

16. The causal power theory of causal inference (Cheng, 1997) is based on exactly this type of metaphysical picture.

17. Remember that the nodes are spatial locations whose values are the objects at that location. So "not moving" just means that the node has the same value for t, t+1, and t+2.

18. One might doubt whether such a model could actually be specified, since "something else" is not necessarily well-defined. I share these doubts but grant (for the sake of argument) the possibility of such a model.

5 Concepts, Categories, and Inference

1. I will also not engage with philosophical analyses of concepts as whatever makes possible various propositional attitudes, as I agree with Machery (2009) that those involve a distinctly different project.

2. Recall that all the mathematical details are provided in section 5.5.

3. Anecdotally, more than one researcher has suggested to me that there is no point in looking at second-order features, since they are deterministic functions, so seemingly cannot provide any real increase in expressive power. The divergence between $\mathbf{GM}_{PC1}$ and $\mathbf{GM}_{PC2}$ clearly shows that this claim is false.

4. There are various technical caveats on the claims in this paragraph; see section 5.5 for details.

5. Cases when "importance" depends on what other concepts are possible at a moment will be modeled as aspects of categorization behavior.

6. Recall that the "|" symbol in a probability statement should be read as "given" or "conditional on."

7. As I noted, this issue concerns distinctively causal reasoning and so could equally well have been discussed in section 4.3. I would have made the same observations and arguments if we had examined it there.

8. The idea of translating psychological categorization into optimal distribution choice has previously been explored (Ashby & Alfonso-Reese, 1995; Ashby & Maddox, 1993; Myung, 1994; Nosofsky, 1990; Rosseel, 2002). The novel aspect here is the use of graphical models.

9. As an aside, notice that categorization can now be understood as "simple" inference of the value of this new variable. That is, categorization looks like a type of feature inference, though the relevant feature is special in many ways.

10. This model is similar in many respects to Heit's (1998) Bayesian model.

11. This model also easily captures empirical results about how people incorporate novel causal laws into existing concepts (Hadjichristidis, Sloman, Stevenson, & Over, 2004; Rehder, 2009).

12. This extension to second-order features is stronger than is strictly required. If we have second-order features, then we can weaken condition (b) of the definition of proper similarity function: we only need the prototype point to be a global maximum, not a maximum along each dimension. In practice, however, the stronger condition is always satisfied, and it makes the presentation significantly simpler.

13. This qualification is necessary because it is technically possible for there to be "parameter balancing" resulting in two different features being independent in the similarity function, though both depend on the exemplars. For more details, see the proof.

14. Recall that a double Laplace (exponential) distribution is $P(x) = \frac{1}{\sigma\sqrt{2}} e^{-\frac{\sqrt{2}|x-\mu|}{\sigma}}$, and the Gaussian (normal) distribution is $P(x) = \frac{1}{\sigma\sqrt{2}} e^{-\frac{(x-\mu)^2}{2\sigma^2}}$.

15. For GCMs with $d = 2$, the general equation for Gaussian variance is $\sigma_i^2 = m/2c\alpha_i$.

16. There is a complication here: optimal categorization requires that I compute $P(C \mid X)$, but then my *decision* should be whichever concept is most probable; I should not optimally or rationally "probability match" by choosing probabilistically based on $P(C \mid X)$. Given that people (sometimes) probability match in this way, we need to either explain why people are only "partially rational" or else provide a normative justification of probability matching (Eberhardt & Danks, 2011). As I am not particularly focused here on the normativity of human cognition, I will simply note this issue, rather than attempt to solve it.

17. F might also be the child or parent of some other feature(s) in G. I leave aside that complication.

6 Decision Making via Graphical Models

1. As a simple example, suppose the graph is $C \rightarrow T$, and both are binary variables. In that case, the cue validity of C is $P(T \mid C)(1 - P(T \mid \neg C))$, and those two probabilities are parameters in the full graphical model.

2. As noted in previous discussions of interventions, I focus in the main text on "hard" interventions, rather than the broader class of "soft" ones (Eberhardt & Scheines, 2007). Human ability to make decisions about such soft interventions is almost completely unexplored.

3. "Acceptable" can be defined in many ways, whether simply exceeding some fixed threshold or a more sophisticated stopping rule, such as selecting the first "anomalously high" expected value. Importantly, this algorithm does *not* instantiate

the so-called secretary problem, since the sequence of action values is not one of samples from a random variable; the sequence is (deliberately) biased to have higher values earlier in the sequence. As a result, stopping rules for the secretary problem (e.g., Bruss, 1984) would need to be modified to fit this case.

4. This statement can be made precise and proven correct under natural assumptions, but the theorem is significantly more complicated than this sentence and requires substantial technical machinery that would distract from the main point.

7 Unifying Cognition

1. Machery (2010, p. 237) provides a clear statement of worry about this possible confusion.

2. The notion of "silo" here is not the same as a "module" in the style of Fodor (1983) and others. This chapter focuses solely on the extent to which there are shared representations, so no commitments are made (in any direction) with respect to properties such as automaticity, informational encapsulation, and so forth. I revisit issues of modularity in section 9.1.

3. As this restriction suggests, even the "one/no silo" view considered here restricts the scope of processes in certain ways. For example, I am principally concerned with "higher-level" cognition rather than, say, low-level auditory processing.

4. Some of those experiments are being conducted right now.

5. Waldmann and Hagmayer suggest that there could be a dynamic process in which the concept is revised if its use leads to suboptimal (in some sense) causal structures. Their data do not really speak to this possibility, though, so we cannot draw any conclusions about it from their paper.

6. Unsupervised concept learning involves the construction of concepts from unlabeled instances, usually based on the statistics of the observed features. Most psychological experiments on concept learning use supervised concept learning in which participants are provided with labeled instances (e.g., "this one is a dax!").

7. Experimentally, it is not quite this simple, since we also have to match the difficulty of the two different learning tasks, which can be nontrivial (Zhu & Danks, 2007).

8. As with all cognitive science experiments, alternative interpretations are possible. For example, perhaps people engage in explicit recall of instances of M_1 and M_2 during learning and thereby construct the explicit contrasts in a dynamic fashion. The goal of this (and other) experiments is not to produce incontrovertible evidence that the shared representational store view *must* be correct, since that goal is presumably impossible. Rather, the intention is simply to constrain the possibility space in such a way that the single-store view is the most plausible or natural one.

9. Presumably, people do learn distinctively causal structures when they are explicitly told that the relations that underlie the category are causal.

10. Statistical data alone do not suffice to distinguish between the true causal structure $A \rightarrow X \rightarrow B$ and the two structures $A \leftarrow X \rightarrow B$ and $A \leftarrow X \leftarrow B$. However, the true causal structure is learnable with minimal additional assumptions, such as (i) the temporal information that A occurs before X, or (ii) the constraint that the exogenous variable is the only one that ever occurs spontaneously.

11. One might object that the minimalist should predict only that medical professionals will be indifferent between the causal structures. Given that one structure was known to be true, people have a good reason to use that one, and so (the objection concludes) the minimalist should actually predict that people will believe the (known-to-be) true causal structure. This objection overstates the minimalist's commitments, however, since there could be multiple reasons to resolve the indifference in one direction or the other. In particular, Feltovich et al. (1989) argue that the "backward" conception coheres much better with other everyday causal beliefs and thus can justifiably be preferred.

8 Alternative Approaches

1. As a result, one could argue (as does Anderson, 2007) that schema-centered unifications are not really cognitive architectures, since they do not specify a shared cognitive machinery. Leaving aside that terminological issue, these accounts are clearly motivated by a desire to figure out what "binds" (in some sense) cognition together.

2. Neural plausibility can be justified in multiple ways, such as using neuronlike elements in the model or exhibiting appropriate behavioral changes when the model experiences a simulated "lesion." See section 8.2.1.

3. Proponents of Soar sometimes use the slogan "Behavior = Architecture + Content," where "Architecture" refers to Soar itself (Lehman, Laird, & Rosenbloom, 2006). Their hope is that if we get the process architecture right, then we can generate behavior just by plugging in the content that happens to obtain in a particular case. In the language of this slogan, my view can partly be understood as saying "Content matters."

4. In particular, I make almost no effort to engage with the broader questions—particularly in philosophy of science, mind, and psychology—raised by connectionism. Many excellent books explore these issues, including some that collect a variety of viewpoints (Horgan & Tienson, 1996, 1991; Ramsey, Stich, & Rumelhart, 1991).

5. This is a little too quick, since the graph alone determines only a factorization of the joint probability distribution, not the actual data likelihoods. In practice, one

typically provides a parametric family for the model and a probability distribution over those parameters and then integrates them out to determine the likelihood.

6. I will use these two terms relatively interchangeably, though *generative* is arguably the more general (and more useful) one.

7. More specifically, those realist commitments would be rejected by proponents of Bayesian models who stay at the computational level. As noted earlier, some research programs are beginning to focus on understanding the representations and processes that actually underlie the (approximately) Bayesian behavior.

8. There is an interesting similarity between this constraint and my theoretical arguments in chapter 7 in favor of a single-process view.

9. One issue that I will *not* discuss is whether they can account for the same empirical data. Sigma can presumably account for almost all the same data as Soar (Laird, 2012), though an exact mapping that subsumes Soar under Sigma does not yet seem to have been provided. Sigma has also been applied to several more realistic tasks (Chen et al., 2011; Rosenbloom et al., 2013) and has shown great promise. It has not, however, been systematically connected with the cognitive psychology data that have been the empirical focus of this book. Thus whether one outperforms the other is simply unclear.

10. One needs to be careful here about what is considered a "distinct process." Feature inference and categorization (see chap. 5), for example, are not necessarily distinct processes, since both can be understood as conditional probability estimation. In contrast, inference given observation and inference given intervention are truly distinct processes, since the latter has a step that the former does not have.

9 Broader Implications

1. The answers are partial because almost all the learning accounts show only how to extract relevance relations for a predefined set of variables, events, or other entities corresponding to the graphical model nodes. The accounts do not say why the learner focused on that particular set of entities in the first place, so they do not provide a full account of how relevance relations can be learned. A fully developed account of relevance learning would likely have to incorporate other cognitive processes, such as generalized attentional mechanisms.

2. We can also build webs for concepts that are not mutually exclusive, but it gets a bit more complicated.

3. See Glymour (2007) or Woodward (2006) for more about just what it means to be the "right" causal variable in some situation.

4. A different diagnosis of these problems is that we do not understand what is required to properly specify an intervention (Eberhardt, 2014). That might explain

the issues in these examples, but inference problems arise for multiple edge types even when we are not trying to perform an intervention.

5. Neuropsychology primarily involves investigating the behavior of individuals who have had brain lesions to try to determine both which cognitive processes are separable from one another and where certain types of processing are likely to occur.

6. One natural idea is to have populations of neurons code for variable values, and then inference consists in something like spreading activation. There are massive interconnections throughout the brain; it is not just a feed-forward machine, and that interconnectivity could be the means by which many types of inference are carried out. Of course, much more work needs to be done to make this idea fully formed, including an explanation of why inference is sometimes blocked, such as after an intervention.

References

Ahn, W.-K., & Bailenson, J. (1996). Causal attribution as a search for underlying mechanisms: An explanation of the conjunction fallacy and the discounting principle. *Cognitive Psychology, 31*, 82–123.

Ahn, W.-K., Kalish, C. W., Medin, D. L., & Gelman, S. A. (1995). The role of covariation versus mechanism information in causal attribution. *Cognition, 54*, 299–352.

Ahn, W.-K., Kim, N. S., Lassaline, M. E., & Dennis, M. J. (2000). Causal status as a determinant of feature centrality. *Cognitive Psychology, 41*(4), 361–416.

Aizawa, K. (2009). Neuroscience and multiple realization: A reply to Bechtel and Mundale. *Synthese, 167*, 493–510.

Alchourrón, C. E., Gärdenfors, P., & Makinson, D. (1985). On the logic of theory change: Partial meet contraction and revision functions. *Journal of Symbolic Logic, 50*(2), 510–530.

Alicke, M. (1992). Culpable causation. *Journal of Personality and Social Psychology, 36*, 368–378.

Anderson, J. R. (1990). *The adaptive character of thought.* Hillsdale, NJ: Erlbaum.

Anderson, J. R. (1991a). Is human cognition adaptive? *Behavioral and Brain Sciences, 14*, 471–484.

Anderson, J. R. (1991b). The adaptive nature of human categorization. *Psychological Review, 98*, 409–429.

Anderson, J. R. (2005). Human symbol manipulation within an integrated cognitive architecture. *Cognitive Science, 29*, 313–341.

Anderson, J. R. (2007). *How can the human mind occur in the physical universe?* New York: Oxford University Press.

Anderson, J. R., & Betz, J. (2001). A hybrid model of categorization. *Psychonomic Bulletin and Review, 8*(4), 629–647.

Anderson, J. R., Bothell, D., Byrne, M. D., Douglass, S., Lebiere, C., & Qin, Y. (2004). An integrated theory of the mind. *Psychological Review, 111*(4), 1036–1060.

Anderson, J. R., Carter, C. S., Fincham, J. M., Qin, Y., Ravizza, S. M., & Rosenberg-Lee, M. (2008). Using fMRI to test models of complex cognition. *Cognitive Science, 32*, 1323–1348.

Anderson, J. R., Qin, Y., Jung, K.-J., & Carter, C. S. (2007). Information-processing modules and their relative modality specificity. *Cognitive Psychology, 54*, 185–217.

Andersson, S. A., Madigan, D., & Perlman, M. D. (1996). An alternative Markov property for chain graphs. In F. V. Jensen & E. Horvitz (Eds.), *Proceedings of the 12th Annual Conference on Uncertainty in Artificial Intelligence* (pp. 40–48). San Francisco: Morgan Kaufmann.

Ariely, D. (2008). *Predictably irrational: The hidden forces that shape our decisions*. New York: Harper Collins.

Ashby, F. G., & Alfonso-Reese, L. A. (1995). Categorization as probability density estimation. *Journal of Mathematical Psychology, 39*, 216–233.

Ashby, F. G., Alfonso-Reese, L. A., Turken, A. U., & Waldron, E. M. (1998). A neuropsychological theory of multiple systems in category learning. *Psychological Review, 105*(3), 442–481.

Ashby, F. G., & Maddox, W. T. (1993). Relations between prototype, exemplar, and decision bound models of categorization. *Journal of Mathematical Psychology, 37*, 372–400.

Ashby, F. G., & Waldron, E. M. (2000). The neuropsychological bases of category learning. *Current Directions in Psychological Science, 9*(1), 10–14.

Bailenson, J. N., Shum, M. S., Atran, S., Medin, D. L., & Coley, J. D. (2002). A bird's eye view: Biological categorization and reasoning within and across cultures. *Cognition, 84*, 1–53.

Baker, C. L., Saxe, R., & Tenenbaum, J. B. (2009). Action understanding as inverse planning. *Cognition, 113*, 329–349.

Balzer, W., Moulines, C. U., & Sneed, J. D. (1987). *An architectonic for science*. Dordrecht: Reidel.

Barendregt, M., & van Rappard, J. F. H. (2004). Reductionism revisited: On the role of reduction in psychology. *Theory and Psychology, 14*(4), 453–474.

Barrett, H. C., & Kurzban, R. (2006). Modularity in cognition: Framing the debate. *Psychological Review, 113*(3), 628–647.

Barsalou, L. W. (1999). Perceptual symbol systems. *Behavioral and Brain Sciences, 22*, 577–660.

Barsalou, L. W. (2008). Grounded cognition. *Annual Review of Psychology, 59,* 617–645.

Batterman, R. W. (2002). *The devil in the details: Asymptotic reasoning in explanation, reduction, and emergence.* Oxford: Oxford University Press.

Bechara, A., Damasio, A. R., Damasio, H., & Anderson, S. W. (1994). Insensitivity to future consequences following damage to human prefrontal cortex. *Cognition, 50*(1–3), 7–15. doi:http://dx.doi.org/10.1016/0010-0277(94)90018-3.

Bechara, A., Tranel, D., & Damasio, H. (2000). Characterization of the decision-making deficit of patients with ventromedial prefrontal cortex lesions. *Brain, 123*(11), 2189–2202.

Bechlivanidis, C., & Lagnado, D. A. (2013). Does the "why" tell us the "when"? *Psychological Science, 24*(8), 1563–1572.

Bechtel, W., & Mundale, J. (1999). Multiple realizability revisited: Linking cognitive and neural states. *Philosophy of Science, 66,* 175–207.

Beukema, P. (2011). *Causal inference with a recurrent neural network.* (M.S. Thesis). Philosophy Department, Carnegie Mellon University, Pittsburgh, PA.

Bickle, J. (1998). *Psychoneural reduction: The new wave.* Cambridge, MA: MIT Press.

Bickle, J. (2002). Concepts structured through reduction: A structuralist resource illuminates the consolidation-long-term potentiation (LTP) link. *Synthese, 130,* 123–133.

Bickle, J. (2003). *Philosophy and neuroscience: A ruthlessly reductive account.* Dordrecht: Kluwer Academic.

Bishop, C. M. (2006). *Pattern recognition and machine learning.* Springer.

Blaisdell, A. P., Sawa, K., Leising, K. J., & Waldmann, M. R. (2006). Causal reasoning in rats. *Science, 311,* 1020–1022.

Blakemore, S.-J., Fonlupt, P., Pachot-Clouard, M., Darmon, C., Boyer, P., Meltzoff, A. N., et al. (2001). How the brain perceives causality: An event-related fMRI study. *Neuroreport, 12*(17), 3741–3746.

Bollen, K. A. (1989). *Structural equations with latent variables.* New York: John Wiley & Sons.

Bonawitz, E. B., Griffiths, T. L., & Schulz, L. E. (2006). Modeling cross-domain causal learning in preschoolers as Bayesian inference. In R. Sun & N. Miyake (Eds.), *Proceedings of the 28th Annual Conference of the Cognitive Science Society* (pp. 89–94). Mahwah, NJ: Erlbaum.

Boutilier, C., Friedman, N., Goldszmidt, M., & Koller, D. (1996). Context-specific independence in Bayesian networks. In *Proceedings of the 12th Annual Conference on Uncertainty in Artificial Intelligence* (pp. 115–123). San Francisco: Morgan Kaufmann.

Bovens, L., & Hartmann, S. (2003). *Bayesian epistemology*. Oxford: Oxford University Press.

Broder, A. (2000). Assessing the empirical validity of the "take-the-best" heuristic as a model of human probabilistic inference. *Journal of Experimental Psychology: Learning, Memory, and Cognition, 26*(5), 1332–1346.

Bruss, F. T. (1984). A unified approach to a class of best choice problems with an unknown number of options. *Annals of Probability, 12*, 882–889.

Butts, C., & Carley, K. (2007). Structural change and homeostasis in organizations: A decision-theoretic approach. *Journal of Mathematical Sociology, 31*(4), 295–321.

Cacioppo, J. T., & Petty, R. E. (1982). The need for cognition. *Journal of Personality and Social Psychology, 42*(1), 116–131.

Cacioppo, J. T., Petty, R. E., & Kao, C. F. (1984). The efficient assessment of need for cognition. *Journal of Personality Assessment, 48*(3), 306–307.

Carey, S. (1985). *Conceptual change in childhood*. Cambridge, MA: MIT Press.

Carruthers, P. (2006). *The architecture of the mind*. Oxford: Oxford University Press.

Cartwright, N. (1983). *How the laws of physics lie*. New York: Clarendon.

Cartwright, N. (1989). *Nature's capacities and their measurement*. Oxford: Oxford University Press.

Cartwright, N. (2002). Against modularity, the causal Markov condition, and any link between the two: Comments on Hausman and Woodward. *British Journal for the Philosophy of Science, 53*, 411–453.

Catena, A., Maldonado, A., & Candido, A. (1998). The effect of the frequency of judgment and the type of trials on covariation learning. *Journal of Experimental Psychology: Human Perception and Performance, 24*(2), 481–495.

Chater, N., & Oaksford, M. (Eds.). (2008). *The probabilistic mind: Prospects for Bayesian cognitive science*. Oxford: Oxford University Press.

Chater, N., Oaksford, M., Nakisa, R., & Redington, M. (2003). Fast, frugal, and rational: How rational norms explain behavior. *Organizational Behavior and Human Decision Processes, 90*, 63–86.

Chater, N., Tenenbaum, J. B., & Yuille, A. (2006). Probabilistic models of cognition: Conceptual foundations. *Trends in Cognitive Sciences, 10*(7), 287–291.

Chen, J., Demski, A., Han, T., Morency, L.-P., Pynadath, D. V., Rafidi, N., et al. (2011). Fusing symbolic and decision-theoretic problem solving + perception in a graphical cognitive architecture. In A. V. Samsonovich & K. R. Jóhannsdóttir (Eds.), *Proceedings of the 2nd International Conference on Biologically Inspired Cognitive Architecture (BICA-2011)* (pp. 64–72). Amsterdam: IOS Press.

Chen, Y., & Welling, M. (2012). Bayesian structure learning for Markov random fields with a spike and slab prior. In N. de Freitas & K. Murphy (Eds.), *Proceedings of the 28th Annual Conference on Uncertainty in Artificial Intelligence (UAI-2012)* (pp. 174–184). Corvallis, OR: AUAI Press.

Cheng, P. W. (1997). From covariation to causation: A causal power theory. *Psychological Review, 104*, 367–405.

Cheng, P. W., & Novick, L. R. (1992). Covariation in natural causal induction. *Psychological Review, 99*(2), 365–382.

Chickering, D. M. (2002). Optimal structure identification with greedy search. *Journal of Machine Learning Research, 3*, 507–554.

Chin-Parker, S., & Ross, B. H. (2002). The effect of category learning on sensitivity to within-category correlations. *Memory and Cognition, 30*, 353–362.

Chin-Parker, S., & Ross, B. H. (2004). Diagnosticity and prototypicality in category learning: A comparison of inference learning and classification learning. *Journal of Experimental Psychology: Learning, Memory, and Cognition, 30*, 216–226.

Cho, B., Rosenbloom, P. S., & Dolan, C. P. (1991). Neuro-Soar: A neural-network architecture for goal-oriented behavior. In K. J. Hammond & D. Gentner (Eds.), *Proceedings of the Thirteenth Annual Conference of the Cognitive Science Society* (pp. 673–677). Hillsdale, NJ: Erlbaum.

Choi, H., & Scholl, B. J. (2004). Effects of grouping and attention on the perception of causality. *Perception and Psychophysics, 66*(6), 926–942.

Choi, H., & Scholl, B. J. (2006). Perceiving causality after the fact: Postdiction in the temporal dynamics of causal perception. *Perception, 35*, 385–399.

Chu, T., & Glymour, C. (2008). Search for additive time series causal models. *Journal of Machine Learning Research, 9*, 967–991.

Churchland, P. M. (1981). Eliminative materialism and the propositional attitudes. *Journal of Philosophy, 78*, 67–90.

Churchland, P. M. (1985). Reduction, qualia, and the direct introspection of brain states. *Journal of Philosophy, 82*, 1–22.

Collins, D. J., & Shanks, D. R. (2006). Conformity to the Power PC theory of causal induction depends on the type of probe question. *Quarterly Journal of Experimental Psychology, 59*(2), 225–232.

Cormier, S. M., & Hagman, J. D. (Eds.). (1987). *Transfer of learning: Contemporary research and applications*. San Diego, CA: Academic Press.

Corrado, G., & Doya, K. (2007). Understanding neural coding through the model-based analysis of decision making. *Journal of Neuroscience, 27*(31), 8178–8180.

Cosmides, L., & Tooby, J. (1992). Cognitive adaptations for social exchange. In J. H. Barkow, L. Cosmides, & J. Tooby (Eds.), *The adapted mind: Evolutionary psychology and the generation of culture* (pp. 163–228). Oxford: Oxford University Press.

Craver, C. F. (2007). *Explaining the brain: Mechanisms and the mosaic unity of neuroscience*. Oxford: Oxford University Press.

Csibra, G., Gergely, G., Biro, S., Koos, O., & Brockbank, M. (1999). Goal attribution without agency cues: The perception of "pure reason" in infancy. *Cognition, 72*, 237–267.

Danks, D. (2003). Equilibria of the Rescorla-Wagner model. *Journal of Mathematical Psychology, 47*, 109–121.

Danks, D. (2004). Constraint-based human causal learning. In M. Lovett, C. Schunn, C. Leviere, & P. Munro (Eds.), *Proceedings of the 6th International Conference on Cognitive Modeling* (pp. 342–343). Mahwah, NJ: Erlbaum.

Danks, D. (2007a). Causal learning from observations and manipulations. In M. C. Lovett & P. Shah (Eds.), *Thinking with data* (pp. 359–388). Mahwah, NJ: Erlbaum.

Danks, D. (2007b). Theory unification and graphical models in human categorization. In A. Gopnik & L. E. Schulz (Eds.), *Causal learning: Psychology, philosophy, and computation* (pp. 173–189). Oxford: Oxford University Press.

Danks, D. (2008). Rational analyses, instrumentalism, and implementations. In N. Chater & M. Oaksford (Eds.), *The probabilistic mind: Prospects for Bayesian cognitive science* (pp. 59–75). Oxford: Oxford University Press.

Danks, D. (2009). The psychology of causal perception and reasoning. In H. Beebee, C. Hitchcock, & P. Menzies (Eds.), *Oxford handbook of causation*. Oxford: Oxford University Press.

Danks, D. (2014). Functions and cognitive bases for the concept of actual causation. *Erkenntnis*. doi:10.1007/s10670-013-9439-2.

Danks, D., Griffiths, T. L., & Tenenbaum, J. B. (2003). Dynamical causal learning. In S. Becker, S. Thrun, & K. Obermayer (Eds.), *Advances in neural information processing systems* (Vol. 15, pp. 67–74). Cambridge, MA: MIT Press.

Daw, N. D., Niv, Y., & Dayan, P. (2005). Uncertainty-based competition between prefrontal and dorsolateral striatal systems for behavioral control. *Nature Neuroscience, 8*, 1704–1711.

Deneve, S., Latham, P. E., & Pouget, A. (2001). Efficient computation and cue integration with noisy population codes. *Nature Neuroscience, 4*(8), 826–831.

Denison, S., Bonawitz, E. B., Gopnik, A., & Griffiths, T. L. (2013). Rational variability in children's causal inferences: The Sampling Hypothesis. *Cognition, 126*(2), 285–300.

Desimone, R., & Duncan, J. (1995). Neural mechanisms of selective visual attention. *Annual Review of Neuroscience, 18*, 193–222.

Dizadji-Bahmani, F., Frigg, R., & Hartmann, S. (2010). Who's afraid of Nagelian reduction? *Erkenntnis, 73*, 393–412.

Doumas, L. A. A., Hummel, J. E., & Sandhofer, C. M. (2008). A theory of the discovery and predication of relational concepts. *Psychological Review, 115*(1), 1–43.

Dowe, P. (2007). *Physical causation*. Cambridge: Cambridge University Press.

Downing, P. E. (2000). Interactions between visual working memory and selective attention. *Psychological Science, 11*, 467–473.

Doya, K., Ishii, S., Pouget, A., & Rao, R. P. N. (Eds.). (2007). *Bayesian brain: Probabilistic approaches to neural coding*. Cambridge, MA: MIT Press.

Dretske, F. (1981). *Knowledge and the flow of information*. Cambridge, MA: MIT Press.

Dretske, F. (1988). *Explaining behavior: Reasons in a world of causes*. Cambridge, MA: MIT Press.

Drewitz, U., & Brandenburg, S. (2012). Memory and contextual change in causal learning. In N. Rußwinkel, U. Drewitz, & H. van Rijn (Eds.), *Proceedings of the 11th International Conference on Cognitive Modeling (ICCM-2012)* (pp. 265–270). Berlin: Universitätsverlag der TU Berlin.

Eberhardt, F. (2014). Direct causes and the trouble with soft interventions. *Erkenntnis*.

Eberhardt, F., & Danks, D. (2011). Confirmation in the cognitive sciences: The problematic case of Bayesian models. *Minds and Machines, 21*(3), 389–410.

Eberhardt, F., & Scheines, R. (2007). Interventions and causal inference. *Philosophy of Science, 74*(5), 981–995.

Eliasmith, C., & Anderson, C. H. (2002). *Neural engineering: Computation, representation, and dynamics in neurobiological systems*. Cambridge, MA: MIT Press.

Eliasmith, C., Stewart, T. C., Choo, X., Bekolay, T., DeWolf, T., Tang, Y., et al. (2012). A large-scale model of the functioning brain. *Science, 338*(6111), 1202–1205.

Elman, J. L. (1991). Distributed representations, simple recurrent networks, and grammatical structure. *Machine Learning, 7*, 194–220.

Feltovich, P. J., Spiro, R. J., & Coulson, R. L. (1989). The nature of conceptual understanding in biomedicine: The deep structure of complex ideas and the development of misconceptions. In D. A. Evans & V. L. Patel (Eds.), *Cognitive science in medicine: Biomedical modeling* (pp. 113–172). Cambridge, MA: MIT Press.

Fernbach, P. M., Hagmayer, Y., & Sloman, S. A. (2014). Effort denial in self-deception. *Organizational Behavior and Human Decision Processes, 123*, 1–8.

Fernbach, P. M., & Sloman, S. A. (2009). Causal learning with local computations. *Journal of Experimental Psychology: Learning, Memory, and Cognition, 35*(3), 678–693.

Fodor, J. A. (1974). Special sciences: Or the disunity of science as a working hypothesis. *Synthese, 28*, 97–115.

Fodor, J. A. (1983). *The modularity of mind.* Cambridge, MA: MIT Press.

Fodor, J. A. (1997). Special sciences: Still autonomous after all these years. *Noûs, 31*, 149–163.

Fodor, J. A. (2001). *The mind doesn't work that way: The scope and limits of computational psychology.* Cambridge, MA: MIT Press.

Fodor, J. A., & Pylyshyn, Z. W. (1988). Connectionism and cognitive architecture: A critical analysis. *Cognition, 78*, 3–71.

Frank, M. C., & Goodman, N. D. (2012). Predicting pragmatic reasoning in language games. *Science, 336*(6084), 998.

Frank, M. J., & Claus, E. D. (2006). Anatomy of a decision: Striato-orbitofrontal interactions in reinforcement learning. *Psychological Review, 113*(2), 300–326.

Frey, B. J., & Kschischang, F. R. (1996). Probability propagation and iterative decoding. In S. P. Meyn & W. K. Jenkins (Eds.), *Proceedings of the 34th Allerton Conference on Communications, Control, and Computing* (pp. 482–493). Champaign-Urbana, IL: University of Illinois.

Gaifman, H., & Snir, M. (1982). Probabilities over rich languages, testing, and randomness. *Journal of Symbolic Logic, 47*(3), 495–548.

Gao, T., Newman, G. E., & Scholl, B. J. (2009). The psychophysics of chasing: A case study in the perception of animacy. *Cognitive Psychology, 59*, 154–179.

Garcia-Retamero, R., & Hoffrage, U. (2006). How causal knowledge simplifies decision-making. *Minds and Machines, 16*, 365–380.

Garcia-Retamero, R., Muller, S. M., Cantena, A., & Maldonado, A. (2009). The power of causal beliefs and conflicting evidence on causal judgments and decision making. *Learning and Motivation, 40*(3), 284–297.

Garcia-Retamero, R., Wallin, A., & Dieckmann, A. (2007). Does causal knowledge help us be faster and more frugal in our decisions? *Memory and Cognition, 35*(6), 1399–1409.

Gärdenfors, P. (Ed.). (2003). *Belief revision.* Cambridge: Cambridge University Press.

Geiger, D., Verma, T., & Pearl, J. (1989). D-separation: From theorems to algorithms. In M. Henrion, R. Shachter, L. Kanal, & J. Lemmer (Eds.), *Proceedings of the 5th Annual Conference on Uncertainty in Artificial Intelligence* (pp. 118–125). New York: Elsevier Science.

Gelman, S. A. (1988). The development of induction within natural kind and artifact categories. *Cognitive Psychology, 20*(1), 65–95.

Gelman, S. A., & O'Reilly, A. W. (1988). Children's inductive inferences within superordinate categories: The role of language and category structure. *Child Development, 59*(4), 876–887.

Gergely, G., Nadasdy, Z., Csibra, G., & Biro, S. (1995). Taking the intentional stance at 12 months of age. *Cognition, 56*, 165–193.

Gerstenberg, T., Goodman, N. D., Lagnado, D. A., & Tenenbaum, J. B. (2012). Noisy Newtons: Unifying process and dependency accounts of causal attribution. In N. Miyake, D. Peebles, & R. P. Cooper (Eds.), *Proceedings of the 34th Annual Conference of the Cognitive Science Society* (pp. 378–383). Austin, TX: Cognitive Science Society.

Gigerenzer, G. (2000). *Adaptive thinking: Rationality in the real world.* New York: Oxford University Press.

Gigerenzer, G., Czerlinski, J., & Martignon, L. (1999). How good are fast and frugal heuristics? In J. Shanteau, B. Mellers, & D. Schum (Eds.), *Decision research from Bayesian approaches to normative systems* (pp. 81–103). Norwell, MA: Kluwer.

Gigerenzer, G., & Goldstein, D. G. (1996). Reasoning the fast and frugal way: Models of bounded rationality. *Psychological Review, 103*, 650–669.

Glimcher, P. W., & Rustichini, A. (2004). Neuroeconomics: The consilience of brain and decision. *Science, 306*, 447–452.

Gluck, M. A., & Bower, G. H. (1988). From conditioning to category learning: An adaptive network model. *Journal of Experimental Psychology: General, 117*, 227–247.

Glymour, C. (1998). Learning causes: Psychological explanations of causal explanation. *Minds and Machines, 8*, 39–60.

Glymour, C. (1999). Rabbit hunting. *Synthese, 121*, 55–78.

Glymour, C. (2002). *The mind's arrows: Bayes nets and graphical causal models in psychology*. Cambridge, MA: MIT Press.

Glymour, C. (2003). Learning, prediction, and causal Bayes nets. *Trends in Cognitive Sciences, 7*(1), 43–48.

Glymour, C. (2007). When is a brain like the planet? *Philosophy of Science, 74*, 330–347.

Glymour, C., & Danks, D. (2007). Reasons as causes in Bayesian epistemology. *Journal of Philosophy, 104*(9), 464–474.

Glymour, C., & Meek, C. (1994). Conditioning and intervening. *British Journal for the Philosophy of Science, 45*(4), 1001–1021.

Gold, J. I., & Shadlen, M. N. (2007). The neural basis of decision making. *Annual Review of Neuroscience, 30*, 535–574.

Goldstein, D. G., & Gigerenzer, G. (1999). The recognition heuristic: How ignorance makes us smart. In G. Gigerenzer & P. M. Todd (Eds.), *Simple heuristics that make us smart* (pp. 37–58). New York: Oxford University Press.

Goodman, N. D., Tenenbaum, J. B., Feldman, J., & Griffiths, T. L. (2008). A rational analysis of rule-based concept learning. *Cognitive Science, 32*(1), 108–154.

Gopnik, A. (1988). Conceptual and semantic development as theory change. *Mind and Language, 3*, 197–217.

Gopnik, A., Glymour, C., Sobel, D. M., Schulz, L. E., Kushnir, T., & Danks, D. (2004). A theory of causal learning in children: Causal maps and Bayes nets. *Psychological Review, 111*(1), 3–32.

Gopnik, A., & Meltzoff, A. N. (1997). *Words, thoughts, and theories*. Cambridge, MA: MIT Press.

Gorski, N. A., & Laird, J. E. (2011). Learning to use episodic memory. *Cognitive Systems Research, 12*, 144–153.

Gravier, G., & Sigelle, M. (1999). Markov random field modeling for speech recognition. *Australian Journal of Intelligent Information Processing Systems, 5*, 245–252.

Griffiths, T. L., Chater, N., Kemp, C., Perfors, A., & Tenenbaum, J. B. (2010). Probabilistic models of cognition: Exploring representations and inductive biases. *Trends in Cognitive Sciences, 14*, 357–364.

Griffiths, T. L., Kemp, C., & Tenenbaum, J. B. (2008). Bayesian models of cognition. In R. Sun (Ed.), *The Cambridge handbook of computational cognitive modeling*. Cambridge: Cambridge University Press.

Griffiths, T. L., & Tenenbaum, J. B. (2005). Structure and strength in causal induction. *Cognitive Psychology, 51*(4), 334–384.

Griffiths, T. L., Vul, E., & Sanborn, A. N. (2012). Bridging levels of analysis for probabilistic models of cognition. *Current Directions in Psychological Science, 21*(4), 263–268.

Grossman, M., Smith, E. E., Koenig, P., Glosser, G., DeVita, C., Moore, P., et al. (2002). The neural basis for categorization in semantic memory. *NeuroImage, 17*, 1549–1561.

Grush, R. (1997). The architecture of representation. *Philosophical Psychology, 10*(1), 5–23.

Gunetti, P., Dodd, T., & Thompson, H. (2013). Simulation of a Soar-based autonomous mission management system for unmanned aircraft. *Journal of Aerospace Information Systems, 10*(2), 53–70.

Gunetti, P., & Thompson, H. (2008). A Soar-based planning agent for gas-turbine engine control and health management. In M. J. Chung & P. Misra (Eds.), *Proceedings of the 17th World Congress of the International Federation of Automatic Control* (pp. 2200–2205). Oxford: Pergamon Press.

Hadjichristidis, C., Sloman, S., Stevenson, R., & Over, D. (2004). Feature centrality and property induction. *Cognitive Science, 28*, 45–74.

Hagmayer, Y., & Meder, B. (2013). Repeated causal decision making. *Journal of Experimental Psychology: Learning, Memory, and Cognition, 39*(1), 33–50.

Hagmayer, Y., Meder, B., Osman, M., Mangold, S., & Lagnado, D. A. (2010). Spontaneous causal learning while controlling a dynamic system. *Open Psychology Journal, 3*, 145–162.

Hagmayer, Y., & Sloman, S. A. (2006). Causal vs. evidential decision making in Newcomb's Paradox. In R. Sun & N. Miyake (Eds.), *Proceedings of the 28th Annual Conference of the Cognitive Science Society* (p. 2497). Mahwah, NJ: Erlbaum.

Hagmayer, Y., & Sloman, S. A. (2009). Decision makers conceive of their choices as interventions. *Journal of Experimental Psychology: General, 138*(1), 22–38.

Hamlin, J. K., Ullman, T., Tenenbaum, J., Goodman, N., & Baker, C. (2013). The mentalistic basis of core social cognition: Experiments in preverbal infants and a computational model. *Developmental Science, 16*(2), 209–226. doi:10.1111/desc.12017.

Hammersley, J. M., & Clifford, P. E. (1971). Markov fields on finite graphs and lattices. Unpublished manuscript.

Harlow, L. L., Muliak, S. A., & Steiger, J. H. (Eds.). (1997). *What if there were no significance tests?* Mahwah, NJ: Erlbaum.

Harnad, S. (1994). Computation is just interpretable symbol manipulation; cognition isn't. *Minds and Machines, 4*, 379–390.

Haskell, R. E. (2000). *Transfer of learning: Cognition, instruction, and reasoning.* San Diego, CA: Academic Press.

Hattori, M., & Oaksford, M. (2007). Adaptive non-interventional heuristics for covariation detection in causal induction: Model comparison and rational analysis. *Cognitive Science, 31*, 765–814.

Hausman, D. M., & Woodward, J. (1999). Independence, invariance and the causal Markov condition. *British Journal for the Philosophy of Science, 50*, 521–583.

Hausman, D. M., & Woodward, J. (2004). Modularity and the causal Markov assumption: A restatement. *British Journal for the Philosophy of Science, 55*(1), 147–161.

Heckerman, D. (1998). A tutorial on learning with Bayesian networks. In M. I. Jordan (Ed.), *Learning in graphical models* (pp. 301–354). Cambridge, MA: MIT Press.

Heider, F., & Simmel, M.-A. (1944). An experimental study of apparent behavior. *American Journal of Psychology, 57*, 243–249.

Heit, E. (1998). A Bayesian analysis of some forms of inductive reasoning. In M. Oaksford & N. Chater (Eds.), *Rational models of cognition* (pp. 248–274). New York: Oxford University Press.

Heit, E. (2000). Properties of inductive reasoning. *Psychonomic Bulletin and Review, 7*(4), 569–592.

Heit, E., & Rubinstein, J. (1994). Similarity and property effects in inductive reasoning. *Journal of Experimental Psychology: Learning, Memory, and Cognition, 20*(2), 411–422.

Hinton, G. E., & Shallice, T. (1991). Lesioning an attractor network: Investigations of acquired dyslexia. *Psychological Review, 98*(1), 74–95.

Hitchcock, C., & Knobe, J. (2009). Cause and norm. *Journal of Philosophy, 106*(11), 587–612.

Hoffman, A. B., & Rehder, B. (2010). The costs of supervised classification: The effect of learning task on conceptual flexibility. *Journal of Experimental Psychology: General, 139*(2), 319–340.

Hogarth, R. M., & Karelaia, N. (2006). "Take-the-best" and other simple strategies: Why and when they work "well" with binary cues. *Theory and Decision, 61*, 205–249.

Holroyd, C. B., & Coles, M. G. H. (2002). The neural basis of human error processing: Reinforcement learning, dopamine, and the error-related negativity. *Psychological Review, 109*(4), 679–709.

Holyoak, K. J., & Cheng, P. W. (2011). Causal learning and inference as a rational process: The new synthesis. *Annual Review of Psychology, 62*, 135–163.

Hooker, C. A. (1981a). Towards a general theory of reduction, part I: Historical and scientific setting. *Dialogue, 20*, 38–59.

Hooker, C. A. (1981b). Towards a general theory of reduction, part II: Identity in reduction. *Dialogue, 20*, 201–236.

Horgan, T., & Tienson, J. (Eds.). (1991). *Connectionism and the philosophy of mind*. New York: Springer.

Horgan, T., & Tienson, J. (1996). *Connectionism and the philosophy of psychology*. Cambridge, MA: MIT Press.

Hornik, K., Stinchcombe, M., & White, H. (1989). Multilayer feedforward networks are universal approximators. *Neural Networks, 2*(5), 359–366.

Howard, R. A., & Matheson, J. E. (1981). Influence diagrams. *Decision Analysis, 2,* 127–143.

Huang, L., & Pashler, H. (2007). Working memory and the guidance of visual attention: Consonance-driven orienting. *Psychonomic Bulletin and Review, 14*(1), 148–153.

Hummel, J. E., & Holyoak, K. J. (2003). A symbolic-connectionist theory of relational inference and generalization. *Psychological Review, 110,* 220–264.

Humphreys, G. W., & Forde, E. M. E. (2001). Hierarchies, similarity, and interactivity in object recognition: "Category-specific" neuropsychological deficits. *Behavioral and Brain Sciences, 24,* 453–476.

Jee, B. D., & Wiley, J. (2007). How goals affect the organization and use of domain knowledge. *Memory and Cognition, 35*(5), 837–851.

Jeffrey, R. (1965). *The logic of decision.* New York: McGraw-Hill.

Jern, A., & Kemp, C. (2011). Decision factors that support preference learning. In *Proceedings of the 33rd Annual Conference of the Cognitive Science Society.* Austin, TX: Cognitive Science Society.

Jern, A., Lucas, C. G., & Kemp, C. (2011). Evaluating the inverse decision-making approach to preference learning. In J. Shawe-Taylor, R. S. Zemel, P. Bartlett, F. Pereira, & K. Q. Weinberger (Eds.), *Advances in neural information processing systems* (Vol. 24, pp. 2276–2284). La Jolla, CA: The NIPS Foundation.

Johansen, M. K., & Kruschke, J. K. (2005). Category representation for classification and feature inference. *Journal of Experimental Psychology: Learning, Memory, and Cognition, 31*(6), 1433–1458.

Johnson, K. E., & Mervis, C. B. (1997). Effects of varying levels of expertise on the basic level of categorization. *Journal of Experimental Psychology: General, 126*(3), 248–277.

Jones, M., & Love, B. C. (2011). Bayesian fundamentalism or enlightenment? On the explanatory status and theoretical contributions of Bayesian models of cognition. *Behavioral and Brain Sciences, 34*(4), 169–188.

Joyce, J. M. (1999). *The foundations of causal decision theory.* Cambridge: Cambridge University Press.

Joyce, J. M. (2002). Levi on causal decision theory and the possibility of predicting one's own actions. *Philosophical Studies, 110,* 69–102.

Kaplan, D. (2009). *Structural equation modeling: Foundations and extensions* (2nd ed.). Thousand Oaks, CA: Sage Publications.

Kelley, H. H. (1973). The processes of causal attribution. *American Psychologist, 28,* 107–128.

Kemp, C., Perfors, A., & Tenenbaum, J. B. (2007). Learning overhypotheses with hierarchical Bayesian models. *Developmental Science, 10*(3), 307–321.

Kersten, D., & Yuille, A. (2003). Bayesian models of object perception. *Current Opinion in Neurobiology, 13,* 1–9.

Kim, J. (1992). Multiple realization and the metaphysics of reduction. *Philosophy and Phenomenological Research, 52,* 1–26.

Kitcher, P. (2001). *Science, truth, and democracy*. New York: Oxford University Press.

Knill, D. C., & Pouget, A. (2004). The Bayesian brain: The role of uncertainty in neural coding and computation. *Trends in Neurosciences, 27*(12), 712–719.

Knobe, J., & Fraser, B. (2008). Causal judgment and moral judgment: Two experiments. In W. Sinnott-Armstrong (Ed.), *Moral psychology* (pp. 441–448). Cambridge, MA: MIT Press.

Knorr-Held, L., & Rue, H. V. (2002). On block updating in Markov random field models for disease mapping. *Scandinavian Journal of Statistics, 29*(4), 597–614.

Knutson, B., Taylor, J., Kaufman, M., Peterson, R., & Glover, G. (2005). Distributed neural representation of expected value. *Journal of Neuroscience, 25*(19), 4806–4812.

Koller, D., & Friedman, N. (2009). *Probabilistic graphical models: Principles and techniques*. Cambridge, MA: MIT Press.

Kording, K. P., & Wolpert, D. M. (2006). Bayesian decision theory in sensorimotor control. *Trends in Cognitive Sciences, 10*(7), 319–326.

Kruschke, J. K. (1992). ALCOVE: An exemplar-based connectionist model of category learning. *Psychological Review, 99,* 22–44.

Kruschke, J. K. (2006). Locally Bayesian learning with applications to retrospective revaluation and highlighting. *Psychological Review, 113*(4), 677–699.

Kschischang, F. R., Frey, B. J., & Loeliger, H.-A. (2001). Factor graphs and the sum-product algorithm. *IEEE Transactions on Information Theory, 47*(2), 498–519.

Kusser, A., & Spohn, W. (1992). The utility of pleasure is a pain for decision theory. *Journal of Philosophy, 89,* 10–29.

Lafferty, J., McCallum, A., & Pereira, F. C. N. (2001). Conditional random fields: Probabilistic models for segmenting and labeling sequence data. In C. E. Brodley & A. P. Danyluk (Eds.), *Proceedings of the 18th International Conference on Machine Learning (ICML 2001)* (pp. 282–289). San Francisco: Morgan Kaufmann.

Lagnado, D. A., Waldmann, M. R., Hagmayer, Y., & Sloman, S. A. (2007). Beyond covariation: Cues to causal structure. In A. Gopnik & L. E. Schulz (Eds.), *Causal learning: Psychology, philosophy, and computation* (pp. 154–172). Oxford: Oxford University Press.

Laird, J. E. (2012). *The Soar cognitive architecture*. Cambridge, MA: MIT Press.

Laird, J. E., Derbinsky, N., & Tinkerhess, M. (2011). A case study in integrating probabilistic decision making and learning in a symbolic cognitive architecture: Soar plays dice. In *Advances in cognitive systems: Papers from the 2011 AAAI Fall Symposium*. Menlo Park, CA: AAAI Press.

Laird, J. E., Newell, A., & Rosenbloom, P. S. (1987). Soar: An architecture for general intelligence. *Artificial Intelligence, 33*, 1–64.

Laird, J. E., Rosenbloom, P. S., & Newell, A. (1986). Chunking in Soar: The anatomy of a general learning mechanism. *Machine Learning, 1*(1), 11–46.

Lamberts, K. (1998). The time course of categorization. *Journal of Experimental Psychology: Learning, Memory, and Cognition, 24*, 695–711.

Lamberts, K. (2000). Information accumulation theory of categorization response times. *Psychological Review, 107*, 227–260.

Langley, P., Laird, J. E., & Rogers, S. (2009). Cognitive architectures: Research issues and challenges. *Cognitive Systems Research, 10*(2), 141–160.

Lauritzen, S. L. (1996). *Graphical models*. Oxford: Clarendon Press.

Lauritzen, S. L., & Richardson, T. S. (2002). Chain graph models and their causal interpretation. *Journal of the Royal Statistical Society, Series B: Methodological, 64*, 321–361.

Lauritzen, S. L., & Wermuth, N. (1989). Graphical models for association between variables, some of which are qualitative and some quantitative. *Annals of Statistics, 17*, 31–57.

Lee, M. D. (2006). A hierarchical Bayesian model of human decision-making on an optimal stopping problem. *Cognitive Science, 30*, 1–26.

Lee, S.-I., Ganapathi, V., & Koller, D. (2007). Efficient structure learning of Markov networks using L1 regularization. In B. Scholkopf, J. Platt, & T. Hoffman (Eds.), *Advances in neural information processing systems* (Vol. 19, pp. 817–824). Cambridge, MA: MIT Press.

Lee, T. S., & Mumford, D. (2003). Hierarchical Bayesian inference in the visual cortex. *Journal of the Optical Society of America, A: Optics, Image Science, and Vision, 20*(7), 1434–1448.

Lehman, J. F., Laird, J. E., & Rosenbloom, P. S. (2006, October 16). A gentle introduction to Soar, an architecture for human cognition: 2006 update. *ai.eecs.umich.edu*. Retrieved October 16, 2013, from http://ai.eecs.umich.edu/soar/sitemaker/docs/misc/GentleIntroduction-2006.pdf.

Leising, K. J., Wong, J., Waldmann, M. R., & Blaisdell, A. P. (2008). The special status of actions in causal reasoning in rats. *Journal of Experimental Psychology: General, 137*(3), 514–527.

Lerner, U., Moses, B., Scott, M., McIlraith, S., & Koller, D. (2002). Monitoring a complex physical system using a hybrid dynamic Bayes net. In A. Darwiche & N. Friedman (Eds.), *Proceedings of the 18th Conference on Uncertainty in Artificial Intelligence* (pp. 301–310). San Francisco: Morgan Kaufmann.

Leslie, A. M. (1982). The perception of causality in infants. *Perception, 11*(2), 173–186.

Levi, I. (1991). *The fixation of belief and its undoing: Changing beliefs through inquiry*. Cambridge: Cambridge University Press.

Levi, I. (1997). *The covenant of reason*. Cambridge: Cambridge University Press.

Levi, I. (2000). Review essay: *The foundations of causal decision theory*. *Journal of Philosophy, 97*, 387–402.

Levi, I. (2004). *Mild contraction: Evaluating loss of information due to loss of belief*. Oxford: Clarendon Press.

Levi, I. (2007). Deliberation does crowd out prediction. In T. Ronnow-Rasmussen, B. Petersson, J. Josefsson, & D. Egonsson (Eds.), *Hommage a Wlodek: Philosophical papers dedicated to Wlodek Rabinowicz*. Retrieved from http://www.fil.lu.se/hommageawlodek.

Lewis, D. (1981). Causal decision theory. *Australasian Journal of Philosophy, 59*(1), 5–30.

Lewis, R. L. (1993). An architecturally-based theory of human sentence comprehension. In W. Kintsch (Ed.), *Proceedings of the 15th Annual Conference of the Cognitive Science Society* (pp. 108–113). Hillsdale, NJ: Erlbaum.

Li, S. Z. (2009). *Markov random field modeling in image analysis* (3rd ed.). London: Springer.

Lien, Y., & Cheng, P. W. (2000). Distinguishing genuine from spurious causes: A coherence hypothesis. *Cognitive Psychology, 40*, 87–137.

Lin, Z., Zhao, X., Ismail, K. M., & Carley, K. M. (2006). Organizational design and restructuring in response to crises: Lessons from computational modeling and real-world cases. *Organization Science, 17*(5), 598–618.

Logan, G. D. (2004). Cumulative progress in formal theories of attention. *Annual Review of Psychology, 55*, 207–234.

Love, B. C., Medin, D. L., & Gureckis, T. M. (2004). SUSTAIN: A network model of category learning. *Psychological Review, 111*, 309–332.

Lucas, C. G., & Griffiths, T. L. (2010). Learning the form of causal relationships using hierarchical Bayesian models. *Cognitive Science, 34*, 113–147.

Luce, R. D. (1959). *Individual choice behavior: A theoretical analysis*. New York: Wiley.

Luce, R. D. (1963). Detection and recognition. In R. D. Luce, R. R. Bush, & E. Galanter (Eds.), *Handbook of mathematical psychology*. New York: Wiley.

Lycan, W. G. (1981). Form, function, and feel. *Journal of Philosophy, 78*(1), 24–50.

Machamer, P., Darden, L., & Craver, C. F. (2000). Thinking about mechanisms. *Philosophy of Science, 67*(1), 1–25.

Machery, E. (2009). *Doing without concepts*. Oxford: Oxford University Press.

Machery, E. (2010). The heterogeneity of knowledge representation and the elimination of concept. *Behavioral and Brain Sciences, 33*(2–3), 231–244.

Mangold, S., & Hagmayer, Y. (2011). Unconscious vs. conscious thought in causal decision making. In C. H. Carlson & T. Shipley (Eds.), *Proceedings of the 33rd Annual Conference of the Cognitive Science Society* (pp. 3104–3109). Austin, TX: Cognitive Science Society.

Markman, Art B., & Ross, B. H. (2003). Category use and category learning. *Psychological Bulletin, 129*, 592–613.

Markman, Art B., & Wisniewski, E. J. (1997). Similar and different: The differentiation of basic-level categories. *Journal of Experimental Psychology: Learning, Memory, and Cognition, 23*(1), 54–70.

Marr, D. (1982). *Vision*. San Francisco: W. H. Freeman.

Martignon, L., & Hoffrage, U. (1999). Where and why is take the best fast, frugal, and fit? In G. Gigerenzer & P. M. Todd (Eds.), *Simple heuristics that make us smart* (pp. 119–140). Oxford: Oxford University Press.

Mayor, J., & Plunkett, K. (2010). A neurocomputational account of taxonomic responding and fast mapping in early word learning. *Psychological Review, 117*(1), 1–31.

Mayrhofer, R., Goodman, N. D., Waldmann, M. R., & Tenenbaum, J. B. (2008). Structured correlation from the causal background. In B. C. Love, K. McRae, & V. M. Sloutsky (Eds.), *Proceedings of the 30th Annual Conference of the Cognitive Science Society* (pp. 303–308). Austin, TX: Cognitive Science Society.

Mayrhofer, R., Hagmayer, Y., & Waldmann, M. R. (2010). Agents and causes: A Bayesian error attribution model of causal reasoning. In S. Ohlsson & R. Catrambone (Eds.), *Proceedings of the 32nd Annual Meeting of the Cognitive Science Society* (pp. 925–930). Austin, TX: Cognitive Science Society.

McCallum, A., Freitag, D., & Pereira, F. C. N. (2000). Maximum entropy Markov models for information extraction and segmentation. In P. Langley (Ed.), *Proceedings of the 17th International Conference on Machine Learning (ICML 2000)* (pp. 591–598). San Francisco: Morgan Kaufmann.

McCauley, R. N., & Henrich, J. (2006). Susceptibility to the Müller-Lyer illusion, theory-neutral observation, and the diachronic penetrability of the visual input system. *Philosophical Psychology, 19*(1), 79–101.

McClelland, J. L., Botvinick, M. M., Noelle, D. C., Plaut, D. C., Rogers, T. T., Seidenberg, M. S., et al. (2010). Letting structure emerge: Connectionist and dynamical systems approaches to cognition. *Trends in Cognitive Sciences, 14*(8), 348–356.

McClelland, J. L., McNaughton, B. L., & O'Reilly, R. C. (1995). Why there are complementary learning systems in the hippocampus and neocortex: Insights from the successes and failures of connectionist models of learning and memory. *Psychological Review, 102*(3), 419–457.

McGurk, H., & MacDonald, J. (1976). Hearing lips and seeing voices. *Nature, 264*, 746–748.

Meder, B., Gerstenberg, T., Hagmayer, Y., & Waldmann, M. R. (2010). Observing and intervening: Rational and heuristic models of causal decision making. *Open Psychology Journal, 3*, 119–135.

Meder, B., & Hagmayer, Y. (2009). Causal induction enables adaptive decision making. In N. A. Taatgen & H. van Rijn (Eds.), *Proceedings of the 31st Annual Conference of the Cognitive Science Society* (pp. 1651–1656). Austin, TX: Cognitive Science Society.

Medin, D. L., & Schaffer, M. M. (1978). Context theory of classification learning. *Psychological Review, 85*, 207–238.

Meek, C. (1995). Strong completeness and faithfulness in Bayesian networks. In P. Besnard & S. Hanks (Eds.), *Proceedings of the 11th Annual Conference on Uncertainty in Artificial Intelligence* (pp. 411–418). San Francisco: Morgan Kaufmann.

Melz, E. R., Cheng, P. W., Holyoak, K. J., & Waldmann, M. R. (1993). Cue competition in human categorization: Contingency or the Rescorla-Wagner learning rule? Comment on Shanks (1991). *Journal of Experimental Psychology: Learning, Memory, and Cognition, 19*(6), 1398–1410.

Michotte, A. (1946). *La perception de la causalité*. Louvain: Etudes de Psychologie.

Millikan, R. G. (1984). *Language, thought, and other biological categories*. Cambridge, MA: MIT Press.

Minda, J. P., & Smith, J. D. (2001). Prototypes in category learning: The effects of category size, category structure, and stimulus complexity. *Journal of Experimental Psychology: Learning, Memory, and Cognition, 27*, 775–799.

Minda, J. P., & Smith, J. D. (2002). Comparing prototype-based and exemplar-based accounts of category learning and attentional allocation. *Journal of Experimental Psychology: Learning, Memory, and Cognition, 28*, 275–292.

Minsky, M., & Papert, S. (1969). *Perceptrons: An introduction to computational geometry*. Cambridge, MA: MIT Press.

Mischel, W., & Shoda, Y. (1995). A cognitive-affective system theory of personality: Reconceptualizing situations, dispositions, dynamics, and invariance in personality structure. *Psychological Review, 102*(2), 246–268.

Mitchell, T. M. (1997). *Machine learning*. New York: McGraw-Hill.

Montague, P. R., Dayan, P., & Sejnowski, T. J. (1996). A framework for mesencephalic dopamine systems based on predictive Hebbian learning. *Journal of Neuroscience, 16*(5), 1936–1947.

Moulines, C. U. (1984). Ontological reduction in the natural sciences. In W. Balzer, D. Pearce, & H.-J. Schmidt (Eds.), *Reduction in science* (pp. 51–70). Dordrecht: Reidel.

Moulines, C. U. (1996). Structuralism: The basic ideas. In W. Balzer & C. U. Moulines (Eds.), *Structuralist theory of science: Focal issues, new results* (pp. 1–13). Berlin: Walter de Gruyter.

Moulines, C. U., & Polanski, M. (1996). Bridges, constraints, and links. In W. Balzer & C. U. Moulines (Eds.), *Structuralist theory of science: Focal issues, new results* (pp. 219–232). Berlin: Walter de Gruyter.

Moussouris, J. (1974). Gibbs and Markov random systems with constraints. *Journal of Statistical Physics, 10*, 11–33.

Murphy, G. L. (1993). Theories and concept formation. In I. V. Mechelen, J. Hampton, R. Michalski, & P. Theuns (Eds.), *Categories and concepts: Theoretical views and inductive data analysis* (pp. 173–200). London: Academic Press.

Murphy, G. L. (2004). *The big book of concepts*. Cambridge, MA: Bradford.

Murphy, G. L., & Lassaline, M. E. (1997). Hierarchical structure in concepts and the basic level of categorization. In K. Lamberts & D. R. Shanks (Eds.), *Knowledge, concepts, and categories: Studies in cognition* (pp. 93–131). Cambridge, MA: MIT Press.

Myung, I. J. (1994). Maximum entropy interpretation of decision bound and context models of categorization. *Journal of Mathematical Psychology, 38*, 335–365.

Nagel, E. (1961). *The structure of science: Problems in the logic of scientific explanation.* New York: Harcourt.

Nason, S., & Laird, J. E. (2005). Soar-RL: Integrating reinforcement learning with Soar. *Cognitive Systems Research, 6*(1), 51–59.

Neumann, P. G. (1974). An attribute frequency model for the abstraction of prototypes. *Memory and Cognition, 2*, 241–248.

Newell, A. (1990). *Unified theories of cognition.* Cambridge, MA: Harvard University Press.

Newell, B. R., & Shanks, D. R. (2003). Take the best or look at the rest? Factors influencing "one-reason" decision making. *Journal of Experimental Psychology: Learning, Memory, and Cognition, 29*(1), 53–65.

Nichols, W., & Danks, D. (2007). Decision making using learned causal structures. In D. S. McNamara & J. G. Trafton (Eds.), *Proceedings of the 29th Annual Meeting of the Cognitive Science Society* (pp. 1343–1348). Austin, TX: Cognitive Science Society.

Nickles, T. (1973). Two concepts of intertheoretic reduction. *Journal of Philosophy, 70*(7), 181–201.

Nodelman, U., Shelton, C. R., & Koller, D. (2002). Continuous time Bayesian networks. In A. Darwiche & N. Friedman (Eds.), *Proceedings of the 18th Conference on Uncertainty in Artificial Intelligence* (pp. 378–387). San Francisco: Morgan Kaufmann.

Nodelman, U., Shelton, C. R., & Koller, D. (2003). Learning continuous time Bayesian networks. In C. Meek & U. Kjaerulff (Eds.), *Proceedings of the 19th International Conference on Uncertainty in Artificial Intelligence* (pp. 451–458). San Francisco: Morgan Kaufmann.

Norenzayan, A., Choi, I., & Nisbett, R. E. (2002). Cultural similarities and differences in social inference: Evidence from behavioral predictions and lay theories of behavior. *Personality and Social Psychology Bulletin, 28*, 109–120.

Nosofsky, R. M. (1984). Choice, similarity, and the context theory of classification. *Journal of Experimental Psychology: Learning, Memory, and Cognition, 10*, 104–114.

Nosofsky, R. M. (1986). Attention, similarity, and the identification-categorization relationship. *Journal of Experimental Psychology: General, 115*, 39–57.

Nosofsky, R. M. (1990). Relations between exemplar-similarity and likelihood models of classification. *Journal of Mathematical Psychology, 34*, 393–418.

Nosofsky, R. M. (1991). Tests of an exemplar model for relating perceptual classification and recognition memory. *Journal of Experimental Psychology: Human Perception and Performance, 17*, 3–27.

Nosofsky, R. M., & Palmeri, T. J. (1997). An exemplar-based random walk model of speeded classification. *Psychological Review, 104*, 266–300.

Nosofsky, R. M., & Zaki, S. R. (2002). Exemplar and prototype models revisited: Response strategies, selective attention, and stimulus generalization. *Journal of Experimental Psychology: Learning, Memory, and Cognition, 28*, 924–940.

Novick, L. R., & Cheng, P. W. (2004). Assessing interactive causal influence. *Psychological Review, 111*(2), 455–485.

Nozick, R. (1970). Newcomb's problem and two principles of choice. In N. Rescher (Ed.), *Essays in honor of Carl G. Hempel* (pp. 114–146). Dordrecht: Reidel.

Nuxoll, A. M., & Laird, J. E. (2012). Enhancing intelligent agents with episodic memory. *Cognitive Systems Research, 17–18*, 34–48.

Oakes, L. M., & Cohen, L. B. (1990). Infant perception of a causal event. *Cognitive Development, 5*, 193–207.

Oaksford, M., & Chater, N. (2007). *Bayesian rationality: The probabilistic approach to human reasoning*. Oxford: Oxford University Press.

Okamoto, M. (1973). Distinctness of the eigenvalues of a quadratic form in a multivariate sample. *Annals of Statistics, 1*(4), 763–765.

Oppenheimer, D. M., Tenenbaum, J. B., & Krynski, T. R. (2013). Categorization as causal explanation: Discounting and augmenting in a Bayesian framework. *Psychology of Learning and Motivation, 58*, 203–231.

Osherson, D. N., Smith, E. E., Wilkie, O., Lopez, A., & Shafir, E. (1990). Category-based induction. *Psychological Review, 97*(2), 185–200.

Park, J., & Sloman, S. A. (2013). Mechanistic beliefs determine adherence to the Markov property in causal reasoning. *Cognitive Psychology, 67*(4), 186–216.

Pashler, H., & Harris, C. R. (2001). Spontaneous allocation of visual attention: Dominant role of uniqueness. *Psychonomic Bulletin and Review, 8*(4), 747–752.

Patalano, A. L., Smith, E. E., Jonides, J., & Koeppe, R. A. (2001). PET evidence for multiple strategies of categorization. *Cognitive, Affective, and Behavioral Neuroscience, 1*(4), 360–370.

Paulin, M. G. (2005). Evolution of the cerebellum as a neuronal machine for Bayesian state estimation. *Journal of Neural Engineering, 2*, S219–S234.

Pearce, J. M. (1987). A model for stimulus generalization in Pavlovian conditioning. *Psychological Review, 94*(1), 61–73.

Pearl, J. (1988). *Probabilistic reasoning in intelligent systems: Networks of plausible inference*. San Francisco: Morgan Kaufmann.

Pearl, J. (2000). *Causality: Models, reasoning, and inference*. Cambridge: Cambridge University Press.

Penn, D. C., Holyoak, K. J., & Povinelli, D. J. (2008). Darwin's mistake: Explaining the discontinuity between human and nonhuman minds. *Behavioral and Brain Sciences, 31*, 109–130.

Perales, J. C., & Shanks, D. R. (2007). Models of covariation-based causal judgment: A review and synthesis. *Psychonomic Bulletin and Review, 14*(4), 577–596.

Perfors, A., Tenenbaum, J. B., Griffiths, T. L., & Xu, F. (2011). A tutorial introduction to Bayesian models of cognitive development. *Cognition, 120*(3), 302–321.

Piantadosi, S. T., Tenenbaum, J. B., & Goodman, N. D. (2012). Bootstrapping in a language of thought: A formal model of numerical concept learning. *Cognition, 123*, 199–217.

Pinker, S. (1997). *How the mind works*. New York: W. W. Norton.

Plaut, D. C., & Shallice, T. (1993). Deep dyslexia: A case study of connectionist neuropsychology. *Cognitive Neuropsychology, 10*, 377–500.

Poggio, T. (2012). The Levels of Understanding framework, revised. *Perception, 41*(9), 1017–1023.

Poldrack, R. A., & Packard, M. G. (2003). Competition among multiple memory systems: Converging evidence from animal and human brain studies. *Neuropsychologia, 41*, 245–251.

Poole, D., & Zhang, N. L. (2003). Exploiting contextual independence in probabilistic inference. *Journal of Artificial Intelligence Research, 18*, 263–313.

Port, R. F., & van Gelder, T. (1995). *Mind as motion: Explorations in the dynamics of cognition*. Cambridge, MA: MIT Press.

Posner, M. I., & Keele, S. W. (1968). On the genesis of abstract ideas. *Journal of Experimental Psychology, 77*, 353–363.

Pothos, E. M., & Wills, A. J. (Eds.). (2011). *Formal approaches in categorization*. Cambridge: Cambridge University Press.

Pouget, A., Beck, J. M., Ma, W. J., & Latham, P. E. (2013). Probabilistic brains: Knowns and unknowns. *Nature Neuroscience, 16*, 1170–1178.

Putnam, H. (1975). Philosophy and our mental life. In *Mind, language, and Reality: Philosophical papers* (Vol. 2, pp. 291–303). Cambridge, MA: Cambridge University Press.

Rabiner, L. R. (1989). A tutorial on hidden Markov models and selected applications in speech recognition. *Proceedings of the IEEE, 77*(2), 257–286.

Rabinowicz, W. (2002). Does practical deliberation crowd out self-prediction? *Erkenntnis, 57*, 91–122.

Ramsey, W. M. (2007). *Representation reconsidered*. Cambridge: Cambridge University Press.

Ramsey, W., Stich, S. P., & Rumelhart, D. E. (Eds.). (1991). *Philosophy and connectionist theory*. Oxford: Psychology Press.

Rao, R. P. N. (2005). Bayesian inference and attentional modulation in the visual cortex. *Cognitive Neuroscience and Neuropsychology, 16*(16), 1843–1848.

Reed, S. K. (1972). Pattern recognition and categorization. *Cognitive Psychology, 3*, 382–407.

Rehder, B. (2003a). A causal-model theory of conceptual representation and categorization. *Journal of Experimental Psychology: Learning, Memory, and Cognition, 29*, 1141–1159.

Rehder, B. (2003b). Categorization as causal reasoning. *Cognitive Science, 27*, 709–748.

Rehder, B. (2006). When similarity and causality compete in category-based property generalization. *Memory and Cognition, 34*(1), 3–16.

Rehder, B. (2009). Causal-based property generalization. *Cognitive Science, 33*, 301–344.

Rehder, B., & Burnett, R. C. (2005). Feature inference and the causal structure of categories. *Cognitive Psychology, 50*(3), 264–314.

Rehder, B., Colner, R. M., & Hoffman, A. B. (2009). Feature inference learning and eyetracking. *Journal of Memory and Language, 60*, 393–419.

Rehder, B., & Hastie, R. (2004). Category coherence and category-based property induction. *Cognition, 91*, 113–153.

Rehder, B., & Kim, S. (2006). How causal knowledge affects classification: A generative theory of categorization. *Journal of Experimental Psychology: Learning, Memory, and Cognition, 32*(4), 659–683.

Rehder, B., & Kim, S. (2010). Causal status and coherence in causal-based categorization. *Journal of Experimental Psychology: Learning, Memory, and Cognition, 36*(5), 1171–1206.

Rescorla, R. A., & Wagner, A. R. (1972). A theory of Pavlovian conditioning: Variations in the effectiveness of reinforcement and nonreinforcement. In A. H. Black & W. F. Prokasy (Eds.), *Classical conditioning II: Current research and theory* (pp. 64–99). New York: Appleton-Century-Crofts.

Richardson, T. S. (1996). A discovery algorithm for directed cyclic graphs. In E. Horvitz & F. Jensen (Eds.), *Proceedings of the 12th Conference on Uncertainty in Artificial Intelligence* (pp. 454–461). San Francisco: Morgan Kaufmann.

Richardson, T. S. (1997). A characterization of Markov equivalence for directed cyclic graphs. *International Journal of Approximate Reasoning, 17*(2–3), 107–162.

Richardson, T. S. (1998). Chain graphs and symmetric associations. In M. I. Jordan (Ed.), *Learning in graphical models* (pp. 231–259). Cambridge, MA: MIT Press.

Richardson, T. S. (2003). Markov properties for acyclic directed mixed graphs. *Scandinavian Journal of Statistics, 30*(1), 145–157.

Richardson, T. S., & Spirtes, P. (2002). Ancestral graph Markov models. *Annals of Statistics, 30*(4), 962–1030.

Rips, L. J. (2011). Causation from perception. *Perspectives on Psychological Science, 6*, 77–97.

Rogers, T. T., & McClelland, J. L. (2004). *Semantic cognition: A parallel distributed processing approach.* Cambridge, MA: MIT Press.

Rolls, E. T., McCabe, C., & Redoute, J. (2008). Expected value, reward outcome, and temporal difference error representations in a probabilistic decision task. *Cerebral Cortex, 18*(3), 652–663.

Rosch, E. (1973). Natural categories. *Cognitive Psychology, 4*(3), 328–350.

Rosch, E., Mervis, C. B., Gray, W. D., Johnson, D. M., & Boyes-Braem, P. (1976). Basic objects in natural categories. *Cognitive Psychology, 8*(3), 382–439.

Rose, D., & Danks, D. (2012 Causation: Empirical trends and future directions. *Philosophy Compass, 7*(9), 643–653.

Rose, M. R., & Lauder, G. V. (Eds.). (1996). *Adaptation.* San Diego, CA: Academic Press.

Rosenbloom, P. S. (2006). A cognitive odyssey: From the power law of practice to a general learning mechanism and beyond. *Tutorials in Quantitative Methods for Psychology, 2*, 43–51.

Rosenbloom, P. S. (2009a). A graphical rethinking of the cognitive inner loop. In *Proceedings of the 1st IJCAI Workshop on Graph Structures for Knowledge Representation and Reasoning* (pp. 33–38). Pasadena, CA: IJCAI.

Rosenbloom, P. S. (2009b). Towards a new cognitive hourglass: Uniform implementation of cognitive architecture via factor graphs. In A. Howes, D. Peebles, & R. P. Cooper (Eds.), *Proceedings of the 9th International Conference on Cognitive Modeling (ICCM-2009)* (pp. 116–121). Manchester, UK: University of Manchester.

Rosenbloom, P. S. (2010). Combining procedural and declarative knowledge in a graphical architecture. In D. D. Salvucci & G. Gunzelmann (Eds.), *Proceedings of the 10th International Conference on Cognitive Modeling (ICCM-2010)* (pp. 205–210). Philadelphia, PA: Drexel University.

Rosenbloom, P. S. (2011). Rethinking cognitive architecture via graphical models. *Cognitive Systems Research, 12,* 198–209.

Rosenbloom, P. S. (2012). Towards a 50 msec cognitive cycle in a graphical architecture. In N. Rußwinkel, U. Drewitz, & H. van Rijn (Eds.), *Proceedings of the 11th International Conference on Cognitive Modeling (ICCM-2012)* (pp. 305–310). Berlin: Universitätsverlag der TU Berlin.

Rosenbloom, P. S., Demski, A., Han, T., & Ustun, V. (2013). Learning via gradient descent in Sigma. In R. L. West & T. C. Stewart (Eds.), *Proceedings of the 12th International Conference on Cognitive Modeling (ICCM-2013)* (pp. 35–40). Ottawa, Canada: Carleton University.

Rosenbloom, P. S., Laird, J. E., & Newell, A. (1993). *The Soar papers: Research on integrated intelligence.* Cambridge, MA: MIT Press.

Roser, M. E., Fugelsang, J. A., Dunbar, K. N., Corballis, P. M., & Gazzaniga, M. S. (2005). Dissociating processes supporting causal perception and causal inference in the brain. *Neuropsychology, 19*(5), 591–602.

Ross, B. H. (1997). The use of categories affects classification. *Journal of Memory and Language, 37,* 240–267.

Ross, B. H. (1999). Postclassification category use: The effects of learning to use categories after learning to classify. *Journal of Experimental Psychology: Learning, Memory, and Cognition, 25*(3), 743–757.

Ross, B. H. (2000). The effects of category use on learned categories. *Memory and Cognition, 28*(1), 51–63.

Ross, B. H., & Murphy, G. L. (1999). Food for thought: Cross-classification and category organization in a complex real-world domain. *Cognitive Psychology, 38,* 495–553.

Rosseel, Y. (2002). Mixture models of categorization. *Journal of Mathematical Psychology, 46,* 178–210.

Rottman, B. M., & Hastie, R. (2014). Reasoning about causal relationships: Inferences on causal networks. *Psychological Bulletin, 140*(1), 109–139.

Rozenblit, L., & Keil, F. C. (2002). The misunderstood limits of folk science: An illusion of explanatory depth. *Cognitive Science, 26,* 521–562.

Rubinoff, R., & Lehman, J. F. (1994). Real-time natural language generation in NL-Soar. In *Proceedings of the Seventh International Workshop on Natural Language Generation* (pp. 199–206). Association for Computational Linguistics.

Rue, Håvard, & Held, Leonhard. (2005). *Gaussian Markov random fields: Theory and applications*. Boca Raton, FL: Chapman & Hall.

Rueger, A. (2001). Explanations at multiple levels. *Minds and Machines, 11*, 503–520.

Rueger, A. (2005). Perspectival models and theory unification. *British Journal for the Philosophy of Science, 56*, 579–594.

Rumelhart, D. E., McClelland, J. L., & the PDP Research Group. (1986). *Parallel distributed processing: Explorations in the microstructure of cognition: Foundations* (Vol. 1). Cambridge, MA: MIT Press.

Salvucci, D. (2006). Modeling driver behavior in a cognitive architecture. *Human Factors, 48*, 362–380.

Samuels, R. (1998). Evolutionary psychology and the massive modularity hypothesis. *British Journal for the Philosophy of Science, 49*(4), 575–602.

Samuels, R. (2010). Classical computationalism and the many problems of cognitive relevance. *Studies in History and Philosophy of Science, 41*, 280–293.

Satpute, A. B., Fenker, D. B., Waldmann, M. R., Tabibnia, G., Holyoak, K. J., & Lieberman, M. D. (2005). An fMRI study of causal judgments. *European Journal of Neuroscience, 22*, 1233–1238.

Schaffner, K. (1967). Approaches to reduction. *Philosophy of Science, 34*, 137–147.

Schervish, M. J., Seidenfeld, T., & Kadane, J. B. (2003). Measures of incoherence: How not to gamble if you must. In J. M. Bernardo, M. J. Bayarri, A. P. Dawid, J. O. Berger, D. Heckerman, A. F. M. Smith, & M. West (Eds.), *Bayesian statistics 7: Proceedings of the 7th Valencia Conference on Bayesian Statistics* (pp. 349–363). Oxford: Oxford University Press.

Schlottmann, A. (2000). Is perception of causality modular? *Trends in Cognitive Sciences, 4*(12), 441–442.

Schlottmann, A., & Anderson, N. H. (1993). An information integration approach to phenomenal causality. *Memory and Cognition, 21*(6), 785–801.

Schlottmann, A., & Shanks, D. R. (1992). Evidence for a distinction between judged and perceived causality. *Quarterly Journal of Experimental Psychology, 44A*, 321–342.

Scholl, B. J., & Nakayama, K. (2002). Causal capture: Contextual effects on the perception of collision events. *Psychological Science, 13*(6), 493–498.

Scholl, B. J., & Nakayama, K. (2004). Illusory causal crescents: Misperceived spatial relations due to perceived causality. *Perception, 33*, 455–469.

Scholl, B. J., & Tremoulet, P. D. (2000). Perceptual causality and animacy. *Trends in Cognitive Sciences, 4*(8), 299–309.

Schooler, L. J., Shiffrin, R. M., & Raaijmakers, J. G. W. (2001). A Bayesian model for implicit effects in perceptual identification. *Psychological Review, 108*(1), 257–272.

Schoppek, W. (2001). The influence of causal interpretation on memory for system states. In J. D. Moore & K. Stenning (Eds.), *Proceedings of the 23rd Annual Conference of the Cognitive Science Society* (pp. 904–909). Mahwah, NJ: Erlbaum.

Schouten, M. K. D., & de Jong, H. L. (Eds.). (2012). *The matter of the mind: Philosophical essays on psychology, neuroscience and reduction*. London: Wiley-Blackwell.

Schulte, O. (1999). The logic of reliable and efficient inquiry. *Journal of Philosophical Logic, 28*, 399–438.

Schultz, W. (2006). Behavioral theories and the neurophysiology of reward. *Annual Review of Psychology, 57*, 87–115.

Scott, J. P. (2000). *Social network analysis: A handbook* (2nd ed.). London: Sage Publications.

Searle, J. (1980). Minds, brains, and programs. *Behavioral and Brain Sciences, 3*, 417–424.

Shachter, R. D. (1986). Evaluating influence diagrams. *Operations Research, 34*, 871–882.

Shachter, R. D. (1988). Probabilistic inference and influence diagrams. *Operations Research, 36*, 589–604.

Shafto, P., & Coley, J. D. (2003). Development of categorization and reasoning in the natural world: Novices to experts, naive similarity to ecological knowledge. *Journal of Experimental Psychology: Learning, Memory, and Cognition, 29*, 641–649.

Shagrir, O. (2012). Structural representations and the brain. *British Journal for the Philosophy of Science, 63*(3), 519–545.

Shallice, T., & Burgess, P. W. (1991). Deficits in strategy application following frontal lobe damage in man. *Brain, 114*(2), 727–741.

Shanks, D. R. (1991). Categorization by a connectionist network. *Journal of Experimental Psychology: Learning, Memory, and Cognition, 17*(3), 433–443.

Shanks, D. R. (1993). Associative versus contingency accounts of causal learning: Reply to Melz, Cheng, Holyoak, and Waldmann (1993). *Journal of Experimental Psychology: Learning, Memory, and Cognition, 19*(6), 1411–1423.

Shanks, D. R. (1995). Is human learning rational? *Quarterly Journal of Experimental Psychology, 48A*(2), 257–279.

Shanks, D. R., & Dickinson, A. (1987). Associative accounts of causality judgment. In G. H. Bower (Ed.), *The psychology of learning and motivation* (Vol. 21, pp. 229–261). San Diego, CA: Academic Press.

Shepard, R. N. (1957). Stimulus and response generalization: A stochastic model relating generalization to distance in psychological space. *Psychometrika, 22*, 325–345.

Shi, L., & Griffiths, T. L. (2009). Neural implementation of hierarchical Bayesian inference by importance sampling. In Y. Bengio, D. Schuurmans, J. Lafferty, C. Williams, & A. Culotta (Eds.), *Advances in neural information processing systems* (Vol. 22, pp. 1669–1677). La Jolla, CA: The NIPS Foundation.

Shiffrin, R. M., & Steyvers, M. (1997). A model for recognition memory: REM-retrieving effectively from memory. *Psychonomic Bulletin and Review, 4*, 145–166.

Shimizu, S., Hoyer, P. O., Hyvärinen, A., & Kerminen, A. (2006). A linear non-Gaussian acyclic model for causal discovery. *Journal of Machine Learning Research, 7*, 2003–2030.

Singley, M. K., & Anderson, J. R. (1989). *The transfer of cognitive skill*. Cambridge, MA: Harvard University Press.

Sloman, S. A. (1998). Categorical inference is not a tree: The myth of inheritance hierarchies. *Cognitive Psychology, 35*(1), 1–33.

Sloman, S. A. (2005). *Causal models: How people think about the world and its alternatives*. Oxford: Oxford University Press.

Sloman, S. A., Fernbach, P. M., & Hagmayer, Y. (2010). Self-deception requires vagueness. *Cognition, 115*, 268–281.

Sloman, S. A., & Hagmayer, Y. (2006). The causal psycho-logic of choice. *Trends in Cognitive Sciences, 10*, 407–412.

Sloman, S. A., & Lagnado, D. A. (2005). Do we "do"? *Cognitive Science, 29*, 5–39.

Sloman, S. A., Love, B. C., & Ahn, W.-K. (1998). Feature centrality and conceptual coherence. *Cognitive Science, 22*(2), 189–228.

Smith, N. J., & Levy, R. (2013). The effect of word predictability on reading time is logarithmic. *Cognition, 128*, 302–319.

Sneed, J. D. (1971). *The logical structure of mathematical physics*. Dordrecht: Reidel.

Sobel, D. M., Tenenbaum, J. B., & Gopnik, A. (2004). Children's causal inferences from indirect evidence: Backwards blocking and Bayesian reasoning in preschoolers. *Cognitive Science, 28*, 303–333.

Solway, A., & Botvinick, M. M. (2012). Goal-directed decision making as probabilistic inference: A computational framework and potential neural correlates. *Psychological Review, 119*(1), 120–154.

Spirtes, P., Glymour, C., & Scheines, R. (2000). *Causation, prediction, and search* (2nd ed.). Cambridge, MA: MIT Press.

Spirtes, P., & Scheines, R. (2004). Causal inference of ambiguous manipulations. *Philosophy of Science, 71*, 833–845.

Stegmuller, W. (1976). *The structure and dynamics of theories*. Berlin: Springer.

Sterelny, K. (2003). *Thought in a hostile world: The evolution of human cognition*. London: Wiley-Blackwell.

Steyvers, M., Tenenbaum, J. B., Wagenmakers, E.-J., & Blum, B. (2003). Inferring causal networks from observations and interventions. *Cognitive Science, 27*, 453–489.

Stich, S. (1983). *From folk psychology to cognitive science*. Cambridge, MA: MIT Press.

Stich, S. (1992). What is a theory of mental representation? *Mind, 101*(402), 243–261.

Studeny, M. (1995). Description of structures of stochastic conditional independence by means of faces and imsets. 3rd part: Examples of use and appendices. *International Journal of General Systems, 23*(4), 323–341.

Sutton, C., & McCallum, A. (2007). An introduction to conditional random fields for relational learning. In L. Getoor & B. Taskar (Eds.), *Introduction to statistical relational learning* (pp. 93–126). Cambridge, MA: MIT Press.

Sytsma, J., Livengood, J., & Rose, D. (2012). Two types of typicality: Rethinking the role of statistical typicality in ordinary causal attributions. *Studies in History and Philosophy of Biological and Biomedical Sciences, 43*(4), 814–820.

Talmy, L. (1988). Force dynamics in language and cognition. *Cognitive Science, 12*, 49–100.

Taskar, B., Guestrin, C., & Koller, D. (2004). Max-margin Markov networks. In S. Thrun, L. Saul, & B. Scholkopf (Eds.), *Advances in neural information processing systems* (Vol. 16). Cambridge, MA: MIT Press.

Tassoni, C. J. (1995). The least mean squares network with information coding: A model of cue learning. *Journal of Experimental Psychology: Learning, Memory, and Cognition, 21*, 193–204.

Teller, P. (1973). Conditionalization and observation. *Synthese, 26*, 218–238.

Teller, P. (1976). Conditionalization, observation, and change of preference. In W. L. Harper & C. A. Hooker (Eds.), *Foundations of probability theory, statistical inference, and statistical theories of science* (Vol. 1, pp. 205–259). Dordrecht: Reidel.

Tenenbaum, J. B., & Griffiths, T. L. (2001). Structure learning in human causal induction. In T. Leen, T. Deitterich, & V. Tresp (Eds.), *Advances in neural information processing systems* (Vol. 13, pp. 59–65). Cambridge, MA: MIT Press.

Tillman, R. E., Danks, D., & Glymour, C. (2008). Integrating locally learned causal structures with overlapping variables. In D. Koller, D. Schuurmans, Y. Bengio, & L. Bottou (Eds.), *Advances in neural information processing systems* (Vol. 21, pp. 1665–1672). La Jolla, CA: The NIPS Foundation.

Tillman, R. E., Gretton, A., & Spirtes, P. (2010). Nonlinear directed acyclic structure learning with weakly additive noise models. In Y. Bengio, D. Schuurmans, J. Lafferty, C. K. I. Williams, & A. Culotta (Eds.), *Advances in neural information processing systems* (Vol. 22, pp. 1847-1855). La Jolla, CA: The NIPS Foundation.

Tooby, J., & Cosmides, L. (1992). The psychological foundations of culture. In J. H. Barkow, L. Cosmides, & J. Tooby (Eds.), *The adapted mind: Evolutionary psychology and the generation of culture* (pp. 19–136). Oxford: Oxford University Press.

Ullman, T., Baker, C., Macindoe, O., Evans, O., Goodman, N., & Tenenbaum, J. (2009). Help or hinder: Bayesian models of social goal inference. In Y. Bengio, D. Schuurmans, J. Lafferty, C. K. I. Williams, & A. Culotta (Eds.), *Advances in neural information processing systems* (Vol. 22, pp. 1874–1882). La Jolla, CA: The NIPS Foundation.

Van Hamme, L. J., & Wasserman, E. A. (1994). Cue competition in causality judgments: The role of nonpresentation of compound stimulus elements. *Learning and Motivation, 25*, 127–151.

Van Overwalle, F., & Van Rooy, D. (2001). How one cause discounts or augments another: A connectionist account of causal competition. *Personality and Social Psychology Bulletin, 27*(12), 1613–1626.

Vul, E., Goodman, N. D., Griffiths, T. L., & Tenenbaum, J. B. (2009). One and done? Optimal decisions from very few samples. In N. A. Taatgen & H. van Rijn (Eds.), *Proceedings of the 31st Annual Conference of the Cognitive Science Society* (pp. 148–153). Austin, TX: Cognitive Science Society.

Vul, E., Hanus, D., & Kanwisher, N. (2009). Attention as inference: Selection is probabilistic; responses are all-or-none samples. *Journal of Experimental Psychology: General, 138*(4), 540–560.

Waldmann, M. R. (1996). Knowledge-based causal induction. In D. R. Shanks, K. J. Holyoak, & D. L. Medin (Eds.), *Causal learning: The psychology of learning and motivation* (Vol. 34, pp. 47–88). San Diego, CA: Academic Press.

Waldmann, M. R., Cheng, P. W., Hagmayer, Y., & Blaisdell, A. P. (2008). Causal learning in rats and humans: A minimal rational model. In N. Chater & M. Oaksford (Eds.), *The probabilistic mind: Prospects for Bayesian cognitive science* (pp. 453–484). Oxford: Oxford University Press.

Waldmann, M. R., & Hagmayer, Y. (2005). Seeing versus doing: Two modes of accessing causal knowledge. *Journal of Experimental Psychology: Learning, Memory, and Cognition, 31*(2), 216–227.

Waldmann, M. R., & Hagmayer, Y. (2006). Categories and causality: The neglected direction. *Cognitive Psychology, 53*, 27–58.

Waller, L. A., Carlin, B. P., Xia, H., & Gelfand, A. E. (1997). Hierarchical spatio-temporal mapping of disease rates. *Journal of the American Statistical Association, 92*, 607–617.

Walsh, C., & Sloman, S. A. (2007). Updating beliefs with causal models: Violations of screening off. In M. A. Gluck, J. R. Anderson, & S. M. Kosslyn (Eds.), *Memory and mind* (pp. 345–358). New York: Erlbaum.

Wang, C., Blei, D., & Heckerman, D. (2008). Continuous time dynamic topic models. In D. A. McAllester & P. Myllymaki (Eds.), *Proceedings of the 24th Conference on Uncertainty in Artificial Intelligence* (pp. 579–586). Corvallis, OR: AUAI Press.

Wasserman, S., & Faust, K. (1995). *Social network analysis: Methods and applications*. Cambridge: Cambridge University Press.

Wattenmaker, W. D., Dewey, G. I., Murphy, T. D., & Medin, D. L. (1986). Linear separability and concept learning: Context, relational properties, and concept naturalness. *Cognitive Psychology, 18*, 158–194.

Watts, D. J., Dodds, P. S., & Newman, M. E. J. (2002). Identity and search in social networks. *Science, 296*(5571), 1302–1305.

Wellen, S., & Danks, D. (2012). Learning causal structure through local prediction-error learning. In N. Miyake, D. Peebles, & R. P. Cooper (Eds.), *Proceedings of the 34th Annual Conference of the Cognitive Science Society* (pp. 2529–2534). Austin, TX: Cognitive Science Society.

White, P. A. (2003a). Making causal judgments from the proportion of confirming instances: The pCI rule. *Journal of Experimental Psychology: Learning, Memory, and Cognition, 29*(4), 710–727.

White, P. A. (2003b). Causal judgement as evaluation of evidence: The use of confirmatory and disconfirmatory information. *Quarterly Journal of Experimental Psychology, 56A*(3), 491–513.

White, P. A. (2009). Perception of forces exerted by objects in collision events. *Psychological Review, 116*(3), 580–601.

White, P. A. (2012). The experience of force: The role of haptic experience of forces in visual perception of object motion and interactions, mental simulation, and motion-related judgments. *Psychological Bulletin, 138*(4), 589–615.

White, P. A., & Milne, A. (1997). Phenomenal causality: Impressions of pulling in the visual perception of objects in motion. *American Journal of Psychology, 110,* 573–602.

White, P. A., & Milne, A. (1999). Impressions of enforced disintegration and bursting in the visual perception of collision events. *Journal of Experimental Psychology: General, 128,* 499–516.

Wickens, J. R., Horvitz, J. C., Costa, R. M., & Killcross, S. (2007). Dopaminergic mechanisms in actions and habits. *Journal of Neuroscience, 27*(31), 8181–8183.

Williams, J. J., & Lombrozo, T. (2010). The role of explanation in discovery and generalization: Evidence from category learning. *Cognitive Science, 34*(5), 776–806.

Wolff, P. (2007). Representing causation. *Journal of Experimental Psychology: General, 136*(1), 82–111.

Wolff, P., & Song, G. (2003). Models of causation and the semantics of causal verbs. *Cognitive Psychology, 47,* 276–332.

Wolpert, D. M., & Kawato, M. (1998). Multiple paired forward and inverse models for motor control. *Neural Networks, 11,* 1317–1329.

Woodward, J. (2003). *Making things happen: A theory of causal explanation.* Oxford: Oxford University Press.

Woodward, J. (2006). Sensitive and insensitive causation. *Philosophical Review, 115*(1), 1–50.

Wray, R. E., Laird, J. E., Nuxoll, A. M., Stokes, D., & Kerfoot, A. (2005). Synthetic adversaries for urban combat training. *AI Magazine, 26*(3), 82–92.

Yamauchi, T., Love, B. C., & Markman, A. B. (2002). Learning nonlinearly separable categories by inference and classification. *Journal of Experimental Psychology: Learning, Memory, and Cognition, 28*(3), 585–593.

Yamauchi, T., & Markman, A. B. (1998). Category learning by inference and classification. *Journal of Memory and Language, 39,* 124–148.

Yamauchi, T., & Markman, A. B. (2000). Inference using categories. *Journal of Experimental Psychology: Learning, Memory, and Cognition, 26,* 776–795.

Young, R. M., & Lewis, R. L. (1999). The Soar cognitive architecture and human working memory. In A. Miyake & P. Shah (Eds.), *Models of working memory: Mechanisms of active maintenance and executive control* (pp. 224–256). Cambridge: Cambridge University Press.

Zaki, S. R., Nosofsky, R. M., Stanton, R. D., & Cohen, A. L. (2003). Prototype and exemplar accounts of category learning and attentional allocation: A reassessment.

Journal of Experimental Psychology: Learning, Memory, and Cognition, 29(6), 1160–1173.

Zhang, N. L., & Poole, D. (1999). On the role of context-specific independence in probabilistic inference. In *Proceedings of the 16th International Joint Conference on Artificial Intelligence* (pp. 1288–1293). San Francisco: Morgan Kaufmann.

Zhu, H., & Danks, D. (2007). Task influences on category learning. In D. S. McNamara & J. G. Trafton (Eds.), *Proceedings of the 29th Annual Meeting of the Cognitive Science Society* (pp. 1677–1682). Austin, TX: Cognitive Science Society.

Index